"America's leading source of self-help legal information." ★★★★

—YAHOO!

W9-CAZ-604

LEGAL INFORMATION ONLINE ANYTIME

24 hours a day

www.nolo.com

AT THE NOLO.COM SELF-HELP LAW CENTER, YOU'LL FIND

- **Nolo's comprehensive Legal Encyclopedia** filled with plain-English information on a variety of legal topics
- **Nolo's Law Dictionary**—legal terms <u>without</u> the legalese
- **Auntie Nolo**—if you've got questions, Auntie's got answers
- **The Law Store**—over 250 self-help legal products including: Downloadable Software, Books, Form Kits and eGuides
- **Legal and product updates**
- **Frequently Asked Questions**
- **NoloBriefs, our free monthly email newsletter**
- **Legal Research Center,** for access to state and federal statutes
- **Our ever-popular lawyer jokes**

✓ITHDRAWN

Quality LAW BOOKS & SOFTWARE FOR EVERYONE

Nolo's user-friendly products are consistently first-rate. Here's why:

- A dozen in-house legal editors, working with highly skilled authors, ensure that our products are accurate, up-to-date and easy to use
- We continually update every book and software program to keep up with changes in the law
- Our commitment to a more democratic legal system informs all of our work
- We appreciate & listen to your feedback. Please fill out and return the card at the back of this book.

OUR "NO-HASSLE" GUARANTEE

Return anything you buy directly from Nolo for any reason and we'll cheerfully refund your purchase price. No ifs, ands or buts.

Read This First

The information in this book is as up-to-date and accurate as we can make it. But it's important to realize that the law changes frequently, as do fees, forms, and procedures. If you handle your own legal matters, it's up to you to be sure that all information you use—including the information in this book—is accurate. Here are some suggestions to help you:

First, make sure you've got the most recent edition of this book. To learn whether a later edition is available, check the edition number on the book's spine and then go to Nolo's online Law Store at www.nolo.com or call Nolo's Customer Service Department at 800-728-3555.

Next, even if you have a current edition, you need to be sure it's fully up-to-date. The law can change overnight. At www.nolo.com, we post notices of major legal and practical changes that affect the latest edition of a book. To check for updates, find your book in the Law Store on Nolo's website (you can use the "A to Z Product List" and click the book's title). If you see an "Updates" link on the left side of the page, click it. If you don't see a link, that means we haven't posted any updates. (But check back regularly.)

Finally, we believe accurate and current legal information should help you solve many of your own legal problems on a cost-efficient basis. But this text is not a substitute for personalized advice from a knowledgeable lawyer. If you want the help of a trained professional, consult an attorney licensed to practice in your state.

Acknowledgments

Many thanks to:

Amy DelPo, for her encouragement and suggestions.

Rich Stim, for his excellent editing and his sharp eye for the noir detail.

Ella Hirst and Stan Jacobson, for their research assistance.

Susan Putney, for her wonderful cover and book design.

Joe Sadusky, for the meticulous proofreading.

Dedication

For my parents, whose five children gave them plenty to investigate.

In loving memory.

WITHDRAWN

Table of Contents

4 Make and Document Your Decision

PART TWO
Investigating Common Workplace Problems

5 Investigating Discrimination

6 Investigating Harassment

7 Investigating Workplace Theft

8   Investigating Threats and Violence

PART I

Investigation Basics

CHAPTER

Workplace Investigations: An Overview

Chances are good that you picked up this book because something has gone seriously awry in your workplace—and you're not quite sure how to handle it. Maybe you've received a complaint or report of misconduct that sounds something like this:

> "Every time I go into John's office, he's looking at porn on the Internet—it's really starting to offend me and some of the other women in the office."

> "We've finished our internal audit, and the numbers just don't add up. I think we may have a thief on our payroll."

> "I've been passed over for promotion three times, and each time the job has gone to a younger person who doesn't have my experience or training. I feel like I'm being discriminated against."

> "Mark has been really angry lately—he keeps talking about his gun collection, and yesterday he told me that 'management is about to get what's coming to them.' I'm afraid he's going to shoot someone."

You suddenly have to deal with a serious workplace problem, and now you're facing some very tough decisions: Whom should I believe? What really happened and why? How serious is this problem? What should I do about it? Can I handle this situation without ending up in court?

A complete, impartial, and timely investigation can answer all these questions and more. In fact, a proper investigation is one of the most important tools an employer has for maintaining a safe and productive workplace—and staying out of legal trouble. Handled properly, an investigation can help you manage misconduct, assure workers that their complaints, concerns, and safety are taken seriously, underline the importance of following workplace rules, and even provide a valuable defense to an employee lawsuit.

What a Good Investigation Can Do for You

Very few employers are pleased to learn that they have a workplace problem serious enough to require an investigation. However, you can turn this negative into a positive by investigating in a way that strengthens and protects your company. Among its many benefits, a proper investigation will help you:

Figure out what happened. The immediate aim of any investigation is to get to the bottom of a problem. After all, you won't know how to handle a situation until you know what really happened. And acting before you have all the facts could lead you to discipline the wrong employee, let a wrongdoer off the hook, or allow a workplace problem to fester unchecked.

Nip employee problems in the bud. An investigation will help you figure out who's behind your workplace problems, so you can take action before things get any worse. If you are dealing with a problem employee, you can discipline that worker. If you discover that employees are breaking the rules because they don't know what you expect from them, you can implement training programs, work harder to publicize and distribute your policies, and make sure your managers are enforcing the rules.

Enforce company policies. If you don't enforce your own policies, your workers will quickly come to realize that they don't have to follow the rules. Showing your employees that there are consequences for misconduct will help deter future trouble and keep your workers on the straight and narrow.

Encourage reporting. Investigating and dealing with problems quickly will encourage workers to come forward with their issues and concerns. This means that you'll hear about workplace trouble right away, before it has a chance to grow into a serious problem.

Avoid or counter bad publicity. When you ignore complaints and problems, you give the impression that you don't care about your workers or the law. And if your failure to deal with a problem becomes public knowledge—through a lawsuit, for example—it could really hurt your reputation and drive away business.

Protect your company from lawsuits. A solid investigation is a kind of insurance policy, protecting the decisions you make now from legal challenges in the future. If someone who is injured by workplace misconduct—an employee who is sexually harassed, for example—sues your company, you can argue that you took action as soon as you learned of the problem, which will protect you from liability in many cases. If an employee who was disciplined or fired as a result of your investigation files a lawsuit challenging your actions, you will be able to show that you acted reasonably and in good faith, which will go a long way towards defeating the employee's claims.

By the same token, however, a slipshod investigation can *lead* to employee lawsuits, by giving employees the ammunition they need to demonstrate that you were careless, that you discriminated, that you spread false information, or that you treated employees poorly, among other things. And failing to investigate at all is even worse—if an employee can show that you knew about a problem and didn't do anything about it, you will be legally responsible for any harm that employee suffered.

So how do you conduct the right kind of investigation? By being fair and thorough and making good-faith efforts to get to the truth. Even if you come to the wrong conclusion, you are legally entitled to take action (for example, to discipline or fire an employee) based on the results of your investigation, as long as you investigated properly and your decisions were reasonable based on the information available to you.

EXAMPLE: Ralph was accused of sexually harassing two female coworkers. The company immediately performed a complete investigation, interviewing the women, Ralph, and a number of witnesses—including five Ralph suggested. Based on these interviews, the company concluded that Ralph was guilty as charged and fired him.

Ralph later sued the company, claiming that he had a consensual affair with both women, no harassment had occurred, and the women were angry with him for two-timing them. (Ralph did not tell any of this to the company's investigator.) The jury found in Ralph's favor. However, an appeals court decided that it didn't matter what really happened—as long as the company conducted a fair and thorough investigation and reached a good-faith conclusion based on the information available to it at the time, it could not be sued for firing Ralph based on the investigation's results.

This book gives you the tools and information you need to conduct a successful investigation. Part I (Chapters 1 through 4) describes in detail the ten steps to a successful investigation of any kind of workplace problem. Part II (Chapters 5 through 8) takes a closer look at four common workplace problems—discrimination, harassment, theft, and violence—and explains how to meet the special investigation challenges posed by each.

This chapter will help you get started. Section A introduces the basic components of a proper workplace investigation, including the actions you will have to take—and decisions you will have to make—along the way. (Each of these steps is covered in detail in Chapters 2 through 4.) Section B explains some common investigation mistakes that can lead to legal trouble—and tips that will help careful employers avoid them.

Who Are You?

This book addresses two audiences: the employer and the investigator. If you run a small business, you may fill both of these roles—and this book is always speaking to "you." You will perform the traditional task of the investigator: figuring out what happened. And you will also play the employer's part: deciding whether an investigation is warranted and what actions to take based on the results of the investigation.

In larger companies, however, the employer will choose an investigator, most often a human resources specialist, to conduct the investigation. In this situation, each of you may have separate tasks—for example, one may conduct interviews and examine documents, and the other may decide how to discipline the wrongdoer and prevent similar problems in this future. This book always addresses the person handling a given task, so if you divide up the responsibilities, the discussion will sometimes speak to "you," the employer, and sometimes to "you," the investigator.

A. Ten Steps to a Successful Investigation

The best way to tackle an investigation—like any other project—is to divide it up into manageable tasks. Fortunately, most workplace investigations follow a pretty similar pattern, although the details can vary considerably. Once you become aware of a problem or complaint, you'll have to:

1. decide whether to investigate
2. take immediate action, if necessary
3. choose an investigator
4. plan the investigation
5. interview
6. gather documents and other evidence
7. evaluate the evidence
8. take action
9. document the investigation, and
10. follow up.

Investigations Require Judgment Calls

Although most investigations will require you to at least consider each of these ten steps, every situation is a little bit different. Workplace problems rarely land on your desk in a tidy package with an obvious solution. Instead, you'll often be faced with conflicting stories, documents that are open to different interpretations, and no clear answers about what happened and what you should do about it. You'll have to decide which problems merit a closer look, whom to interview, and what documents to review—and when your investigation is complete, you'll have to decide what you think really happened.

All of these decisions are judgment calls, and no book can tell you how to handle every possible scenario you might face. However, if you follow the guidelines in the chapters that follow, keep an open mind, and use your best judgment, you'll be able to untangle most of the problems that come your way.

1. Decide Whether to Investigate

When you learn of a problem or a complaint of workplace wrongdoing, you must first decide whether to investigate. There are some situations when an investigation won't be necessary. For example, if everyone involved in the problem agrees about what happened, you usually won't need to do any fact-finding—you can move on to figuring out what actions to take (if any) to handle the situation. Similarly, if the problem appears to be minor—for example, one employee accuses another of playing the radio too loudly in a common workspace—you can simply talk to the employees involved and clear things up quickly.

Generally, however, you should err on the side of conducting an investigation. If the problem is more serious than it seemed, failing to investigate can lead to legal trouble. (See Section B1, below.) And sometimes, you won't know how widespread or substantial a problem is until you do a little poking around.

What's more, if you don't investigate complaints or situations that trouble your employees, you will send the message that you aren't concerned about your workers—and that you will turn a deaf ear to their problems. This can damage your relationship to your workers, diminish workplace morale, and deprive you of valuable legal defenses, should you face an employee lawsuit.

If you aren't sure whether a problem merits investigation, you can begin to investigate by interviewing the employees who are directly involved in the situation. If the problem is straightforward and easy to resolve, you can wrap up your work quickly. But if the issues seem more complicated than they first appeared, you can expand the investigation accordingly. For more on deciding whether to investigate, see Chapter 2, Section B.

2. Take Immediate Action, If Necessary

Once you decide that an investigation is warranted, you'll have to decide whether the situation calls for immediate action, even before you begin to investigate. If you are investigating a situation that is volatile or could otherwise cause immediate harm to your business, you might have to act right away. For example, if an employee is accused of sexually assaulting a coworker, stealing trade secrets, or bringing a weapon to work, you'll probably want to act first and ask questions later.

For more detailed information on taking interim measures—including tips that will help you avoid legal claims based on your pre-investigation actions—see Chapter 2, Section C.

3. Choose an Investigator

Once you've dealt with any immediate problems, your next step is to choose an investigator. Who's the right person for the job? Someone who's experienced and/or trained in investigations, is impartial *and* is perceived as impartial by the employees involved, and is capable of acting—and, if necessary, testifying—professionally about the investigation. (For more on each of these requirements, see Chapter 2, Section D.) If you have someone who meets this job description on your payroll, you're in luck. You can tap that person to begin the investigation.

If you don't have any employees who fit the bill, consider hiring an outsider—a professional investigator or lawyer, for example—to investigate for you. See Chapter 2, Section D, for more details on hiring an outsider to investigate, including circumstances in which it might be wise for an employer to bring in outside help.

4. Plan the Investigation

Take some time up front to organize your thoughts and information. This is when you need to start thinking like a detective: What evidence do you have? What evidence do you need to figure out what happened? Who might have relevant information? What's the best way to get that information from them? Doing a little planning ahead of time will help you avoid wasting time—or missing crucial pieces of the puzzle—as you conduct the investigation.

Gather any information you already have about the problem to be investigated. Think about how the situation came to your attention. If an employee made a complaint or a supervisor reported suspicious behavior, you'll have the information from that initial report. Pull together any documents that might be important, such as a company policy relating to the problem (a sexual harassment or workplace violence policy, for example), documents from the accused employee's personnel file, or written materials that are part of the problem (such as x-rated posters or threatening emails).

Using this information as your guide, think about what you'll need to find out during your investigation. Whom will you interview and what will you ask? Are there additional documents that employees or supervisors might have? Is there anyone who witnessed important incidents—or anyone who should have? Once you've plotted your course, you are ready to actually get started. For more on preparing to investigate, see Chapter 2, Section E.

5. Interview

The heart of any investigation is gathering information—and the most basic way to do that is by asking people questions.

Most investigations involve at least two interviews: one of the employee accused of wrongdoing, and another of the employee who complained or was the victim. Sometimes, you will also have to interview witnesses—others who may have seen or heard something important. And sometimes, there won't be any complaining employee—for example, if a worker is suspected of stealing from the company, you might learn of the problem through a supervisor's suspicion or funny accounting records, not through the complaint of a coworker.

When you interview workers, your goal is to get as much information as possible. The best way to do this is by asking open-ended questions that allow the person you're interviewing to tell the story in his or her own words. However, you don't want to give too much away—if you reveal your opinions or important facts about the situation to your interview subjects, you risk affecting their answers to your questions, appearing biased, or violating the privacy rights of other employees. Chapter 3, Section B, explains how to conduct successful interviews, including whom to interview and in what order, questions to ask, and tips that will help you get the information you need.

6. Gather Documents and Other Evidence

Almost every investigation will also include other types of evidence, often documents like personnel files, email messages, company policies, or personal notes. In fact, some investigations hinge on documents—for example, if an employee complains about receiving harassing emails from a supervisor, those messages will play a large role in your investigation.

And as you no doubt know from watching detective shows or reading mysteries, physical evidence—the smoking gun, the blood-stained clothing, or the candlestick in the conservatory with Colonel Mustard—often helps solve a criminal investigation. The same is true of workplace investigations. In some cases, you may have to gather items like drugs, a weapon, photographs, or clothing. Chapter 3, Section C, gives more information on gathering evidence, including a checklist of documents that might be relevant in a workplace investigation.

7. Evaluate the Evidence

The most challenging part of the investigation—especially if witnesses disagree or contradict each other—is figuring out what actually happened. There are some proven methods of figuring out where the truth lies—methods that all of us use in our everyday lives to get to the bottom of things. You'll want to consider, for example, whose story makes the most sense, whose demeanor was more convincing, and who (if anyone) has a motive to mislead you. And in some situations, you may just have to throw up your hands and acknowledge that there isn't enough evidence to decide what happened. Chapter 4, Section A, explains how to sift through the evidence and come to a conclusion, if possible.

8. Take Action

Sometimes, you will conclude that an employee engaged in serious misconduct. In these circumstances, you have to take action—and fast—to avoid legal liability for that employee's behavior and to protect your other employees (and company) from harm. In deciding what to do, you should consider a number of factors, including how serious the actions were and how you have handled similar problems in that past.

In other cases, you may conclude that no serious wrongdoing occurred or that, despite all of your hard work, you simply can't reach any conclusions about what happened. In these situations, you generally won't take any disciplinary action against the accused employee (although you may want to follow up with the employees involved). Chapter 4, Sections B and C, covers taking action following an investigation, including information on how to deliver the news to the employees involved and a checklist of factors to consider if you have to impose discipline.

9. Document the Investigation

Once your investigation is complete, you should write an investigation report that explains what you did and why. This will not only give the company some protection from lawsuits relating to the investigation, but will also provide a written record in case of future misconduct by the same employee(s).

Your report should briefly explain:

- how and when the problem came to the company's attention
- when the investigation began
- whom you interviewed
- what each person you interviewed said
- what other evidence and documents you considered
- what conclusions you reached and why, and
- any disciplinary or other workplace action taken based on the results of the investigation.

Chapter 4, Section D, explains how to write an investigation report.

10. Follow Up

The last step is to follow up with your employees to make sure you've solved the problem that led to the investigation. Talk to the complaining employee to make sure that any misconduct has stopped and that he or she hasn't been ostracized or punished for complaining. Follow through to make sure that the wrongdoer was disciplined appropriately and met any requirements imposed as a result of the investigation (for example, that the employee completed a required training course on sexual harassment or attended mandatory counseling sessions on anger management). You should also consider whether the investigation revealed any systemic workplace problems that you should tackle—such as widespread ignorance of company policies or lack of training on issues like workplace diversity or proper procedures for handling money. Chapter 4, Section E, explains how to follow up after your investigation.

 You'll find a checklist of the ten steps to a successful investigation in Appendix B.

What a Good Investigation Looks Like

By following the ten steps outlined in this chapter (and explained in detail later), you can conduct an investigation that helps you get to the bottom of your workplace problem—and will hold up in court. For example, here's how one California employer won a lawsuit by conducting a timely, thorough, and fair investigation:

Lucky Stores (a supermarket chain) received two complaints by female employees that John Silva had sexually harassed them. After conducting a month-long investigation, Lucky concluded that Silva had committed sexual harassment and fired him. Silva filed a lawsuit against Lucky, claiming that he didn't harass the women and, therefore, that Lucky didn't have the right to fire him.

The court found in Lucky's favor, because it had good reason to believe, based on its investigation, that Silva committed the harassment. The court detailed the qualities that made Lucky's investigation so reliable:

- Lucky chose Jeff Szczesny, a human resources representative who had been trained on how to conduct an investigation, to investigate the complaint. Szczesny was not involved in the underlying incident.

- Szczesny began investigating immediately.

- Szczesny interviewed 15 Lucky employees and documented the interviews. He asked open-ended questions and tried to elicit facts, not opinions. He encouraged the witnesses to contact him if they wanted to talk to him again.

- Szczesny told Silva of the charges against him and gave him a chance to tell his side of the story.

- Szczesny met again with important witnesses, including Silva, to give them a chance to hear new information and to clarify or correct their own statements.

- Szczesny memorialized the investigation in a written report, detailing the conclusions he reached and why.

B. Common Investigation Mistakes—and How to Avoid Them

There are a number of legal traps waiting for the employer who fails to investigate or conducts an improper investigation. Generally, these traps come in the form of potentially ruinous lawsuits brought either by an employee who was a victim of inappropriate behavior in the workplace or by an employee who was disciplined or fired after being accused of misconduct. In either situation, an employer whose investigation was incomplete, biased, sloppy, or late—or who never investigated at all—begins the lawsuit in a fairly deep hole. Not only has the employer ignored its workers' legal rights, but it has also shown a lack of concern for its workers' well-being—a sentiment that jurors (most of whom are or were employees themselves, not employers) generally find extremely distasteful.

In addition to these legal issues, employers who don't investigate problems or who conduct a half-hearted investigation will face practical problems. These employers are sending precisely the wrong signals to their workers, managers, and customers: that they don't want to hear about workplace problems, they don't really care what's going on in their company, and they won't enforce their own workplace rules. That's not exactly a message that will build morale, cement employee and customer loyalty, improve retention, and reduce workplace problems.

Finally, failing to investigate or doing a poor job will exact an emotional cost as well. If you wrongly accuse an employee of serious misconduct, you are not only inviting a lawsuit, but you've also ruined that employee's reputation and relationships with coworkers. As if the legal and practical traps described above aren't bad enough, just imagine how bad you'll feel if you make the wrong call—and your mistake brings unhappiness and anxiety to a blameless employee.

Fortunately, it isn't too hard to avoid these mistakes. By following the strategies outlined in this book—and using a healthy dose of common sense—you can keep your investigation on the right side of the law. Here are some common investigation errors—and tips that will help you avoid them.

1. Failing to Investigate

If you are aware of significant misconduct or dangerous activity in your workplace and you don't do anything about it, you are exposing yourself to tremendous legal risk. Generally, any harm that comes to your employees—and sometimes, to people who aren't on your payroll, such as customers, clients, or bystanders—after you know about the problem will be your legal responsibility. This means, for example, that an employee who suffers sexual harassment or is injured in an incident of workplace violence after you learned that trouble was brewing won't have much difficulty convincing a jury to make you pay.

Retaining a Dangerous Employee Can Lead to a Lawsuit

Someone who is injured by one of your employees might have a legal claim against you if you were careless in supervising or retaining that employee—that is, if you knew or should have known that the employee was unfit for the job, yet you did nothing about it. These are called "negligent retention" or "negligent supervision" claims.

Failing to investigate can give rise to one of these lawsuits. If you failed to perform an investigation that would have revealed that a particular employee posed a danger to others, you could be on the hook for damages if the employee harms someone.

Example: John works at a machine plant. His coworkers notice that John has not been himself lately—his appearance is somewhat disheveled, he seems distracted, and he loses his temper easily. He complains that company management is trying to force him to retire, but that he "won't go quietly." Coworkers bring this to the attention of the human resources department but are told, "That's just John. He complains a lot, but he does high-quality work." A month later, John sabotages a major piece of equipment, which malfunctions and injures several employees and a few students visiting from a local vocational school. The company might face a lawsuit for negligent retention.

Negligent retention and supervision claims can always be brought by outsiders—those who don't work for your company. Your employees, on the other hand, may not be able to sue you for negligence. The workers' compensation insurance system, which guarantees compensation to employees who are injured in the workplace, prohibits employees from suing their employers for injuries that are paid for by workers' comp. For more on this issue, see Chapter 8, Section A3.

You might also face a lawsuit if you fire an employee for workplace wrongdoing without first conducting an investigation. If that employee has an employment contract—whether written, oral, or implied—that limits your right to fire, that employee might sue you for breach of contract if you don't investigate before terminating his or her employment. The lawsuit would claim that (1) the employee didn't commit the misconduct for which he or she was fired; (2) you didn't bother to investigate to figure out what really happened; and, therefore, (3) you didn't have good cause to fire the employee.

Employment Contracts Can Limit Your Right to Fire

An employee with an employment contract that limits your right to fire might have a valid legal claim against you if you fire the employee for wrongdoing without conducting a proper investigation.

Usually, this won't be an issue—most employees don't have employment contracts but instead are "at-will" employees. This means that they can quit at any time, and you can fire them at any time, for any reason that is not illegal (illegal reasons for firing include discrimination and retaliation).

However, some employees have employment contracts that limits the employer's right to fire at will. For example, the contract might state that the employee can only be fired for "good cause"—a common provision—or for specified reasons (such as gross misconduct or financial malfeasance). If you fire the employee for reasons other than those stated in the contract, the employee can sue you for breaching the contract.

Things get a bit trickier if an employee has a contract that hasn't been reduced to writing. For example, some employees have spoken agreements with the employer (known as oral contracts). Whatever the employer and employee agreed to orally will govern the employer's right to fire. In other cases, an employee might have an implied contract: a contract that was never explicitly reduced to words, whether written or spoken, but arose from the conduct and statements of the employer and employee. For example, if an employer tells a worker "as long as you do a good job, we'll keep you on," that could be interpreted as an implied contract restricting the employer's right to fire the employee unless the employee performs poorly.

Employment contracts can get complicated, and the employee's status—whether under contract or at will—affects the types of legal actions you might face for failing to investigate or conducting a poor investigation. If you want to know more about employment contracts, check out *Dealing With Problem Employees*, by Amy DelPo and Lisa Guerin (Nolo).

So how can you avoid these kinds of trouble? By taking workplace problems seriously. Never ignore complaints of wrongdoing. Even if a situation seems simple or straightforward, always do some initial research before deciding that an investigation isn't warranted. And make sure you know all the facts before you take disciplinary action against an employee.

2. Delay

Even if you eventually decide to investigate and do a good job, you can get into legal trouble if you wait too long to get started. If an employee suffers harm—from harassment or workplace violence, for example—after you learned about the problem but before you took action, you will usually be legally responsible to that employee. The longer you postpone the investigation, the more serious your legal liability could be.

EXAMPLE: Kristen worked as a checker at a grocery store. She complained that a coworker sexually harassed her by calling her names, propositioning her, commenting on her physical appearance, and touching her. Kristen complained to the store's assistant manager several times; each time, the manager confronted the coworker, who denied the allegations. After Kristen's fourth complaint—two months after her first complaint—the accused harasser was transferred to a different shift, where he had no further contact with Kristen.

Kristen filed a lawsuit against the grocery store for sexual harassment. The employer tried to have her case thrown out, arguing that it took action to stop the harassment by transferring the alleged harasser. However, the court found that the store's two-month delay before taking action was too long, even if it eventually did the right thing by moving the alleged harasser to another shift. The court allowed Kristen's lawsuit to go forward.

Postponing the investigation could also lead the complaining employee to claim that he or she was retaliated against—disciplined or otherwise treated badly for making the complaint. (For more on avoiding retaliation, see Section B4, below.) Here's why: Once you start your investigation, you will warn everyone involved that retaliation will not be tolerated—and you'll assure any employee who complained or suffered misconduct that retaliation will not be permitted. However, until you get going, the employee who came forward might be mistreated for making a complaint. That employee might be threatened by the wrongdoers, given the cold shoulder by other employees, or even disciplined by a supervisor for coming forward. And all of this mistreatment will be your legal responsibility.

Of course, there's a simple solution: Don't delay your investigation. Once you learn of a serious problem or complaint, get moving right away. If you absolutely have to wait a bit before getting started (because the victim is on vacation, for example), document the reasons for the delay. Chapter 3, Section A, explains how to do this.

3. Inconsistency

Some employers get into trouble by acting inconsistently—that is, by handling similar situations differently. In the employment arena, any kind of inconsistent treatment can lead to claims of discrimination. An employee who feels that he or she was treated differently because of a protected characteristic—an inherent quality, such as race or gender, that cannot legally form the basis for an employment decision—might bring a lawsuit claiming that you discriminated.

What Are Protected Characteristics?

Federal laws prohibits employers from making workplace decisions based on an employee's or applicant's race, color, national origin, sex, religion, age (if the employee is at least 40 years old), or disability. (These laws don't apply to smaller employers; only those employers who have at least 15 employees—or 20 employees, for age discrimination—are required to follow them.) In addition, almost every state has adopted an antidiscrimination law. Although some of these laws mirror the federal rules, some prohibit additional kids of discrimination (based on sexual orientation or marital status, for example) and some apply to smaller employers. For more on discrimination laws and protected characteristics, see Chapter 5, Section A. You'll find information on your state's antidiscrimination laws in Appendix C.

If you aren't even-handed in your investigations, you could risk a discrimination claim. For example, if you decide not to investigate a complaint against a white man for sexual harassment but you do investigate a harassment complaint against an African-American man, you might be accused of race discrimination. Similarly, if you don't investigate a claim of discrimination brought by a Muslim employee, that employee might argue that your decision was based on hostility to her religion.

EXAMPLE: Kwik & Klean, a janitorial company, investigates an incident of sexual harassment. The company concludes that Tom, a white employee on one of the night crews, has been telling x-rated jokes and stories, which have made some of his female coworkers uncomfortable. Tom is given a written warning and counseling, and his manager receives training about sexual harassment.

Several months later, a worker on a different crew complains that Eduardo, a Latino employee, has been talking about his sex life and sexual fantasies to whoever will listen. The company investigates and concludes that the complaint is valid. The company is concerned that it has had two incidents of harassment in the past few months and decides that it has to take steps to demonstrate its commitment to rooting out the problem, so it decides to fire Eduardo.

Eduardo sues, claiming that he was treated more harshly than Tom because of his race. Even if the company's decision wasn't based on the race of either employee, it will have trouble defending its inconsistency in court. Because the employees committed similar offenses, the best course of action is to impose similar discipline. The company can take other steps—like requiring sexual harassment training—to show employees that harassment won't be tolerated.

Avoid discrimination claims by treating similar problems similarly. If you decide to investigate one claim but not another, make sure you have a valid, business-related reason for your decision. If you punish one employee more harshly than another, be prepared to articulate a solid justification for your action. And always check your motives: Most of us don't want to admit to any prejudice, but we all have preconceptions that can affect our decisions. Inconsistency is sometimes justified, but it can also be a sign of unconscious bias at work.

4. Retaliation

You may not take any negative action against an employee for coming forward with a complaint or participating in an investigation. Most conscientious employers are sensible enough to realize that punishing an employee for bringing a workplace problem to your attention is a bad idea, for legal and practical reasons. However, even savvy employers sometimes retaliate against an employee without intending do.

This comes up most often when employees have to be separated for some reason. For example, if one employee is harassing another, your first instinct might be to move one of the workers to another position, so they won't have to work together. However, if you move the worker who complained, that worker might feel that he or she is being punished for complaining—especially if the new position, workspace, or shift is less prestigious or desirable.

To protect against retaliation claims, warn everyone involved in an investigation that retaliation won't be tolerated. Ask the complaining employee to bring any instances of retaliation to your attention immediately. And if you must separate workers, move the worker accused of misconduct—or make sure that the worker who complained is in favor of the change of scene you propose.

 Retaliation lawsuits can outlive the original complaint.

Courts have held that an employee can sue an employer who punishes the employee for making a complaint—even if the conduct the employee complains about doesn't violate the law. For example, an employee files a lawsuit, claiming that she was fired for complaining about sexual harassment by a coworker. The court decides that, although the woman was told an off-color joke, the incident wasn't severe enough to constitute illegal harassment, so her harassment claim is thrown out. (For more on the legal standards for harassment claims, see Chapter 6, Section A.) However, the court might still allow the woman to sue for retaliation—even though she wasn't sexually harassed, it is illegal for the employer to fire her for complaining about it in good faith.

---

5. Half-Hearted Efforts

Performing an incomplete or sloppy investigation—by failing to interview key witnesses, neglecting to review important documents, or ignoring issues that come up during the investigation, for example—can have many of the same negative consequences as failing to investigate at all.

The employee who complained or suffered mistreatment will feel that his or her concerns weren't taken seriously and might sue you for retaliation or for harm that continued during and after the investigation. An employee accused of misconduct might believe that you weren't interested in his or her side of the story or in finding out what really happened, which could lead to a lawsuit for wrongful termination or discrimination. And worse, you won't be able to rely on the results of your investigation in court—once an employee demonstrates that you did an incompetent job, you'll be in an even worse position than if you never investigated in the first place.

This is an easy mistake to avoid. Following the simple strategies and steps in this book will ensure that your investigation is thorough and proper—and will stand up in court.

6. Too Much Talk

Loose lips do more than sink ships—they can also torpedo a workplace investigation. From a practical standpoint, talking too much during the investigation—telling a witness what another witness said, revealing your personal opinion to one of the employees involved, or publicizing the complaint in the workplace, for example—can lead others to doubt your objectivity. They might believe you have already made up your mind and therefore aren't going to investigate fairly. Employees involved in the investigation might change their statements, either subconsciously or intentionally, based on what you say. And you can bet that if you're talking about the investigation, the entire workplace is talking, too—which will lead to a lot of gossip, potential ill will, and lost productivity.

As a legal matter, an employee who believes you have maligned her reputation by spreading false information can sue you for defamation. These claims are sometimes made by the target of the investigation, who argues that the employer falsely accused him or her of wrongdoing, resulting in unfair discipline and a damaged reputation—and perhaps even preventing him or her from getting another job.

EXAMPLE: Tricia was fired from the Reader's Hideaway, a bookstore and café, after her register drawer was short on several occasions. Tricia claims that she didn't steal any money from the store, and that another employee—David, the owner's son—used her register on each day that it was short. David denies taking the money, and the company never talks to other employees about what they've seen or looks into Tricia's claims further. When Tricia applies for other jobs and Reader's Hideaway is called for a reference, the owner says that Tricia was fired for stealing from the company. Tricia sues for defamation.

Defamation claims can also be brought by an employee who makes a workplace complaint, if you conclude that the complaint is false and publicize your belief. In this situation, the employee's claim is that the employer falsely labeled him or her a liar. Even a witness who participated in a workplace investigation could accuse the employer of lying about what he or she said, if the employer's statements damaged the employee's reputation.

Defamation claims start when employers talk too much, or when they say things that they don't know to be true. The best way to avoid this mistake is to reveal information on a need-to-know basis only. Don't talk about the complaint, the investigation, the evidence, or your conclusions with anyone except those who need to be in on the decisions. If you must make a damaging statement about an employee or former employee, stick to the facts and keep it short.

Defamation Defenses

Although employers can be held liable for harming an employee's reputation, the law recognizes that employers sometimes have to talk about former employees and the reasons why they are no longer employed. Here are a few legal defenses that will protect an employer who reveals limited information in good faith:

- **Truth.** If you are telling the truth, you can't be sued for defamation. In other words, if you tell someone that an employee was fired because he pulled a gun on you, you can't be sued for defamation if that's exactly what happened.

- **Good-faith reference to a prospective employer.** Most states will not allow a former employee to sue an employer for defamation if the employer makes statements that it reasonably believes to be true to a prospective employer seeking a reference.

- **Good-faith statement to a government agency.** You generally cannot be sued for responding in good faith to an official request for information about why an employee was fired. For example, you won't face a defamation claim if you tell the unemployment or workers' compensation office your reasons for terminating an employee.

The best way to avoid a defamation claim is to speak only to people who have a legitimate need to know why the employee was fired, and to make only statements that you know to be true. Conducting a proper investigation will help you figure out where the truth lies—and, therefore, what you can safely say about the situation.

7. Losing Objectivity

You've probably developed some personal opinions about most of the people you work with. It's human nature to like some people and dislike others. But you have to put these opinions aside and look objectively at the evidence when you conduct a workplace investigation. If you let your personal feelings and opinions hold sway, you might be accused of discrimination—and the results of your investigation could be called into question.

It can also be tough to stay objective if you have to investigate—and recommend discipline against—people who outrank you on the corporate ladder. If you let the offending employee's position in the company dictate the outcome of the investigation, you aren't doing your job properly.

The best antidote for this problem is to remember your role. When you investigate, you are acting on behalf of the company. If you feel unable to put your personal feelings aside, get some help—ask someone else within the workplace (or hire an outside investigator) to conduct the investigation or get some advice from a lawyer.

8. Strong-Arm Interview Tactics

Some investigators are so intent on getting straight answers from the workers they interview that they restrain workers against their will. For example, an investigator might lock the door to the interview room, physically prevent the employee from leaving, or tell the employee something like "nobody's leaving this room until I find out what really happened." Using physical means to restrain an employee, or taking actions that lead the employee to believe that he or she is not free to go, can lead to a legal claim of false imprisonment.

You can avoid false imprisonment lawsuits by avoiding these bullying tactics. If an employee indicates that he or she wants to leave the room or stop an interview, let him or her go. You are free to take disciplinary action against an employee who refuses to answer legitimate questions or participate in a workplace investigation. However, you can't use physical means or coercion to prevent the employee from leaving.

9. Invading Employee Privacy

Don't become so zealous in your search for the truth that you invade your employees' privacy rights. This can be a tough call for employers; after all, conducting an investigation involves a certain amount of poking around, usually into things that someone doesn't want you to know about. However, if you cross the line from legitimate workplace concerns into private employee property or behavior, you could face a lawsuit for violating an employee's privacy rights.

If an employee files a lawsuit for invasion of privacy, a judge will look at why both sides acted as they did: why the employee expected privacy and why the employer searched, monitored, or otherwise got into an area the employee felt was private. Then, the judge decides whose side of the argument seems most reasonable, in what is aptly called a "balancing test."

a. Searches

When investigating certain types of wrongdoing, you may need to search an employee's work area. For example, if an employee is accused of theft, you may want to look in the employee's desk or locker for the stolen items. You will be on safest legal ground if you have a policy that reserves you the right to search employee workspaces—this type of policy shows that your employees should not have expected the contents of their desks or lockers to be private.

The more intrusive the search, the more compelling your reasons for searching must be. For example, if you want to search something an employee brings on your property, such as a lunch pail or backpack, you must have a fairly strong reason to search. And you probably should not undertake this kind of search unless you have clearly warned your employees, in a written policy, that these items are subject to search. If you want to conduct a really intrusive search—for example, turning out a worker's pockets or searching an employee physically—you are asking for trouble. If your investigation reaches a point where this type of search seems necessary, talk to a lawyer. (For more on workplace searches, see Chapter 7, Section B4.)

b. Electronic Monitoring

As long as you adopt a written policy letting your workers know that you might monitor their email or use of the Internet, you generally have the right to read employee email sent on company equipment or monitor which websites employees visit during work hours. During an investigation, email messages often provide crucial proof of misconduct, such as harassment, discrimination, or threats.

EXAMPLE: Isaac complains that he is being harassed because he is African-American—but he doesn't know who's behind it. He says that someone is sending him racist cartoons and jokes anonymously, using the office email system. The company has a written policy permitting email monitoring. The investigator reads the email messages and asks for the tech department's help in figuring out where they originated. The employee who sent the offensive messages would have a hard time arguing that the company shouldn't have read the email.

Monitoring phone calls is another story. You are legally allowed to monitor employee conversations with customers or clients for quality control (although some state laws require you to inform the parties to the call—either by announcement or by signal—that someone is listening in). However, you cannot monitor personal calls. Once you realize that a particular call is personal, you must immediately stop monitoring.

c. Avoiding Privacy Lawsuits

The best way to avoid trampling on employee's privacy rights is to ask—or search for—only what you need to know. Exercise restraint: Don't search or monitor your employees without a good reason. The further you stray from the complaint (if there is one), the alleged misconduct, or other work-related issues, the more likely you are to invade someone's privacy.

You can reduce your legal exposure by adopting written policies warning employees that you reserve the right to search desks, lockers, and email. If you have a written policy warning that you might search, employees will have a tough time arguing that they reasonably expected those areas to be private.

 Need help developing policies?

You can find sample workplace policies—including policies for electronic monitoring and searches—in *Create Your Own Employee Handbook*, by Lisa Guerin and Amy DelPo (Nolo). The book comes with a CD-ROM, which you can use to cut and paste the sample policies together into a handbook to distribute to your employees.

---

10. Using Polygraphs Improperly

You might believe that the easiest way to get to the bottom of a workplace problem is to require everyone involved to take a lie detector test. In many situations, however, polygraph tests will only lead to trouble. A federal law, the Employee Polygraph Protection Act (29 U.S.C. §§ 2001-2009) strictly limits the circumstances in which an employer can require workers to take a lie detector or polygraph test—and it's not easy to meet the law's requirements.

An employer has to fit within one of the law's narrow exceptions to have the legal right to test. (One of the exceptions applies to theft investigations—see Chapter 7, Section B4, for more information.) And even then, the employer has to meet a long list of technical requirements before it can use the results of the test to make a disciplinary decision about an employee. For example, the employee must receive a variety of written notices, must receive the test questions in advance, cannot be asked certain types of questions, and must receive a copy of the test results, among other things. In addition, the employer may only use a polygraph examiner who meets certain qualifications and reports the results of the test in a particular form.

 Want more information on the Employee Polygraph Protection Act?

Federal Employment Laws, by Amy DelPo and Lisa Guerin (Nolo), explains the law—and 18 other important federal workplace laws—in detail. It includes a summary of the law's provisions, tips for compliance, and resources that will help you sort out your responsibilities.

It can be pretty tough to conduct a legal polygraph test under this law. Even if you meet the legal requirements, you'll have to decide how much weight to give the test results. Experts disagree about how easy (or difficult) it is to "beat" the test. Because of these legal and practical problems, most employers should probably just skip the polygraph testing altogether. If you are still inclined to test, make sure you fall within one of the law's exceptions—and hire a polygraph examiner who is properly certified and understands the law. ■

CHAPTER

Getting Started

Although you can reap a lot of benefits from conducting an effective investigation, that doesn't necessarily mean you'll have a good time doing it. Investigating can be unpleasant work. If you're looking into a sexual harassment complaint, for example, you might see or hear some pretty graphic things. If you're investigating a violence complaint, you might have to make difficult judgments to ensure the safety of your coworkers or employees. And if you're investigating a complaint that involves employees whom you like or work closely with, your investigation may affect those relationships. All the while, you will probably feel some pressure to resolve the situation quickly, without incurring legal liability.

In short, you're likely to experience some anxiety when investigating and dealing with workplace problems. The best way to alleviate this anxiety is through careful planning. You'll find that you can achieve some peace of mind by taking some time before you begin your fact-finding to carefully assess the situation and decide how to handle it.

Careful planning can also help you avoid making mistakes that could come back to haunt you and your company. Sometimes, the worst investigation blunders are made before the investigation starts: a company ignores a complaint, chooses an insensitive or biased investigator, or fails to take immediate steps to prevent further harm to its employees. It's often only in hindsight, after a lawsuit is filed, that the employer realizes that these problems could have been avoided by careful attention to preinvestigation details.

This chapter provides the information you'll need to get ready to conduct a successful investigation:

- **Section A** explains how a problem requiring investigation might come to your attention.

- **Section B** helps you decide whether to investigate.

- **Section C** describes some actions you might have to take right away, even before you begin the investigation.

- **Section D** covers the qualities you should look for when selecting an investigator, including the pros and cons of using an outside investigator or attorney to do the job.

- **Section E** explains how to plan the investigation.

A. Discovering Workplace Problems

The situation that triggers an investigation might come to your attention in any number of ways—but your obligation to investigate doesn't depend on how you find out about the problem. Some employers mistakenly believe that they have a duty to investigate only formal complaints. This is wrong, from both a legal and practical standpoint. No matter how you learn of a serious workplace problem, you generally have a legal duty to take appropriate action to deal with it—and a duty to investigate the situation before taking action, if necessary. As a practical matter, if you hide your head in the sand and ignore misconduct, morale will drop, productivity will suffer, and your employees will quickly learn that they don't have to follow workplace rules.

Some investigations do begin with a formal complaint. But you can't count on your employees to bring every workplace problem to your attention. Employees sometimes choose not to complain, because they don't want to be seen as troublemakers, they fear retaliation, or they simply hope the problem will go away on its own.

In some situations, employees may not even know about the misconduct because they're not being victimized by it. For example, if an employee is stealing from customers, it's possible that no other worker is even aware of the problem. And in some situations, no one wants to come forward because they are all implicated in the misconduct. For example, if employees are selling drugs in the workplace, you probably shouldn't expect their coworkers—who are also their customers—to let you in on the details.

Here are some of the many ways you might find out about a workplace problem requiring an investigation.

1. Formal Complaints

One advantage of starting an investigation with a formal complaint—in which an employee directly reports a problem to the appropriate person—is that you can document the source and nature of the problem. A complaint gives your investigation a natural starting point; you can begin by getting the details directly from the complaining employee.

Use a standard form for recording complaints—and don't require the complaining employee to fill it out.

You should have a form for reporting complaints, with blanks to fill in the complaining employee's name, the date of the complaint, the details of the complaint, and so on. (You'll find a sample complaint form in Appendix B.) Although some companies require the complaining employee to complete a complaint form, this could create problems. Some employees will feel intimidated by having to commit their complaint to writing and will balk at this requirement. And you'll be at the mercy of the complaining employee's writing skills (and ability to pinpoint the problem). It's a better idea to have the person who takes the complaint—often a human resources representative or designated manager—fill in the complaint form.

An employer can encourage formal complaints by instituting well-publicized complaint and open-door policies that encourage employees to come forward with their concerns. These policies can:

- give you an opportunity to deal with workplace problems immediately, before they turn into major disasters

- tell your employees that you care about their concerns

- let your managers know what their responsibilities are if they learn of a problem

- support your other workplace policies (for example, an anti-harassment policy or workplace violence policy) by demonstrating that you will hold employees to these rules, and

- give you some legal protection against harassment and discrimination lawsuits (see Section B, below, for more information).

 Need sample policies?

You'll find more information, including sample policies you can use in your workplace, in Appendix A.

What If the Employee Doesn't Want to File a Complaint?

Most experienced managers have faced this troubling situation: An employee comes to their office, shuts the door, and confides that another employee is causing trouble—perhaps by telling dirty jokes, threatening coworkers, or breaking workplace rules. The confiding employee may want advice, a shoulder to cry on, or simply a safe place to let off some steam about a bad situation. What the employee does not want, unfortunately, is to make a formal complaint.

While a manager might be tempted to act as a friend and respect the employee's request to keep things quiet, that is rarely in the best interests of the company or the complaining employee. Once a manager knows of illegal workplace conduct, the company has notice of the problem—and has an obligation to deal with it, even if the employee doesn't want to file a complaint. And the complaining employee's situation isn't going to improve unless and until the company takes action.

This can be a tough situation for managers, particularly those who are friends with the employees who work for them. Prepare your managers by letting them know that you expect them to bring all complaints to the attention of the appropriate people, even if the complaining employee does not want to come forward. Your managers can tell reluctant complainers, "I know this is hard and you want to keep it quiet. But I have an obligation to report this, so the company can do something about it. That's the only way we can improve this situation."

2. Anonymous Complaints

Sometimes, complaints are made anonymously—an unsigned note in a suggestion box, a letter or memo to a manager, or an unidentified phone message, for example.

An employee might complain anonymously for many reasons. An employee who is being harassed might fear retaliation from the wrongdoer or want to avoid being seen as a complainer. An employee who is threatened with violence or who witnesses illegal activities—such as theft or drug crimes—might fear for his or her physical safety or simply not want to talk to the police.

An anonymous complaint might also come from someone who isn't involved in the situation. For example, a coworker might complain anonymously on behalf of a friend who is too fearful to come forward. A customer, vendor, or client may want to report misconduct but not want to get involved. An anonymous complaint might even be made by someone outside the work environment—for example, a concerned friend, spouse, or partner.

3. Reports by Managers and Supervisors

Managers and supervisors are your eyes and ears in the workplace. Because they are on the front lines, they are most likely to witness developing problems. In some cases, managers or supervisors might hear rumors or gossip about improper activities; sometimes, they hear complaints directly from unhappy workers.

You should train all of your managers to report any employee complaints, incidents of workplace wrongdoing, or even rumors of troublesome behavior. Requiring your managers to report problems will give you the opportunity to remedy the situation early. As a legal matter, once your managers are aware of a problem, the company is generally legally responsible for taking action to deal with the situation. If your managers fail to report serious issues, you may be on the hook for any harm that results—even if you never learn of the problem.

4. Indirect Complaints

Sometimes, an employee who is unwilling to bring a complaint will let you know about a problem indirectly. For example, an employee who receives a poor performance evaluation might explain that he or she has been unable to concentrate at work because of harassment. Or an employee who is interviewed as a witness in an investigation might raise a completely separate problem. Even though these workers are not making formal complaints, they are letting you know about a workplace problem—and it's in your best interests to look into it.

5. Information From Departing Workers

What if you learn of workplace troubles from an employee on the way out the door? For example, say that a worker quits, claiming that she has found another job. However, at her exit interview, the worker says that one reason for her departure is that her boss, whom she once dated, won't stop pressuring her to get back together with him. Once she's gone, do you need to look into this further?

The answer is a resounding "yes." Just because the complaining employee is leaving doesn't mean you don't have a potentially serious problem in your workplace—and it doesn't mean that same departing employee can't sue you for sexual harassment. The accused boss may be harassing others. And even if he's not, you have to take action against those who commit sexual harassment to demonstrate your commitment to rooting out the problem, both to the departing employee and to your other workers. If your investigation reveals that the departing employee was harassed, you should also take steps to make things right for her (and possibly avert a lawsuit), such as giving her a chance to return to her old job.

6. Workplace Observation

Sometimes, a workplace problem is obvious but the source of the problem is not. For example, you might see graffiti on an office wall, pornographic images in the lunch room, threats spray-painted in the parking lot, or money missing from petty cash. In these situations, you'll need to investigate to find the culprit.

7. Third Party Reports

Sometimes, you find out about problems in your workplace from an outsider—such as a customer, a client or vendor, an administrative agency, a lawyer, or even the police. Regardless of how you find out about a problem, your obligations are the same. You must investigate and take action to deal with the situation, if necessary.

However, you might need to adjust your investigation procedures somewhat. For example, you might have an obligation to share what you discover with the police, if they are investigating an alleged crime in your workplace. These issues are covered in more detail in the chapters that follow—for now, simply remember that your obligation to investigate doesn't disappear just because you heard about a problem from an outside source, even if that third party or agency is investigating the situation on its own.

B. Decide Whether to Investigate

Not every workplace problem demands an investigation. To decide whether you should investigate, you'll need to consider several factors, including:

- whether there is a dispute over what happened
- how serious the alleged misconduct is, and
- how similar complaints have been handled in the past.

Scale the Investigation to the Size of the Problem

Sometimes, a problem bears some further looking into but doesn't warrant a full inquisition. While you don't want to ignore a complaint or incident, you should also exercise your common sense about how deep to dig. For example, you should spend more time and resources on a report that one employee has threatened another with a gun than on a report that one employee parked in the other's space in the company lot, unless the facts take you in a different direction.

Although you should generally follow the ten investigation steps in any situation that requires a closer look, that shouldn't take much time in a fairly simple dispute. If the situation turns out to be more complicated, you can slow down and take a more detailed approach.

EXAMPLE: You are investigating the case of the errant parker, above. You decide to investigate, because you don't yet know what the story is. You decide that no immediate actions are necessary, that you (the company owner) will handle the investigation yourself, and that you will start by talking to Marie, the complaining employee. Marie tells you that she doesn't know who's been parking in her spot or why. You go to the parking lot, see that the offending car belongs to Jack, and ask him what's going on. He replies that he was recently assigned a parking space and thought the space was his. He says he will happily move his car to wherever he's supposed to park. The person in charge of facility issues tells you that Jack was assigned space 35, and Marie has space 53. You tell both employees, Jack moves his car, and it's over and done with.

Are you going to interview witnesses who may have seen Jack actually parking his car, ask Jack if he has a learning disability that might cause him to transpose numbers, or review Jack's and Marie's personnel files for signs of previous problems? Of course not. Going into any more detail would be a waste of your time—you've gotten to the bottom of the problem and solved it, and that's that.

Now change the facts a little. What if Marie, during your first interview, said, "I know that's Jack's car in my space. Ever since I told him I wouldn't go out with him, he's been trying to intimidate me. I found a really nasty note on my chair yesterday, and I'm pretty sure he wrote it. One of our coworkers told me that he called me a bitch and said he was going to show me who was boss." This is an entirely different situation. Now, you will have other interviews to consider, you have a document to look at, you will want to spend some time planning how you will question Jack, and you will probably want to review his personnel file.

1. Are the Facts in Dispute?

The first thing to consider is whether there is a disagreement about what really happened. For example, if one employee accuses another of making violent threats and the other employee denies making them, you'll need to investigate to figure out who's telling the truth. On the other hand, if everyone agrees on the basic facts, you can move on to figuring out how to deal with the problem.

Sometimes, employees agree on what was said or done but disagree about what it meant. For example, what seemed like an innocent request for a date to one employee might have seemed like harassment to another. These situations call for a closer look—otherwise, you won't know if the incident was just a miscommunication or is part of a larger pattern of harassment. However, be prepared to adjust the scope of the investigation to fit the facts. If, after completing your interviews of the people involved, you conclude that you're dealing with a simple misunderstanding, that warrants a quicker investigation than if you conclude that the incident is just one example of ongoing misconduct.

2. How Serious Is the Problem?

Sometimes, employees disagree over what happened, but the underlying problem is not serious. Who left the coffeepot on? Who was supposed to show up early to do inventory? In these situations, the simple fact that there's a dispute doesn't mean you have to investigate—just talk to the employees involved and resolve the situation.

3. How Have Similar Problems Been Handled in the Past?

When you are deciding whether an investigation is warranted, think about how your company has handled similar incidents or complaints in the past. If you have generally investigated similar problems, you should consider doing so now. If legal trouble later develops, you want to be able to show that you were fair and consistent with your employees and that you treated their complaints with equal concern.

C. Take Immediate Action, If Necessary

In certain situations, you will need to take some precautionary steps right away, even before the investigation begins. If, for example, an employee complains that her supervisor has fondled her repeatedly, an employee threatens to bring a gun to work, or an employee appears to be stealing company trade secrets to give to a competitor, you don't have the luxury of waiting until your investigation is complete. If the safety of your employees or your company is at risk, you'll have to take some action immediately to prevent further harm.

The actions you take will depend on the situation. In cases of misconduct between two employees (sexual harassment, insubordination, or fighting, for example), an employer might choose to separate the employees until the investigation is finished. By assigning one or both to different shifts, managers, or job responsibilities temporarily, an employer can alleviate the immediate problem and investigate more thoroughly.

 Beware of retaliation.

It is illegal to punish or otherwise take any negative action against an employee who comes forward with a good-faith complaint of harassment, discrimination, illegal conduct, or health and safety violations. The most obvious forms of retaliation are termination, discipline, demotion, pay cuts, or threats of any of these actions. More subtle forms of retaliation may include changing the shift hours or work area of the accuser, changing the accuser's job responsibilities or reporting relationships, and isolating the accuser by leaving her out of meetings and other office functions. Employers can get in trouble here. Although it often makes sense to change the work environment so that the accuser doesn't have to report to or work with the accused, those changes cannot come at the accuser's expense. If one employee must move to a less desirable position temporarily, your best bet is to move the accused employee.

If one employee is accused or suspected of extreme misconduct (such as threatening or harming another employee, sexual assault, or large-scale theft), you'll probably want to suspend that employee, with pay, while you investigate the situation. When you suspend the employee, explain the complaint or behavior at issue and ask to hear the accused employee's side of the story. Assure the employee that you will investigate the incident and reach a decision as quickly as possible.

Avoid Unpaid Suspensions

No matter how egregious the misconduct an employee is accused of committing, it's always a bad idea to suspend employees without pay pending an investigation. From both a practical and legal standpoint, paid suspensions are less risky and less inconvenient for employers—less risky because a paid employee is not as likely to sue as one who isn't being paid, and less inconvenient because you don't have to interrupt your regular payroll system.

In most cases, you cannot suspend salaried employees (those who are not entitled to earn overtime pay) without pay. Even if the employee is entitled to earn overtime pay, however, you can still get in trouble for imposing an unpaid suspension. A suspension without pay signals that you believe the employee is probably guilty—which can cause bad feelings and potential legal problems. If your investigation shows that the employee didn't commit misconduct or that the misconduct was less serious than it appeared, you will probably have to provide retroactive pay anyway—and issue a major apology. It's easier to simply pay the employee for a few days off while you figure out what happened.

D. Choose the Investigator

The person you choose to investigate a problem will depend on various factors, including the size of your company, the identity of the complaining employee and accused employee (if any), and the nature and severity of the problem. Regardless of how these factors play out, however, your investigator must meet a few essential job requirements: experience, impartiality, and professionalism.

Should You Use a Team?

Some companies use a team of two or more investigators to look into workplace problems, rather than relying on one person to handle the job. The benefit of using a team is that you'll have an extra set of eyes, ears, and hands during the investigation. This means, for example, that one investigator can ask questions while the other takes notes, one investigator can gather evidence while the other sets up interviews, the investigators can collaborate when making decisions and recommendations about discipline, and both investigators will be available to testify about the investigation if the employer ends up in court.

However, there are also drawbacks to using a team. For one thing, you'll have two employees pulled away from their usual job responsibilities until the investigation is over, which can be a significant hardship for smaller employers. Some employees may feel intimidated by having to face two questioners, which might make it more difficult to establish rapport during interviews. And there's also the "too many cooks spoil the broth" problem—unless the investigators carefully choreograph who will be responsible for what, there's a danger of duplicated effort and crossed signals.

It's probably best to use a team only for very serious complaints—those that involve many employees, substantial misconduct, and/or a high possibility of legal trouble. You'll reap the greatest benefits (of corroboration and efficiency) in these situations, and they warrant spending a little more time and money to do the job right.

I. Experience

Your investigator should have some experience in investigating complaints, or at least some education and training on the subject. An experienced investigator will know what to look for, how to find it, and how to evaluate what he or she finds—and, therefore, will probably do a better job than someone who hasn't tackled a project like this before.

Experience will also come into play if a complaining party files a lawsuit claiming that the investigation was faulty. If your investigator is inexperienced, a jury is more likely to second-guess his or her decisions, question the quality of the investigation, and, ultimately, disregard the findings altogether.

For larger companies, someone from the human resources department is usually the best bet. HR personnel can get training and educational materials on investigation techniques through professional associations. Often, HR representatives have conducted investigations before and are knowledgeable about employment law.

Smaller companies might not have an experienced investigator on staff. In fact, they often don't have any employees specifically designated as HR representatives. In this case, you can choose a manager who is not involved in the situation to investigate, as long as he or she has experience or training in personnel matters. You can also consider hiring an outside investigator, if the situation warrants the expense.

 Train your investigators ahead of time.

Don't wait until a problem comes up to start training your investigators. You need to be ready to start investigating serious problems as soon as you learn about them. This means that your investigators should be trained and ready to go *before* the trouble starts.

You may also want an investigator with special expertise in certain issues. For example, if the investigation will involve figuring out technical matters (like whether an employee sabotaged a computer program or violated safety rules in a production line) or require advanced knowledge of a particular field (to determine whether an accountant was "cooking the books," for example), you should try to choose an investigator—or make someone available to assist the investigator—who has enough background to understand the details.

2. Impartiality

The person who investigates must be perceived within the workplace—and particularly by the employees involved in the problem—as fair and objective. Someone who supervises, or is supervised by, either the complaining employee or the accused employee should not perform the investigation. Similarly, you shouldn't choose an investigator who has known difficulties with any of the main players.

Who's the Boss?

When you're choosing an investigator, you should consider where the accused employee ranks on the corporate ladder—and pick an investigator whose rank is higher, if possible. That way, you can avoid creating the appearance that the accused employee has any power over the investigator. If your employees (or a jury, if it comes to that) believe that the accused employee can intimidate the investigator or dictate his or her findings, they won't put much stock in the outcome of the investigation.

Once you have come up with a potential investigator, ask the employees involved if they believe that person can be fair and impartial. If they do not, choose someone else. Of course, if you run a small business, you might not have a wide range of potential investigators to choose from. In that case, just make sure that whoever does the job doesn't have an axe to grind with any of the employees involved in the problem.

 Document approval of the investigator.

If the employees involved in the problem agree to the investigator, make a note of it in your file—including the date and time of the conversation. This might be valuable evidence later, if an employee files a lawsuit and argues that the investigator was biased. Some employers also ask the employees to sign a statement verifying that they have no concerns about the investigator's qualifications or impartiality. Although this could also be helpful evidence, it's probably overkill. Your signed statement is evidence of each employee's approval. And an employee who is asked to sign a statement like this may become suspicious that you are more concerned with avoiding a lawsuit than with solving a workplace problem.

Sometimes, the sensitivities of a complaining employee might also influence your choice of investigators. For example, some women might feel more comfortable discussing a sexual harassment complaint with a female investigator. Some larger companies try to make an investigator of each gender available for just this reason.

3. Professionalism

Professionalism is a quality that's sometimes hard to define, but we all know it when we see it. A professional behaves in a businesslike, dependable way, doesn't inject personal feelings or biases into workplace interactions, and remembers that he or she is always representing the company.

A professional demeanor is an essential quality for an investigator for several reasons. First, a good investigator has to keep his or her emotions in check. During any investigation, the investigator will hear or see things—such as x-rated or racist material, threats, or serious misconduct—that are disturbing. The investigator may also bear the brunt of employees' emotions, including anger at being the subject of an investigation, sadness and fear over making a complaint, and so on. In the face of these emotions, a good investigator must remain calm and try to get to the bottom of things.

Second, the investigator must be discreet at all times, to preserve the integrity of the investigation. At some point during an investigation, the investigator will begin to develop some ideas about what really happened—who's lying and who's telling the truth, who committed misconduct and why. Despite these hunches (no matter how well founded they may be), the investigator can't reveal his or her feelings. If the employees involved in the problem believe the investigator has already reached a decision before examining all of the evidence and hearing everyone's statements, they might come to distrust the investigation—and any decisions that are based on it. This can lead to lawsuits challenging the fairness of the investigation. On the other hand, an investigator who conveys that he or she has not reached any decisions and will listen carefully and objectively to everyone's statements builds trust in the investigation and its outcome.

Third, the investigator may have to give testimony about the investigation in the future, to an administrative agency, an employee's lawyer, or even a judge or jury. If this worst-case scenario comes to pass, you'll want your investigator to convey confidence, poise, and objectivity. A professional demeanor will help your investigator convince outsiders that he did the right thing. On the other hand, a jury might have doubts if your investigator is overly nervous, can't answer questions directly, or fails to make eye contact—even if he or she did a bang-up job on the investigation.

4. Hiring an Outside Investigator

In some situations, it makes good sense to ask for professional help to investigate a workplace problem. Many law firms and private consultants will investigate workplace issues for a fee. You might consider bringing in outside help if:

- more than one employee complains about the same serious problem (for example, several women complain that a particular manager is harassing them)

- the accused is a high-ranking official in the business (such as the president or CEO)

- the complaining employee has publicized the complaint in the workplace or in the media

- the complaining employee has hired a lawyer, filed a lawsuit, or filed charges with a government agency, such as the Equal Employment Opportunity Commission, the Occupational Safety and Health Administration, the Wage and Hour Division or a similar state agency

- the accusations are extreme (allegations of rape, assault, threats, or significant theft, for example), or

- for any reason, no one is available to investigate the complaint fairly and objectively.

 Some states require outside investigators to be licensed.

If your state has this type of requirement, make sure that any outside investigator has a current license. Don't just take the investigator's word for it—ask to see and copy the license itself. If your investigator is not properly licensed, you may not be able to rely on the results of the investigation in court.

You can get referrals for professional investigators through management newsletters, trade associations, other business contacts, and even listings in the yellow pages. The American Arbitration Association (AAA), a national provider of dispute resolution services, offers fact-finding services—trained, experienced investigators that are prequalified by the AAA to conduct independent investigations. You can find out more about this service at the AAA's website, www.adr.org. For complaints of discrimination and harassment, your state's Fair

Employment Practices agency may be able to provide referrals. These agencies are listed in Appendix C.

 Your company is responsible for actions you take based on an outside investigator's findings.

Hiring an outside investigator doesn't insulate you from liability for the investigation or the decisions you make based on that investigation (for example, the decision to discipline or fire an employee accused of wrongdoing). In other words, you are ultimately responsible to your employees, even if you hire a professional to do some of the work for you. For this reason, you must work closely with an outside investigator to make sure that he or she receives all relevant information, conducts a thorough and fair investigation, and documents the findings. And although a professional investigator can certainly give you advice about what action to take when the investigation is over, you should always make the final decision.

---

a. Reporting Requirements for Outside Investigators

Until very recently, hiring an outside investigator had a very significant downside (other than the expense): Employers who hired outsiders had to comply with some legal technicalities that had the potential to derail the investigation. Under a law called the Fair Credit Reporting Act, employers who hired an outside investigator had to tell the accused employee that an investigation would be conducted, get the employee's written consent ahead of time, and give a copy of the investigation report to the employee—and wait for a "reasonable period"—before taking any adverse action based on its contents.

These rules were extremely controversial, and were relaxed in 2003. Now, employers who hire an outside investigator are no longer required to warn the accused employee or get the employee's consent. If the employer decides to take action against the employee based on the investigation report, the employer has to give the employee only a summary of the report (which need not identify the employees interviewed). However, the employer must take steps to keep the contents of the report confidential. If you hire an outside investigator, he or she should know about these requirements—and about any steps you will have to follow to make sure that you are in compliance.

b. Hiring a Lawyer to Investigate

There are many good reasons to hire a lawyer to investigate. An experienced employment lawyer will know exactly what to look for—and how to keep your company out of trouble. You can expect your lawyer to know the latest legal developments about investigations and workplace claims, including privacy issues. This specialized knowledge could be a real benefit, especially if your problem is factually or legally complicated.

Another advantage of using a lawyer to investigate is that many (though by no means all) lawyers are experienced in the courtroom. If your investigation is later called into question, your lawyer/investigator should have the presentation skills to come across as a strong witness on your company's behalf.

The fact that your lawyer might have to testify about the investigation illustrates the main drawback to this approach: Your lawyer might have to answer questions about the advice he or she gave you, what you said during the investigation, and other conversations. Usually, when you seek a lawyer's advice about a legal problem, your communications are privileged—which means that no one can force you (or your lawyer) to reveal them. (See "Attorney-Client Privilege," below.) If your lawyer testifies as a witness for your company, however, you will probably lose the protection of this privilege. This means that the lawyer can be asked questions about what you said and did throughout the investigation and about what the lawyer said to you.

Attorney-Client Privilege

Whenever you talk privately to a lawyer about legal matters, that conversation is protected by the attorney-client privilege—which means that no one can force you or the lawyer to reveal what either of you said. The purpose of the privilege is to encourage full disclosure, which allows the lawyer to give a candid assessment of your problem and sound advice about what to do next.

However, you can lose this privilege if you don't honor it. For example, if you tell another person what you said to your lawyer, your conversation with the lawyer is no longer privileged—you waived the privilege by revealing the statement. Similarly, if you put your lawyer on the stand to testify about what a great investigation he or she performed, the lawyer will have to reveal some of your conversations. Once again, you've waived the privilege by allowing these statements to be revealed.

Even if you decide not to use a lawyer to investigate, you can still seek the advice of a lawyer about your investigation.
By doing this, you get the best of both worlds: You'll benefit from the lawyer's expertise, and your conversations will generally be protected by the attorney-client privilege. Of course, you'll also have to pay for the lawyer's time. If you choose to go this route, ask your lawyer—before the investigation begins—how you can make sure that your conversations will stay confidential.

E. Plan the Investigation

Before you start to interview people and sift through documents and other evidence, you should come up with a careful investigation plan that guarantees you won't leave any relevant stones unturned. During your planning, you will review the evidence available to you, then start thinking about what additional evidence might exist that will help you figure out what happened.

1. Start With What You Know

At the outset, you will have some information available—an employee complaint, a report by a manager, or a suspicious situation (an employee who frequently seems to be out of it or money missing from a cash register, for example). Start your planning by figuring out what you already know. What misconduct is suspected or alleged? Your answer to this question will help you figure out what information you will need to decide whether the allegation or suspicion is correct.

Look over any available documents or other evidence related to the misconduct. Review the complaint or report (if applicable), gather and read through any paperwork relevant to the problem (such as personnel files, attendance records, correspondence, or performance reviews), and collect and review any other physical evidence (a weapon, illegal drugs, graphic images, or work materials, for example). Place these documents and items in a locked file cabinet or other safe place.

You should also determine whether any company policies and guidelines might apply to the situation: for example, a sexual harassment policy, workplace violence policy, or noncompetition agreement might be relevant.

Planning for Serious Problems

In some cases, you might have to plan ahead to deal with a major problem. For example, if you suspect an employee of criminal activity (such as embezzlement, rape, or violence), you will have to decide whether to bring in the police. If you are facing issues that could lead to serious legal trouble (like allegations of widespread, egregious harassment or potential workplace violence), this is a good time to get some legal advice. If your workplace problem has been, or might become, publicized in the media, you will need a public relations strategy to handle the situation. If you are facing one of these difficult issues, get some expert advice about how to proceed.

2. Figure Out What You Need to Know

Once you have gotten a sense of the information and evidence already at hand, you can start thinking about what you need to know or find out in order to make a decision about what happened. Whom will you need to interview? What additional evidence might exist? Are there any witnesses or others who might have helpful information?

Then, begin planning the interviews, including:

- **Whom to question.** Make a list of potential interview subjects. In some cases, only the complaining employee and the accused employee should be interviewed—if the complaint is about an incident that no one else witnessed, heard, or was told about later, for example. In other situations, there may be many potential witnesses. If the incident occurred during a staff meeting or company social event, there may be dozens of potential witnesses. In these cases, the investigator should ask both the complaining and the accused employee which workers were most likely to have seen or heard the disputed event.

- **What order to follow.** The complaining employee should be interviewed first, followed generally by the accused employee and the witnesses. This order can be changed to accommodate employees' schedules, in the interests of moving as quickly as possible.

- **What questions to ask.** You need not script every interview question in advance. However, after reviewing Chapter 3, you should take some notes on topics you want to cover in each interview. As you interview each witness, you can review and add to these notes.

Follow the Evidence Wherever It Leads

It's important to plan the investigation ahead of time, but it may be even more important to depart from your plan if new or unexpected information comes up. For example, imagine that an employee complained that her boss had sexually harassed her by repeatedly asking her out on dates. You've planned your investigation to speak to the complaining employee, her boss, and a few witnesses who may have heard or seen the proposals. However, when interviewing the first witness, you learn that the boss has also asked her out on dates. You also learn that the men in this work group routinely tell x-rated jokes, ask their female coworkers about their sex lives, and visit pornographic websites during work hours.

Should you stick to your original plan and just try to get to the bottom of the unwanted date requests? Not if you want to solve what is obviously a significant problem in this work group—and protect yourself from sexual harassment claims. Once you know this additional information, you should revisit your investigation plan. Because the problem is much larger than you thought, you will have to do a more extensive investigation to find out what's going on and who's responsible. ■

CHAPTER

Gathering Information

Once you've decided that an investigation is in order, it's time to get to work. This chapter will explain how to gather the information you need to figure out what happened—and what you should do about it.

Your first priority: Get started right away. Section A explains why delay can derail your investigative efforts and offers some advice for dealing with unavoidable postponements. Section B covers interviews—often your best source of information about workplace problems. Here, you'll find information on how to open and close an interview, sample questions for complaining employees, accused employees, and witnesses, and tips for successful interviewing.

In addition to interviewing, you may also have to do some workplace sleuthing. In some situations, paying a visit to the "scene of the crime"—the place where alleged misconduct occurred—will help you sort out the truth. And in almost every investigation, you'll have to examine documents and other materials, such as inventories, performance evaluations, photographs, or attendance records, to figure out what really happened. Section C explains how to gather evidence of this sort; it includes a checklist of documents that might be relevant to an investigation.

Finally, Section D covers the last stage of information-gathering: follow-up interviews, in which you meet again with the main players to talk about any new information that has surfaced during the investigation.

A. Get Started Right Away

Workplace experts agree that one of the most common—and potentially most costly—investigation mistakes employers make is dragging their feet. Once you become aware of a serious workplace problem that requires an investigation, don't put off the inevitable. Ideally, you should begin investigating within a day or two of receiving the complaint—and complete the investigation within a week or two, depending on how complicated the allegations are. Of course, there will be times when outside circumstances and conflicting schedules lead to unavoidable delays. However, if you dawdle unnecessarily, you will send the message that you don't take the complaint seriously. And if the misconduct continues in the meantime, a court might find you responsible for failing to investigate and take care of the problem right away.

Document unavoidable delays.

If you can't start your investigation right away, write down the reasons why—and include those reasons in the investigation report. (Investigation reports are covered in Chapter 4.) For example, if the accused employee is out tending to a family emergency or the complaining employee is on vacation, make a note of these facts, the date you learned them, and the date the employee will return to work. These notes will help you prove, if necessary, that the company didn't cause the delay.

B. Conducting Interviews

In most investigations, interviews are the main tool employers use to find out what happened. More often than not, employers have to rely solely on statements from the main players and witnesses to get to the truth—and these statements may contradict each other. If the main participants flatly deny each other's claims, you'll have to sort out who is telling the truth.

How can an employer decide whose story is more credible in these "he said, she said" situations? The first step is to conduct interviews designed to elicit as much information as possible. The more information an interviewer can draw out of each witness, the easier it will be to figure out what happened and why. The general interviewing tips that follow will help you elicit the most useful responses—even from the most reluctant or contentious witness. This section also includes specific ideas and questions for interviewing the person who complained (if there is one), the person accused, and witnesses to the wrongdoing.

I. Tips on Conducting Effective Interviews

Conduct the most complete and informative interviews possible by following these tips:

a. Keep an Open Mind

Some employers don't want to believe that misconduct or harassment is taking place right under their noses, and so tend to make light of possible wrongdoing. Other employers jump to the opposite conclusion, assuming that an employee would not complain without good cause.

As an investigator, your job is to avoid making assumptions. No matter how serious the problem or how straightforward the situation appears to be, try not to reach any conclusions until you have gathered and evaluated all the facts. If you start your investigation believing you already know what happened, you will inevitably miss some important details. But if you keep an open mind until your investigation is complete, you will conduct more thorough interviews— and receive more candid answers to your questions.

EXAMPLES

Don't Ask:

Why did you pressure Maria to falsify her time card?

How could you steal from this company?

Ask:

Did you and Maria discuss her time card last week? What did each of you say?

When are your cash register shifts? Do you count the money in your drawer at the start of your shift? Do you count out your drawer at the end of your shift and write that total down for the manager? Your cash register has been short by quite a bit of money several times in the last month. Can you explain why that happened?

b. Ask Open-Ended Questions

Your goal when conducting an interview is to get as much information from your witness as possible. The best way to accomplish this is to ask open-ended questions. If you ask questions that suggest the answer you want to hear or questions that call only for a yes or no answer, you will be the one doing all the talking. Instead, ask the witness to describe what he or she heard, said, or did, and why.

EXAMPLES		
	Don't Ask:	**Ask:**
	Did you arrive at three o'clock?	What time did you arrive?
	Did you hear John tell Ping that she would not be paid for her overtime work unless she agreed to have lunch with him?	Did you hear John and Ping talking last week? Tell me what you heard.

c. Start With the Easy Questions

The employees you interview are likely to be nervous and uncomfortable. Employees suspected of wrongdoing will probably also be defensive, frightened about what may happen, and perhaps willing to lie to save their jobs. If you begin your interview by asking directly about the alleged misconduct, you will aggravate an already tense situation—and probably limit the flow of information. Someone who feels accused or put on the spot is more likely to clam up. Also, if you cut to the chase too soon, you'll miss your chance to find out important details *before* the employee knows why you're asking questions (and, therefore, has an opportunity to tailor the answers accordingly).

The better course of action is to start with basic background questions about the employee's job, coworkers, daily schedule, and so on. You'll have to get to the tough questions eventually, but starting with a few softballs will put the employee at ease and allow you to get a sense of the employee's demeanor. It will also give you the opportunity to ask about seemingly unimportant details that could prove very significant to your investigation.

E X A M P L E S

Don't Start With:

You were seen leaving the workplace very late last Friday, with a bulky package under your coat. On Monday morning, the IT department found that several new modems and some other computer equipment were missing. Did you take these things?

Phyllis says that you refused to promote her to be a floor manager, and that you have never promoted an African-American employee to any management position. Did you refuse to promote her because of her race?

Start With:

Tell me about your usual schedule: What time do you arrive in the morning? What time do you leave at night? Are you often one of the last ones here? Is your schedule fairly regular, or does it vary? What was your schedule like last week? Do you drive to work or take public transportation? Where do you park? Do you usually come in through the main front entrance or use one of the back doors? Which exit do you use when you leave at night?

How long have you worked here? What are your job responsibilities in your current position? Do they include promoting people? To what positions? About how many people have you promoted since you began working here? Tell me what you take into consideration when you're deciding whether to promote someone. Do interested employees have to fill out an application? Do you interview the applicants? Do you look at any documents—work samples, performance evaluations, personnel files? Is there anything else you consider? How do you decide whom to promote?

Dig a little deeper if an employee's reaction seems odd.

If an employee seems much more upset (or much less so) than you would expect, keep asking questions. Although all of us react differently to unpleasant experiences, a response that strikes you as inappropriate could indicate that there's more to the situation than meets the eye.

d. Keep Your Opinions to Yourself

As your investigation progresses, you will inevitably start to develop some opinions about what really happened. You should not share these opinions with your witnesses, however. If you suggest, through your statements or through the tone of your questions, that you have already reached a decision, witnesses will be less likely to speak freely with you. Some witnesses might be afraid of contradicting your version of events; others might feel there is no point in explaining what really happened if you have already made up your mind. In the worst-case scenario, a witness might believe you are conducting an unfair or biased investigation—and challenge the outcome in court. Avoid these problems by keeping your conclusions to yourself until the investigation is complete.

EXAMPLES

Don't Ask:	Ask:
I have already heard from several people that Sameh was absent from last week's mandatory meeting. Is that what you remember?	Did you see Sameh at last week's mandatory meeting?
Can you confirm that Darrell punched Jeff on the loading dock?	Did you work near the loading dock yesterday? Did you see anything unusual? Tell me what happened. (If the witness says she didn't see anything unusual, you might ask, "Did you see an incident between Darrell and Jeff?")

e. Focus on the Facts

On the television series *Dragnet*, Joe Friday had a simple interviewing technique: He asked his subjects to tell him "just the facts." If only it were that easy in real life. Many people have a difficult time distinguishing objective fact from subjective opinion when describing what they have seen and heard. Some witnesses might describe another person's motivations or thoughts, relate rumors as if they were known facts, or exaggerate what they saw or heard. Your job is to separate the wheat from the chaff—that is, to isolate fact from opinion—then find out the basis for the witness's story. By convincing your witnesses to focus on the facts, you can prevent speculation and rumor from affecting your decisions.

EXAMPLES

If You Hear:

Lawrence has been out to get Graciela since the day he started working here. But I'm not surprised; he doesn't like reporting to a woman.

Everyone knew that Evelyn was going to lose her temper and get violent. It was just a matter of time.

You Might Ask:

What have you seen or heard that leads you to believe Lawrence is out to get Graciela? Have you heard him say anything about her? Have you heard Lawrence say anything about reporting to a woman or make any disparaging comments about women in general?

What do you mean by get violent? Have you seen or heard Evelyn do anything that seemed violent or angry? Why did you believe Evelyn was going to lose her temper? What did she say or do to make you think she was on edge? When you say everyone knew, do you mean that you discussed this with others? Whom did you talk to about it, and what did they say?

f. Find Out About Other Witnesses or Evidence

Always look for leads. Ask every person you interview whether they know of other witnesses or physical evidence relating to the incident. If the witness is the accused or complaining employee, ask whether anyone else saw or heard the incidents in question. Ask whether they told anyone about the incident when it happened. Find out if they took any notes about the problem or if any workplace documents—emails, memoranda, or evaluations, for example—relate to the incident.

If You Hear:	You Might Ask:
Robert and I had a loud argument by the elevators. He told me I wouldn't get my raise unless I agreed to withdraw my complaint that he had harassed me. Afterwards, I was so upset that I ran back to my office in tears.	Was anyone else near the elevator when the argument took place? Did anyone hear what Robert said to you? Did you see anyone on your way back to your office? Did you talk to anyone about what happened?
Julie sent me an email apologizing for giving me a bad review. She said her manager made her change my performance appraisal after I filed a workers' compensation claim.	Do you have a copy of Julie's email to you? Did she copy anyone on the email? Did you see the performance appraisal before it was changed? Do you have a copy?

EXAMPLES

g. Ask About Contradictions

Sometimes, one witness contradicts what another has said. The accused and complaining employees are perhaps most likely to contradict each other, but even uninvolved witnesses might give conflicting stories. The best way to get to the bottom of these inconsistencies is to ask about them directly. Once you get down to specifics, you may find that everyone agrees on what happened, but not on whether it was appropriate.

If the witnesses continue to contradict each other even after you have pointed out the conflicts in their stories—if the accused flatly denies the complaining employee's statements, for example—ask each witness why the other might disagree.

EXAMPLES

If You Hear:

I never sexually harassed anyone. I treat the women who work for me with respect.

You Might Ask:

A complaint was made that you touched Tanya's waist and hips several times while she was distributing paperwork to clients, and that you made jokes about her spending the night at her boyfriend's house. Did this happen? Have you ever touched Tanya? Did you say anything that someone might have interpreted in this way? Can you think of any reason why someone might have reported this if it weren't true?

Darnell told us at last week's morning meeting that anyone who complained about safety problems in the warehouse would get in trouble. He basically threatened to fire anyone who reported an accident.

Other people in your work group described that conversation differently. They said that Darnell told all of you he had reported two safety violations to his manager. They said he encouraged you to bring any safety concerns to him, and he would bring them to the company's attention. Did this happen? Did you have a different conversation with Darnell? Why do you think others remember the conversation differently?

h. Keep It Confidential

Complaints can polarize a workplace. Workers will likely side with either the complaining employee or the accused employee, and the rumor mill will start working overtime. Worse, if too many details about the complaint get out, you may be accused of damaging the reputation of the alleged victim or alleged wrongdoer.

Find a Private Interview Room

Interview employees in a private space—one where you won't be seen or overheard by others in the workplace, and where others won't be able to see who comes to be interviewed. For example, a conference room with interior windows, a table in the company break room, or an office that's located in a central place would be a bad choice.

In some particularly volatile situations (for example, if violence is a possibility or employees have been threatened for coming forward), employees may be hesitant to talk to you anywhere in the workplace. In these scenarios, consider meeting an employee offsite, after work hours.

You can minimize these problems by insisting on confidentiality and practicing it in your investigation. Tell each witness only those facts necessary to conduct a thorough interview. For example, accused employees deserve to hear the allegations against them, but peripheral witnesses don't need to know every detail. Caution each witness that the investigation is confidential and should not be discussed with coworkers or friends. Warn everyone you interview that revealing anything about the investigation is against company policy—and can result in discipline. And set a good example by being discreet. Don't discuss the investigation at staff meetings or in the lunchroom, keep your investigation materials in a locked cabinet when you aren't working on them, and avoid gossip at all costs.

E X A M P L E S

Don't Ask:

Sylvia says that Roger asked her out several times and tried to bring her back to his room after the holiday party. She also says that Roger made a lot of X-rated jokes in front of clients, and that you might have heard some of these jokes during the meeting with Pets-Nation. Did you hear any of these jokes?

Fernando has complained that Martin gave him a bad performance evaluation, and he thinks it's because Martin dislikes Latinos. Fernando believes that he has made more successful cold calls than anyone else on his shift. He thought you might be able to confirm this, since you compile the monthly productivity reports. Is this true?

Ask:

Did you attend the pitch meeting with Pets-Nation? Who else was there? Do you remember anyone telling any jokes during this meeting? Tell me what was said.

Do you compile monthly productivity reports? Do these reports contain the cold call success rate for each sales-person? Do you recall who had the highest success rate for the afternoon shift? May I see a copy of these reports for the last year?

i.   Don't Retaliate

It is against the law to punish someone for making a complaint of harassment, discrimination, illegal conduct, or unsafe working conditions. And it is against your best interests to punish any employee who comes forward with an honest complaint, regardless of the subject matter. You want to encourage your employees to bring problems to your attention, so you can resolve disputes before they start draining productivity or stirring up legal trouble. Employees will only come forward if they feel protected from retaliation—and witnesses will only tell you the truth if they know you will not kill the messenger who bears bad news. Assure every person you interview that you want to hear their side of the story and that they will not be retaliated against for coming forward.

<table>
<tr><td>If You Hear:</td><td>You Might Ask:</td></tr>
<tr><td>I'm having some problems working with Maurice, but I don't want to cause trouble.</td><td>I'm glad you brought this issue to my attention. We would really be in trouble if you kept this information to yourself, and your team's work suffered as a result. No one in the company will take any action against you for coming forward. Now, what has been happening with Maurice?</td></tr>
<tr><td>I've seen some pretty heated conversations between Maria and Simone, but it's really none of my business. I don't want Simone to think that I'm not a team player.</td><td>I need to find out what's been going on between Maria and Simone, and anything you can tell me about those conversations will help me get to the bottom of this. If there are problems in your work group, everyone's work suffers and everyone feels uncomfortable. No one will be allowed to retaliate against you for speaking to me. Both Maria and Simone have been told that these issues would be investigated, and they both understand that they cannot retaliate against anyone involved in the investigation. What have your heard Maria and Simone say to each other?</td></tr>
</table>

E X A M P L E S

j. Ask Interviewees to Contact You With New or Additional Information

People sometimes freeze up when they're put on the spot. It's very likely that a witness might remember some significant detail—or learn new information—after the interview is over. To make sure you stay in the loop, close every interview by thanking the witness and asking him or her to contact you if anything else comes to mind.

Some witnesses might intentionally hold back important information during the interview, while trying to decide whether to come clean. If you offer every witness an opportunity to continue the conversation, you are more likely to get the full story. And should your investigation be challenged in court, you will be able to prove that you made every effort to gather all the facts.

EXAMPLE

Don't Say:	Say:
Have you told me everything you remember about these incidents? Because you won't be able to change your statement once I start talking to other witnesses.	Please remember that my door is always open, if you remember anything later or there is something you need to add to your statement. Also, if you learn of any new information that relates to the complaint, please bring it to my attention right away.

k. Write It All Down

Take notes during every interview. Include the date, time, and place of each interview, the name of the witness, and whether anyone else was present. Don't just record the witnesses' conclusions; include all the important facts that the witness relates or denies. Before the interview is over, go back through your notes with the witness to make sure you got it right. These notes will help you remember what each witness said later, when you are making your decision. They will also help you defend yourself in court if the investigation is challenged as biased or incomplete.

Start your notes from each interview on a clean piece of paper. That way, you won't have to worry about the witness seeing your notes from other interviews.

Some investigators ask witnesses to sign and date a written statement of what was said during the interview.

These statements are great evidence of what a witness told you at the time. A witness who later claims to have said something different will have to explain why he or she signed the statement. However, some witnesses are intimidated at the thought of writing up an official statement. If you decide to use a written statement, write the first draft yourself. That way, you can make sure to include all of the important facts the witness told you. Give the draft to the witness and encourage changes, additions, or deletions. (Of course, if the witness makes a change that contradicts an earlier statement to you, you should ask about it.)

EXAMPLE

Don't Write:

I spoke to Joan today. She said that Richard has been acting strange lately but hasn't really seen any fights between him and Sam. She thinks Richard might act out violently sometime soon.

Write:

I interviewed Joan Suzuki today, June 14, 200X, regarding Sam Levine's complaint (see Complaint Form in file). We met in my office at 3 p.m. I asked Joan whether she had seen any incidents between Richard Hart and Sam in the last two weeks. Joan said that she thought Richard has been acting very strange lately When I asked her to explain, she said that Richard seemed distracted and angry, and that he had been complaining to others in the work group about his ex-wife's petition for an increase in child support. Richard told her that Sam had denied his request for a raise, and that Sam was responsible for all of his problems. Joan also said that Richard had made several jokes during shift meetings about about "going postal," and that he told Sam, "You will be the first to go." This is the only incident she has seen between Sam and Richard. Joan said that she was frightened by Richard's change in behavior.

E X A M P L E (con't)

Don't Write: **Write:**

Joan confirmed that Jose, Jocelyn, and LeShawn were at the meetings where Richard made these jokes. I thanked her for her information and encouraged her to come forward with any additional information immedi-ately. I asked her to treat the investigation confidentially. I assured her that Ri chard has been suspended pending the outcome of the investigation, and that the company would act swiftly to deal with the situation as soon as the investigation was complete.

Speak Into the Microphone

You might think it would be easier to dispense with all the written statements and note-taking and just tape your interview sessions, on video or audio. Taping does offer accuracy, but it tends to make things complicated. For one thing, you'll need to know how to operate the equipment (or have someone at the interview who does, which could raise confidentiality concerns). And you'll have to contend with employee anxiety—most employees will be less comfortable (and more nervous) having their interview taped. This means that you'll have to work overtime to build rapport and trust. Finally, when it comes time to use the tape to remember what was said (for example, when you write your report or have to defend your investigation in court), you'll have to fast forward and rewind your way through the conversation until you find the exact statement you need.

For these reasons, most investigators prefer to simply take notes. But this doesn't mean that you should prohibit the employee from taping the interview, at the employee's request. If you refuse to allow an employee to tape, you open the door to later claims that your notes are incomplete or false—and you will start to look a bit shady. ("The investigator didn't write down everything I said—I asked if I could tape the interview, but she wouldn't let me.") If an employee asks to record an interview session, give the OK—but only on the condition that you receive a copy of the tape right away.

Whatever you do, don't tape employees' statements without their knowledge and written consent. In some states (notably California), it is illegal to record a conversation unless both parties consent. Secret taping can lead to an invasion of privacy lawsuit—or even criminal prosecution.

2. Interviewing the Complaining Employee

If the investigation is triggered by a complaint, then you should start by interviewing the complaining employee. Your goals are to put the employee at ease, explain the process, and find out, in as much detail as possible, exactly what happened.

 Handle a distressed complaining employee with care.

If the complaining employee is really upset, you may have to alter your usual interviewing procedures to avoid exacerbating the problem. For example, if the employee wants to take some time off work, you might have to postpone your interview for a few days. Or, you might allow the employee to bring a friend or family member to the interview for moral support. If you do make an accommodation like this, document it in the investigation file—especially if it requires you to delay the investigation.

---

a. Where to Start When No One Complains

In some situations, wrongdoing is clearly taking place, yet no employee has complained. Perhaps the real victim is the company, not any particular employee (as is often the case when employees steal). Or maybe someone has made an anonymous complaint. Who should you interview first when no employee has come forward?

One possibility is to start with someone who has general or background knowledge of the problem. For example, if racist graffiti suddenly started appearing on the walls of a particular work area, you could start by interviewing the manager in charge of those employees to find out who usually works there, what schedules they work, whether there seem to be any racial tensions among the workers, and so on. If money is missing from the cash register, you might start by asking the bookkeeper when and how the problem became apparent and who has access to the cash. Of course, if you don't know who's responsible for the misconduct, the person you interview for background information may turn out to be the perpetrator—and you should keep this in mind when you ask your questions.

Another option is to start by interviewing the suspected wrongdoer, if there is one. For example, if money is missing from a cash register during a particular employee's shift, you could start by interviewing that employee. Or, if a worker is suspected of coming to work drunk or on drugs, you could start by interviewing that person directly.

b. Getting Started

Begin the interview by letting the employee know how the process will work and what to expect. Here are some points you should make at the start of the interview:

- Explain that you will be investigating the employee's complaint by interviewing witnesses and gathering evidence.

- State that you expect the employee to give you complete and accurate information and to answer all of your questions truthfully.

- Explain that, if the investigation reveals misconduct, the company will take appropriate steps to deal with the situation.

- Assure the employee that you will maintain confidentiality to the extent possible, but that it will be necessary to reveal some details of the complaint in order to find out what happened. Make sure the employee knows that you expect him or her to keep the complaint confidential, as well.

- Explain what retaliation is and that the company prohibits it. Ask the employee to come to you immediately with any retaliation concerns.

- Ask whether the employee has any questions or concerns about the process.

Don't compromise your impartiality.

While you want to make sure that the complaining employee feels comfortable and safe coming forward, don't sympathize so strongly that you lose your neutrality. Remember, you haven't decided what happened yet—the complaining employee may be a brave voice crying in the wilderness or may be the boy who cried wolf. Avoid statements implying that you believe the employee is telling the truth—like "What happened to you must have been awful" or "I'm so sorry for what you've been through."

Some investigators begin by thanking the complaining employee for coming forward. While this is an encouraging gesture that can get the interview off on the right foot (and convince the employee to answer your questions fully), it can also improperly signal that you believe the employee's story. If you choose to give thanks, say something like "Thank you for coming forward with this information. We plan to look into it right away."

 Follow up on employee concerns.

If an employee seems overly worried about confidentiality or other employees finding out who complained, find out why. Sometimes, these concerns indicate legitimate fears about retaliation. Ask whether anyone has said the employee shouldn't come forward or threatened to take some retaliatory action. If the employee claims to have been threatened or otherwise warned against complaining, add that to your list of things to be investigated, ask the employee to tell you immediately of any further threats, and monitor the workplace carefully for any sign of retaliation.

c. Sample Questions

Once your introductory statements are out of the way, you'll start your questioning. Of course, the questions you ask will depend on the nature of the complaint. No matter what the complaint is about, however, you'll want to cover the basics: who, what, where, when, how, and (sometimes) why.

Here are some sample questions to consider:

- What happened? If the complaint involves several incidents or a pattern of misconduct over a period of time, start with the most recent problem and work backwards.
- Who was involved? What did that person say or do?
- What was your response or reaction, if any?
- When and where did the incident(s) take place?
- Why did you decide to come forward now (if the incident took place quite a while before the complaint)?
- Did anyone witness the incident(s)?
- Did you tell anyone about the incident(s)?
- Do you know of anyone who might have information about these incidents?
- Have you been affected by the incident(s)? How?
- Do you know of any similar incidents involving other people?
- Do you know of any evidence—documents or otherwise—relating to your complaint?
- How would you like to see this problem resolved?

When Emotions Run High

Employees often find it extremely difficult to come forward with a complaint, especially a complaint about discrimination or harassment. Many employees complain only as a last resort, after trying informally to stop the misconduct. An employee who complains may be wrestling with difficult feelings of embarrassment, anger, sadness, fear—and reluctance to come forward.

When an employee finally does decide to complain, these emotions may spill out during the interview. The worker may cry, become angry, or even try to "take back" the complaint. Your best response is to listen and be understanding. Assure the employee that you know this is difficult and emotional, and that you want to get to the bottom of things. If the complaining worker tries to rescind the complaint, explain that you will have to investigate anyway, and you would like the worker's cooperation. If the employee is afraid of the accused employee, think about what immediate steps you can take to calm these fears, such as separating the workers.

However, don't try so hard to sympathize that you lose your objectivity in the investigation. Remember, your job is to remain impartial, uncover all of the facts, and then make a reasoned, objective decision.

Once you have finished your questions, go back through your notes with the employee to make sure you got everything down correctly. Double check dates, names, and times. If you plan to ask the employee to sign a statement, prepare that document now—you can let the employee take a break while you pull it together.

Conclude the interview by giving the employee some idea what to expect. Tell the employee that you plan to interview the accused worker and any other witnesses, review any additional evidence, and complete the investigation as soon as possible. Ask the employee not to tell anyone about the investigation or talk about the complaint with coworkers. Finally, ask to be contacted with any new or additional information about the complaint.

3. Interviewing the Accused Employee

Imagine what it's like to be accused of wrongdoing in the workplace. If you actually committed misconduct, you probably wouldn't be eager to admit it; if you were wrongly accused, you would likely be upset, even angry. Keep this in mind when interviewing the accused (or suspected) employee. As the investigator, you'll have to assure the employee that you'll make a fair decision while also trying to uncover the truth.

a. Getting Started

As in your interview with the complaining employee, you should start by explaining the process. Here are some topics you should cover at the outset:

- Let the employee know that a complaint has been made (or a problem has come to your attention) and that you will be investigating the situation.

- Assure the accused employee that you have not yet reached any conclusions and that you will listen carefully to everyone involved before taking any action.

- Explain that you expect the employee to give you complete, accurate information and to answer all of your questions truthfully.

- Explain that you will keep the investigation as confidential as possible and that the employee should not talk to coworkers about the investigation or the complaint.

- Tell the employee that retaliation is forbidden, and explain what retaliation is.

- Ask if the employee has any questions or concerns about the investigation.

The Accused Can Bring a Coworker Representative

Since 1975, union members have had the right to bring a union representative to any investigative interview that could result in disciplinary action against the employee. A few years ago, the National Labor Relations Board (NLRB), the federal government agency that oversees issues of union-management relations, held that nonunionized employees also have the right to a representative. The federal Court of Appeals for the District of Columbia upheld this portion of the Board's decision. *Epilepsy Foundation of Northeast Ohio*, 331 NLRB 676 (July 10, 2000), affirmed in part, 268 F.3d 1095 (D.C. Cir. 2001), *cert. denied*, 536 U.S. 904 (2002).

This decision means that any employee can insist, as a condition of participating in an interview, on bringing a representative along. This right applies only to those investigative interviews that the employee reasonably believes will result in disciplinary action — a definition that likely includes any investigation of serious workplace misconduct. Although the employer has no obligation to inform the employee of this right, the employer must allow a representative, if requested by the accused employee, or forgo the interview altogether. In most cases, it will make sense to include the representative in the interview. The representative can help the accused employee remember important facts, ask crucial questions, and present his or her side of the story. Also, the accused employee is more likely to feel fairly treated if you allow a representative. If the representative obstructs the interview or otherwise disrupts the process, you can insist on hearing only from the accused employee.

b. Sample Questions

The questions you ask the accused will, of course, depend on the nature of the complaint and the employee's responses. Remember to begin with the easy questions and background details, then work your way up to the harder issues. Here are some sample questions to consider:

- What is your typical workday like? What time do you arrive, what time do you leave, what are your responsibilities?

- Do you supervise any employees? What are their names and positions?

- What is your response to the complaint or allegations?

- (If the accused employee says the allegations are false) Could someone else have misunderstood your actions or statements? Have you had problems working with anyone? Do you think someone might have made up these incidents? Why?

- (If the accused employee does not completely deny the allegations) What happened? When and where?

- Did anyone witness the incident(s)?

- Did you tell anyone about the incident(s)?

- Do you know of anyone who might have information about these incidents?

- Do you know of any documents or other evidence relating to this situation?

 Silence is golden.

If you're having trouble digging information out of an accused employee, take a page from therapists and counselors—trained experts at getting others to talk about uncomfortable things—and try a little silence. If an employee is giving you short answers and holding back information, let the silence deepen. Instead of immediately asking another question, wait a bit. Look at the employee expectantly. (Those who really want to get into character might even try a "Hmmm" or "I see"). You'll be surprised at how often this prompts employees to add something to a previous answer or try a bit harder to explain their side of the story.

When you're through with your questions, review your notes with the employee to make sure that you didn't miss anything—and that you got everything down correctly. Double check dates, names, and times. If you plan to ask the employee to sign a statement, prepare that document now—you can let the employee take a break while you pull it together.

Again, close the interview by telling the accused employee what will happen next. Explain that you will interview witnesses and review other evidence before reaching a final conclusion. Stress again that retaliation is strictly prohibited. And ask the employee to bring any new or additional information to your attention at once.

4. Interviewing Witnesses

There are many kinds of witnesses; some have seen or heard, firsthand, the misconduct at issue, while others have only heard rumors. Some will be privy to an entire dispute, while others have only a bit of information to share. And some may have an axe to grind (or favor to curry) with either the complaining or the accused employee.

When you interview witnesses, your goal is to find out what they know without revealing any information unnecessarily. While the accused employee has the right to know what allegations have been made, third-party witnesses have no such right—and you have good reasons to maintain confidentiality. If the allegations turn out to be false, you could get into legal trouble for publicizing them unnecessarily. Even if no lawsuit is in the offing, you can cut down on gossip and rumor in the workplace by keeping a tight lid on the investigation.

a. Getting Started

Once again, begin with an opening statement. Here are some topics to include:

- Explain that you are investigating a workplace problem and that you believe the witness might have information that will help you figure out what happened.

- Let the witness know that you have not come to any conclusions about what happened.

- Explain that you expect the witness to give you complete and accurate information and to answer all of your questions truthfully.

- Tell the employee not to talk to anyone at work about the investigation.

- Tell the witness that retaliation is strictly prohibited (and explain what retaliation is). Ask the witness to come to you with any concerns about retaliation for participating in the investigation.

- Ask whether the employee has any questions or concerns about the investigation. (You may find yourself having to explain that you cannot answer some of these questions, particularly if the witness asks who complained or who else is being interviewed.)

b. Sample Questions

When deciding what to ask a witness, think about who suggested the witness and why. Did the complaining employee tell you that the witness saw the misconduct? Did the accused employee tell you that he or she confided in the witness after an incident? Sticking to the facts the witness is supposed to know will help you keep things confidential.

Here are some questions to consider for third-party witnesses:

- Do you work with [the complaining employee or accused employee]?
- If the person may have witnessed the incident, ask what the witness saw or heard. For example, "Were you in the lunch room last Friday? What time? Who else was there? Did you hear Mark and Sarah talking to each other? What did each of them say?"
- When and where did this take place?
- Did you tell anyone about the incident?
- Did [the complaining employee] tell you anything about the incident?
- Did [the accused employee] tell you anything about the incident?
- Have you personally witnessed any other incidents between [the complaining employee] and [the accused employee]?
- Have you heard these issues discussed in the workplace? When, where, and by whom?
- Have you ever had any problems working with [the complaining employee]? [the accused employee]?

As with all interviews, review your notes with the witness when you are through with your questions. Make sure you wrote everything down correctly and that your notes include all of the important details. If you plan to ask the employee to sign a statement, prepare that document now.

When your questions have been answered, thank the witness for participating. Stress that the interview and the investigation must remain confidential; tell the witness not to discuss either with coworkers. And ask the witness to return to you with any further information.

Interviewing Nonemployees

In some situations, you might want to interview someone who doesn't work for the company: a customer who overheard racist comments, a bystander who saw some employees fighting on the street, or a friend or partner in whom an employee confided. Handle these interviews with special care. Talking to someone outside the company can lead to legal and practical problems. From a legal standpoint, an accused employee is more likely to take offense—and possibly contemplate a defamation lawsuit—if people outside the company learn of the allegations. On the practical side, unless the witness is willing to sign a confidentiality agreement, the company has no way to enforce its confidentiality rules against outsiders, which means your dirty laundry might get aired in public.

You may have to run these risks if the witness is crucial to the investigation. For example, if a customer is the only witness to an employee theft or a sexual harassment incident, you need to find out what that person saw. If you find yourself in this situation, stay on your best behavior. Remember, you will be representing the company to the outside world, and you'll want to make it look good. And the witness is under no obligation to talk to you—you're really asking this person to help you out, and you should make that clear from the start.

When interviewing an outside witness, confidentiality is especially important. Conduct the interview offsite, at a place that's convenient for the witness. Don't reveal anything unnecessarily—including the names of the employees involved or what you suspect might have happened. And be sure to thank the witness for helping you get to the bottom of things.

C. Gathering Other Evidence

In some cases, there will be no evidence of wrongdoing other than witness statements. Much workplace misconduct is interpersonal—conducted face to face, rather than in writing. If the alleged misconduct consists of verbal or physical harassment, threats, or violence, there may be no document or other tangible piece of evidence related to the incident.

Sometimes, however, documents and other physical evidence play an important role in the investigation. If one employee accuses the other of sending threatening emails, for example, you'll want to get your hands on those messages. Or if an employee is accused of bringing a weapon to work or drinking on the job, you'll want to look for the "smoking gun" (or the empty bottle).

And in some cases, you might want to play Perry Mason and pay a visit to the scene of the alleged misconduct. This could give you important clues about who's telling the truth—and good ideas of questions to ask and witnesses to interview.

1. Documents

In every investigation, stop and ask yourself, "What documents could help me figure out what happened?" Think about the types of records your company keeps—in personnel files, attendance reports, inventories, computer records, and so on.

In some investigations, documents play a starring role. For example, if an employee claims that her coworkers sexually harassed her by sending X-rated messages and images over the office email system, those messages might be the most important evidence you can gather.

More often, however, documents play a supporting role, by providing important background information. For example, if an employee complains that a supervisor has discriminated against him, you might review the employee's personnel file to see how the supervisor has documented their exchanges. Or, if an employee is accused of stealing company equipment, inventory records can help you figure out exactly when the goods disappeared.

Documents might also help you pin down crucial details. For example, attendance records can corroborate (or contradict) an employee who claims to have been out of the office on a particular day. Or, if an employee accuses a supervisor of changing her performance review after she complained of harassment, you can use documents to find out when the complaint was made, when the performance review was drafted, and whether the review was changed at any time.

Look for documents that are not in official personnel files.

Many supervisors make a habit of keeping their own working files on the employees who report to them. These files often contain documents that never find their way to the employees' official personnel files. For example, a supervisor will probably give an employee's final performance review to the Human Resources department, to place in the employee's personnel file. However, the supervisor might keep old drafts of the review, the employee's comments on the review, and informal notes on the employee's performance in a working file. To make sure that you get your hands on every important document, ask supervisors for all documents they have on the employees involved in the incident, whether or not those documents appear in the employee's personnel file.

Here is a checklist of documents that may figure into your investigation. Of course, not every workplace will use all of these types of documents—and not every document on the list will be relevant to a given investigation. But this list will give you a starting point when you start considering which documents might be helpful:

- ❏ Company policies
- ❏ Email messages
- ❏ Postings to company bulletin boards
  (electronic or corkboard)
- ❏ Correspondence
- ❏ Performance evaluations
- ❏ Work samples
- ❏ Written warnings and other disciplinary records
- ❏ Customer complaints or comments
- ❏ Commendations
- ❏ Documents signed by the employees involved
  (such as hiring agreements, employment contracts, and other agreements)
- ❏ Attendance records
  (for work generally, required meetings, or training sessions, for example)

- ❒ Payroll records
- ❒ Time cards or other records showing hours worked
- ❒ Work schedules
- ❒ Inventory records
- ❒ Expense reports
- ❒ Computer records
  (of Internet sites visited, productivity, and so on)
- ❒ Cash register receipts
- ❒ Purchase orders
- ❒ Productivity reports
  (such as records of sales completed, deadlines met, or projects finished)
- ❒ Sales receipts
- ❒ Equipment logs
- ❒ Notes taken by an employee involved
  (for example, if an employee made a record of threatening or harassing comments by another employee, or kept a diary or journal of workplace incidents)
- ❒ Files from any previous investigations of the same employees or same types of incidents

---

 Keep careful track of your documents.

If you decide a document is relevant to your investigation, take good care of it. Make a record of where you found it and store it in a secure location. If you plan to use the document in your interviews (for example, to show to the accused employee), don't bring the original—make a copy. That way, you won't have to worry about writing on the document or losing it. If you later face a lawsuit relating to the investigation, you will want to be able to prove where important documents came from and, more important, that they have not been altered.

EXAMPLE: Sanjiv is accused of sexually harassing a coworker, Linda. During your investigation, Linda gives you several handwritten notes that Sanjiv gave to her. These notes include sexually explicit comments and threats to harm Linda if she doesn't agree to have a relationship with him. As a result of your investigation, Sanjiv is fired.

Sanjiv sues the company for wrongful termination, claiming that he never harassed Linda and that the company really fired him for complaining about health and safety violations. He claims that the investigation was biased and that the notes were doctored to give the company a reason to fire him. He agrees that he wrote part of the notes but claims that the offensive language and threats were added by someone else. You should be able to defeat these arguments if you can show that you recorded the date you received them, noted that Linda gave them to you, placed them in a secure location, and did not remove them from that location until you were asked to hand them over in the lawsuit.

2. Other Evidence

Misconduct doesn't always leave a paper trail. Sometimes, the path is cluttered with bulkier objects, such as discarded plastic baggies, a knife hidden in a desk drawer, or company data stored on a CD-ROM. In the most extreme cases, you might need to test this evidence to determine its relevance. For example, you may need to check for fingerprints or test for the presence of illegal drugs.

Always consider the range of possible evidence that might exist. If you find evidence like this, store and label it carefully. Indicate when and where you found the evidence, then place it in a secure location. This could prove important later, if you must prove that the evidence has not been tampered with.

 Give contraband to the authorities.

If you come across illegal evidence, such as controlled substances or an unregistered or illegal weapon, report it to the police and contact a lawyer. If you hang on to items that are illegal to possess, you could find yourself facing criminal liability.

---

3. Clues From the Scene

It's often a good idea to visit the place where the alleged misconduct took place. This will give you a better understanding of what the witnesses are describing and give you ideas for additional witnesses or follow-up interview questions. It might even convince you that someone is—or is not—telling the truth.

For example, imagine that an employee has complained that another employee raised his voice to her and threatened to harm her one morning in the hallway outside her office. You go to the hallway at about the time when the incident allegedly happened. You notice that the employee's office is next door to a kitchenette, which employees are allowed to use. During the five minutes you spend there, you see 20 different employees come to get coffee, put their lunches in the refrigerator, or just talk to their coworkers. These are all potential witnesses to the incident—and you should ask the complaining employee if she noticed any of them nearby when she was threatened. If nobody heard the threats, despite all of this traffic, the complaining employee's story starts to sound a bit far-fetched.

On the other hand, imagine that you went to the hallway and noticed that the complaining employee's office was next door not to a kitchenette, but to an equipment room full of noisy machinery. You don't see anyone else while you're investigating. In this situation, it wouldn't hurt the complaining employee's credibility a bit if there were no witnesses to the threats.

D. Follow-Up Interviews

Once you complete your interviews and review any other available evidence, consider setting up another interview with the accused employee—especially if you have heard new allegations or information since you last interviewed the accused worker. If witnesses have added significant details or documents supporting the complaining employee have surfaced, it is probably a good idea to get the accused employee's response to these additional facts. Courts are more likely to find an investigation was fair and thorough—and its outcome reliable—if the accused employee is given the opportunity to respond to all the evidence before the employer makes a final decision.

You should also consider another interview with the complaining employee. If the accused employee or witnesses have denied the complaining employee's allegations or offered reasons why the complaining employee might not be telling the truth, you should let the complaining employee respond. ∎

CHAPTER

Make and Document Your Decision

Now you're facing the hardest part of your job as investigator: figuring out what to do. You have interviewed all the witnesses. You have gathered relevant evidence. But how do you decide who is telling the truth and who is lying? How do you figure out what actually happened?

There is no crystal ball that will tell you the answer, but there are some guidelines that will help you sort through the denials and conflicting stories. This chapter offers some tried and true strategies for evaluating the results of your investigation and reaching a decision.

After you have made your assessments, you must decide whether wrongdoing occurred and what corrective action to take (if any), then document your decisions. And even after the investigation is written up and filed away, you'll want to take a few steps to make sure that you've really dealt with the underlying problem—by following up with the affected employees and thinking about changes you can make in the workplace to avoid similar problems in the future.

A. Evaluate the Evidence

If there is no dispute about what actually happened, you can skip right to Section B, below. However, if there are important disagreements among the witnesses—and particularly if the accused worker denies the facts of the complaint—you will have to figure out where the truth lies.

1. Look at the Facts

To begin, review the evidence you have gathered and your notes from interviews. Are there any facts to which everyone agrees? What are the major points of contention? As to each of these disputes, what did the witnesses say? Are there any documents supporting one version or the other?

Some investigators find it helpful to group the evidence into two categories: disputed facts and undisputed facts. If you can make a decision based solely on the undisputed facts, then you can skip to Section B, below. If the undisputed facts don't give you enough to go on, think about which disputed facts will have to be resolved in order to reach a conclusion. Focus on these facts—and on each witness's version of these facts—as you consider credibility issues (covered in Section 2, below).

EXAMPLE: Mimi is evaluating the evidence she has gathered in her investigation of products missing from an electronics store. Here are the undisputed facts her investigation has revealed:

1. The missing products are all high-ticket items—each is worth several hundred dollars or more.

2. The products were signed for by the receiving department but could not be located on the stock room shelves when customers sought to purchase the items. In other words, the items disappeared from the stock room, not from the showroom floor or in transit between the manufacturer and the electronics store.

3. Franklin and Debbie are the only two employees who were working in the stock room when each of the thefts occurred.

4. Franklin recently bought a new Land Rover and took a cruise to the Bahamas.

Is this enough information for Mimi to decide what happened? Nope. The only fact that points to Franklin as the culprit is his recent change in spending habits, and there could be lots of reasons for that. So Mimi has to move on to consider the many disputed facts. She realizes that these disputed facts are the most important:

1. Debbie claims that Franklin disappeared for an hour or so during each shift when items were taken. Franklin claims that he was asked to work in another area of the store during these intervals.

2. Franklin claims that his wife recently inherited a large sum of money from her deceased grandfather, which paid for their new car and cruise.

3. Several employees claim to have seen Franklin's car parked at the loading dock (which backs onto the stock room) on occasion. Franklin denies that he has ever parked near the loading dock and says these employees must be mistaken.

4. An employee claims to have seen an online ad listing several items that the company carries for sale. The employee recognized Franklin's email address from the ad. Franklin claims to have changed his email address and ISP more than a year ago.

Mimi can now focus her energy on assessing these key disputed facts from every angle, in order to reach her decision.

2. Assess Credibility

When you're faced with conflicting stories—as happens in many investigations—you will have to consider each person's version of the facts. Evaluating credibility and determining who's telling the truth can be difficult, but the following guidelines—along with a healthy dose of common sense—will help you sift through the evidence:

• **Plausibility.** Whose story makes the most sense? Does one person's version of events defy logic or common sense? Based on your visit to the scene (see Chapter 3, Section C), could the employees involved have heard and seen what they claimed to have witnessed? Should they have heard and seen things that they did not admit?

• **Source of information.** Did the witness see or hear the event directly? Did the witness report firsthand knowledge, or rely on secondhand statements from other employees or rumors?

• **Detail.** How general or specific was each person's statement? If a witness gave a detailed statement, were those details supported by other evidence? Did the accused or suspected employee deny the allegations in detail or only generally?

• **Corroboration and conflicting testimony.** Are there witnesses or documents that support one side of the story? Does the evidence contradict one person's statements? Do the witnesses support the person who suggested you interview them? If there are conflicts, are they over minor or significant issues?

• **Contradictions.** Was each person's story consistent throughout your questioning or on a second telling? Did any of the witnesses contradict themselves during your interview? If so, did the change involve a minor issue or a matter of substance?

• **Demeanor.** How did the witnesses act during the interview? Did they appear to be telling the truth or lying? Did the accused employee have a strong reaction to the complaint or no reaction at all? Did the complaining employee seem genuinely upset? Were any witnesses' reactions unusual, based on their usual demeanor or behavior?

• **Omissions.** Did anyone leave out important information during the interview? Is there a sensible explanation for the omission?

- **Prior incidents.** Does the accused employee have a documented history of this type of misconduct? Has the complaining employee made previous complaints? Have there been other incidents between the complaining and the accused employee?

- **Motive.** Does either the complaining worker or the accused worker have a motive to lie about, exaggerate, or deny the incident? Is there any history between these employees that affects their credibility? Do any of the witnesses have a special loyalty to—or a grudge against—any of the employees involved?

 Reopen the investigation, if necessary.

Sometimes, your evaluation of the facts and credibility assessments will lead you to only one definite conclusion: You need more information. In the example of Mimi and Franklin, above, Mimi might decide to go back and gather more evidence that could shed light on the disputed facts—for example, she might decide to interview Franklin's supervisor to find out if he asked Franklin to work elsewhere in the store during shifts when the thefts occurred, or she might do a public records search to see whether she can confirm that Franklin's grandfather-in-law passed away. Or, if your credibility assessments reveal that one witness left something important out or described an event in a different way than everyone else you talked to, you might decide to go back and re-interview the witness.

---

3. Put It All Together

Once you've examined all of the facts and weighed each witness's credibility, you will probably begin to see the real story—or at least, the way that things are most likely to have played out. Often, investigators find that one version of events is really implausible or that it makes a lot less sense than the other. In investigations as in science, the adage holds true: The most obvious explanation is usually correct.

However, the web may remain hopelessly tangled even after you've held every detail up to the magnifying glass. In that case, you might have to end the investigation by admitting that you cannot figure out what really happened. If there is evidence on both sides and it really could have happened either way, it's better to throw up your hands than to take disciplinary action that isn't supported by the evidence. Section B, below, explains how to handle these situations.

EXAMPLE: Stuart complained that Marcus had threatened to fire him for reporting to jury duty. Stuart said that Marcus made this threat in the lunch room on April 28, 200X. Marcus seemed very surprised by this allegation; he agreed that he spoke to Stuart in the lunch room about his jury summons but said only that he hoped Stuart didn't get picked to sit on a jury because jury duty can be so boring. Marcus suggested that the investigator speak to several witnesses, all of whom confirmed his side of the story. Marcus also said that Stuart had seemed upset since his last performance review, when Marcus noted that Stuart hadn't met several of his performance goals for the year. When the investigator interviewed Stuart a second time to get his reaction to this, Stuart admitted that the witnesses were there but insisted that they must have misunderstood what Marcus said. He also admitted his bad feelings about the performance review.

In this case, the investigator can conclude that there was no wrongdoing. All of the witnesses support Marcus's version of events. Stuart cannot explain this discrepancy. Marcus has also offered a reason for Stuart's complaint, which Stuart has not denied.

EXAMPLE: Same as above, but one witness (a friend of Marcus's) confirms Marcus's version of the conversation and one witness (a coworker with whom Stuart often eats lunch) confirms Stuart's version. Although Stuart admits his bad feelings about the performance review, he points out that he went to Marcus's manager shortly after his evaluation to talk about the review. The manager confirmed Marcus's opinion of Stuart's performance and explained how Stuart could improve. Stuart says that he felt more comfortable with the evaluation after this conversation, although Marcus was upset that Stuart went over his head and complained. Marcus denies being upset about this.

What should the investigator do now? Without more evidence, the investigator cannot reach a conclusion. Both Stuart and Marcus claim that the other had a motive to lie, and both claim to be telling the truth. In short, this one could go either way.

Get a Second Opinion

Except in the most clear cut situations, it's a good idea to ask someone else to review your investigation and the conclusions you've reached. This will help you make sure that you've considered all the angles, documented everything properly, and made an objective decision based on the evidence.

If possible, choose someone who is fairly high up in the company and has some distance from the situation—for example, a manager of a different facility or a human resources director for a different region. You might also ask a lawyer to review your decision. Give this person all of your investigative documents and evidence, then ask whether your decision seems justified. This person may point out gaps in your documentation or ask questions that you hadn't considered

B. Decide Whether Misconduct Occurred

Once you have evaluated the evidence and reached some factual conclusions, you will have to decide whether company policies were violated or misconduct occurred. This decision will dictate what further actions you should take and what you should tell the employees involved.

At this point, you may be wondering what, exactly, constitutes misconduct. For the most part, it isn't hard to tell whether an employee has crossed the line that separates eccentric behavior, jokes, or silliness from actions that are worthy of discipline. However, there are some gray areas—situations in which it's tough to distinguish misconduct from a misunderstanding.

EXAMPLE: Over the course of several months, $300 has gone missing from petty cash. Numerous employees see Claude taking money from the petty cash drawer on three separate occasions. When you ask Claude about it, he denies taking the money and calls his coworkers liars. Claude has clearly committed misconduct.

Now assume that employees have seen Claude taking the money, but they've also seen Claude putting money back into the drawer. No money is missing from the petty cash account. When you ask Claude about it, he immediately admits taking the money but says that he always paid it back. He assumed that this was OK because his supervisor also borrows from petty cash. Now, the situation is less clear. Claude hasn't lied, and technically he hasn't stolen. He may have exercised poor judgment, but his supervisor's actions led him to believe his actions were OK. He should be told that he has violated company policy and perhaps given a warning, but severe disciplinary measures aren't called for.

Section C, below, explains what to do once you've decided that wrongdoing did or did not occur, or you've decided that you can't reach a conclusion. If you're having trouble making these distinctions, however, here are some guidelines that may help:

- **The law.** Are the employee's actions illegal? Has the employee committed actionable harassment, stolen from the company or from customers, or threatened to harm someone?

- **Written company policies.** Does the employee's conduct violate company policies, as expressed in the employee handbook or in other documents that are distributed to employees?

- **Company practices and procedures.** Did the employee violate a rule that is known in the workplace, even if it isn't written down?

- **Common sense.** Was the employee's action obviously inappropriate or dangerous, even if it isn't illegal or explicitly prohibited by company policies? For example, an employee decides to play a prank on the supervisor who just gave him a bad review by disassembling the supervisor's car and reassembling it on the factory floor, which disrupts an entire shift of work and creates a hazard for employees on the floor. It's not clear that this is illegal, and many companies won't have had the foresight to explicitly prohibit car assembly in the workspace, but this employee's conduct is deserving of discipline.

What these criteria have in common is that, in each case, employees have fair notice of what constitutes misconduct. If actions are prohibited by law, violate written or understood company policy, or don't pass the blush test ("I didn't know I'd get in trouble for calling in a false fire alarm when our biggest client was here—that's not in the company handbook!"), then it's fair to label those actions misconduct and take appropriate corrective action. On the other hand, if an employee's actions are not illegal, against company policy, or obviously inappropriate (like Claude's loans from the petty cash drawer, in the example above), it might not be fair to take action against the employee.

Misconduct and Discipline: Who Decides?

In many larger companies with dedicated human resources departments, the investigator is responsible only for reaching factual conclusions about the situation under investigation—that is, for deciding what probably happened—not for deciding whether discipline should be imposed. Even in smaller companies, the investigator won't always be responsible for discipline. The person who chooses an appropriate response to misconduct must be someone with experience in disciplinary matters and knowledge of the company's policies (and past disciplinary decisions). If you hire an outside investigator, or your investigator does not occupy a fairly high rank on the company ladder, that person should not be making decisions about discipline.

C. Take Action

After you have decided whether wrongdoing occurred, you will have to take action based on your findings. This section describes how to handle each of the three conclusions you might reach:

- no misconduct occurred (see Section 1, below)

- you can't decide whether misconduct occurred (see Section 2, below), or

- misconduct occurred (see Section 3, below).

1. No Misconduct

There are several situations in which you might find that no misconduct occurred. If there was some incident between the complaining and the accused employee, but nothing happened that is illegal or prohibited by your company policies, you might find that no misconduct occurred. In these situations, you should consider whether the accused employee's behavior (and/or the complaining worker's conduct) warrants counseling or warning.

EXAMPLE: Sabine complains that Henry, a coworker, asked her to go out on a date with him, then seemed unhappy when she turned him down. Henry agrees that this happened, acknowledges that he was disappointed when Sabine declined, but says that he has not asked her out or had any social interaction with her since. Both agree that the incident has not affected their ability to work together. This is not misconduct, but you might want to make sure Henry knows that any further advances towards Sabine could constitute sexual harassment.

In rare cases, you might conclude that the complaint was false. If the complaining employee acted in good faith but was mistaken (for example, if he or she misunderstood an incident or was confused about the accused employee's actions), you probably won't have to take any further action—except to clear up the misunderstanding. On the other hand, if the complaining employee acted maliciously—that is, the employee lied rather than making a mistake—discipline against the complaining worker is in order. Consider the employee's motives, how serious the allegations were, and the disruptions to your workplace in determining an appropriate response. In the most egregious cases, termination might be warranted.

Handling False Complaints

Sometimes, an employee makes a complaint that turns out, after a thorough investigation, to be false or unfounded. Some employers are tempted to punish the complaining employee in this situation—after all, investigations disrupt the workplace, take time and money, and can cause considerable stress for employees wrongly accused of bad conduct. But think twice (or even three times) before taking action against an employee who brings a complaint. If the employee had a good-faith reason for complaining, any disciplinary action against that employee might constitute retaliation.

A complaint is in good faith if the employee honestly and reasonably believes the complaint to be true. Even if an investigation proves that the employee was mistaken, you cannot take action unless the complaining employee acted maliciously or recklessly. For example, imagine that Sarah accuses Bernice of stealing from the cash register. If Sarah made up the allegation to get back at Bernice for dating Sarah's former boyfriend, Sarah should be disciplined for making the complaint. However, if Sarah saw Bernice taking money from the register and reasonably believed that Bernice was stealing, Sarah should not be disciplined if it turns out that Bernice had permission to take the money to purchase company supplies.

Savvy employers discipline complaining employees only when they can prove that the complaint was false, was motivated by bad intentions, and caused the company or another employee harm (including damage to a falsely accused employee's reputation). An employee who is disciplined for complaining might turn around and sue you for retaliation. Even if you believe you had good reason for imposing discipline, a jury might see it otherwise. And juries are quite willing to make employers pay for retaliation—some of the highest damages awards in employment cases go to employees claiming retaliation.

2. Inconclusive Results

In some cases, you may be unable to figure out what happened. If the results of your investigation are inconclusive, you should tell both the complaining and the accused employee why you hit a dead end. You might also remind the accused worker of the rule he or she allegedly violated, to make sure everyone understands what is expected of them going forward. If your investigation uncovered confusion about a particular policy (such as what constitutes sexual harassment or what is required under a safety rule), some workplace training might be in order. (See Section E, below.)

EXAMPLE: Jon claims that his boss, Maureen, said she wouldn't give him a raise because he refused to clock her in each morning at 8 a.m. (when she sometimes arrived at work ten to fifteen minutes late). Maureen denies Jon's claims but admits that she has been warned about her tardiness and that she has joked with Jon about clocking her in. Maureen also says that she does not plan to give Jon a raise because his work performance has been slipping—her statement is supported by productivity records. No witnesses have seen or heard anything relevant. In this situation, it's not clear what happened. You might want to warn Maureen that having another worker clock her in is a violation of company policy that will result in discipline, but otherwise there isn't much you can do.

3. Misconduct

You may find that the accused employee engaged in misconduct that requires discipline. If so, choose a corrective action that will be effective in ending the wrongdoing—and in signaling that the company takes it seriously. And no matter what disciplinary measures you come up with, implement them immediately.

Here are some factors to consider when trying to decide on an appropriate corrective action:

- **Severity.** How serious was the misconduct? If there was a victim (for example, an employee who was harassed or threatened), how was the victim affected by the accused employee's actions? What effect did the accused employee's actions have on the workplace?

- **Consistency.** Have other employees committed similar types of misconduct in the past? How were these incidents handled? Being consistent when you discipline employees will help you avoid charges of discrimination and unfair treatment.

- **Policy.** Does the company have a progressive discipline policy, in which you spell out the types of misconduct that might result in particular disciplinary consequences? Where does this misconduct—and this employee—fall on your company's scale?

- **History.** Have there been any similar prior incidents involving this employee? Does the employee have a history of disciplinary problems?

- **Knowledge.** Did the employee know that his conduct was prohibited? Did workplace rules and policies clearly spell out the company's expectations? An employee who knowingly violates a rule often deserves harsher discipline that an employee who wasn't aware of his transgression.

- **Evidence.** How strong is the evidence of wrongdoing? Remember, you may have to defend whatever action you take in court. Do you have strong, first-hand, corroborated evidence of wrongdoing? If you are going to take harsh disciplinary measures, make sure the evidence you've gathered will support your decision.

Once you have decided how to discipline the wrongdoer, take care of it immediately. Meet with the employee to inform him or her of the results of the investigation and the discipline, that will be imposed.

You must also meet with the complaining employee. Explain what you discovered in your investigation, let the employee know that the wrongdoer has been disciplined, and describe any future steps you will take to prevent further problems. Give assurances that the employee can come to you with any concerns about the situation.

Some employers apologize to the complaining employee for the misconduct. This is a nice gesture, and one that can go a long way towards making employees feel that their concerns—and suffering—were taken seriously. However, if you offer an apology, choose your words with care. Avoid saying things that could be construed as admitting that what happened is the company's fault. There is a world of difference between "We're so sorry that this happened" and "We're so sorry that we allowed this to happen."

If the Complaining Employee Is Unhappy

Even if you take immediate and effective action against the wrongdoer, the complaining employee may be upset. Perhaps the complaining employee believes a harsher punishment should have been imposed, has suffered damage to reputation and/or work opportunities because of the complaint, or does not believe the wrongdoer will shape up.

Your company is under no obligation to impose the punishment your complaining employee favors. Your obligation is to the company, the accused employee, and the rest of your workforce to be fair and reasonable. However, you should listen carefully to the complaining employee's concerns. Perhaps the employee who claims that the wrongdoer will never change is worried about retaliation or further misconduct; if so, you can assure the complaining employee that you will deal swiftly with any such behavior. An employee who claims to have suffered because of the misconduct may have a point: If the employee was unfairly denied a promotion, raise, or time off, for example, you should consider conferring these benefits retroactively.

Although complaining employees may well have their own axes to grind, they can also help you figure out whether you have chosen an effective remedy. If the resolution you've chosen isn't going to work, better to hear about it now when you can fix the problem than later in a lawsuit.

D. Document Your Decision

If you've followed the advice in this book, you've already documented every step of your investigation. At this point, you should have:

- a written complaint or your notes from meeting with the complaining employee, if there is one (if the investigation was based on something other than a complaint—for example, the bookkeeper noticed missing funds or sexist graffiti appeared at a worksite—you should have notes about the incident)

- notes from your other interviews (or written statements from the witnesses), and

- copies of any relevant documents, policies, or other physical evidence relating to the investigation.

You should also make a note of any proposed witness who was not interviewed and the reasons why no interview was conducted. For example, if an employee accused of sexual harassment suggests that you speak to his friend and coworker, who can attest that he "wouldn't sexually harass anyone," you could reasonably choose to save your interviews for those who actually know something about the incident.

Some investigators, particularly consultants who specialize in conducting investigations, prepare formal investigative records. Although you don't have to prepare a formal document with index tabs and footnotes, you should preserve your notes from the investigation and create a brief report of what you did and why. Remember, you might have to prove to a jury that you acted reasonably and your conclusions were sound. If you have documented the reasons for your decision, you will have an easier time remembering the details—and convincing the jury that you considered all the angles before taking action. You will also have a contemporaneous record (that is, one made at the time of the investigation) of what you did and why. This type of document is much more persuasive to a jury than one you create after the fact to present in a courtroom.

I. Prepare an Investigation Report

When you sit down to write your investigation report, remember your audience. If your company is sued for anything related to the investigation—for example, because of the underlying incident or because of the punishment imposed on the wrongdoer—the document you write today could end up in the hands of a lawyer suing your company (and later, in the hands of a judge or jury). If this worst-case scenario comes to pass, you'd better believe that your report will be put under a microscope. Any important omissions, inappropriate comments, or random musings could come back to haunt you.

Because of the unfortunate possibility that your report might be evidence in a lawsuit someday, it can be hard to figure out how much detail to include. Your documentation doesn't have to memorialize every thought that crossed your mind during the investigation—nor should it. If you include a lot of extraneous detail, the jury might have trouble following your decision-making process. But make sure to write down all of the major decisions you made and why.

For example, if you did not believe a witness's statement, make a note of that and the reasons for your skepticism. Similarly, if you concluded that no misconduct occurred, write down all of the reasons for your decision. If you write extensive notes but later claim to have left out an important detail, the jury may well believe that you are trying to build a case after the fact.

If you conclude that the employee committed misconduct, you should certainly say so. However, you should avoid saying that the employee broke the law or committed a legal violation (for example, that the employee sexually harassed someone). The reason is simple: In many cases, the company can be liable for an employee's illegal conduct. If you admit, in an investigation report, that an employee committed an illegal act, you might be handing a silver bullet to any victims of that act. You're far better off simply saying that the employee committed misconduct, violated company policies, acted inappropriately, or used poor judgment.

If the results of your investigation were inconclusive, you should document the reasons why you were unable to sort things out. Note the conflicting evidence carefully. This documentation will be invaluable if similar allegations are later made against the accused employee. You will have a record of previous problems to support any discipline you might impose.

Your documents should include a notation of the discipline (if any) you imposed on the wrongdoer. This information should also go in the wrongdoer's personnel file. If your meeting with either the wrongdoer or the complaining employee was eventful (for example, there was heated argument or significant commentary), you might want to include some notes from that meeting as well.

Investigation Report Checklist

Here are some important facts your investigation report might include, if applicable:

❑ the date of the incident under investigation

❑ if there is a complaint, the date of the complaint and name of the employee who complained

❑ why the investigation was initiated (for example, an employee complained, a fight broke out, or an employee was suspected of being under the influence of drugs at work) and the basic facts to be investigated

❑ who conducted the investigation

❑ when the investigation began

❑ what documents or other evidence were gathered

❑ where documents or evidence were found (for example, in an employee's personnel file, pinned to the company bulletin board, or in an employee's desk drawer)

❑ when documents or evidence were gathered

❑ any company policies that are relevant to the incident under investigation

❑ who was interviewed

❑ the date of each interview

❑ a summary of each witness's statement

❑ a summary of any other important facts (for example, things you may have noticed when visiting the scene of the incident)

❑ your conclusions and how you came to them

❑ any important issues left unresolved

❑ any action taken in the workplace (for example, discipline against the wrongdoer or workplace training)

Sample Written Investigation Report

I completed my investigation of Cynthia Smith's complaint against Jackie Starr on August 27, 200X. Cynthia said that Jackie had made jokes about her wheelchair at a team meeting on August 3 and complained about having to make the restroom wheelchair-accessible on August 5. (See notes from my interview with Cynthia on August 19, 200X).

I spoke to Jackie on August 20, 200X. Notes from this interview are in the file. Jackie denied treating Cynthia any differently from her other direct reports. However, Jackie admitted that she had joked about Cynthia's wheelchair when her team was planning the company picnic; Jackie said she made these jokes because she felt bad that Cynthia would not be able to participate in some of the activities. She said Cynthia laughed, and she was surprised to hear that Cynthia was upset. Jackie also said that she made jokes about having to wait in line to use the women's restroom because a stall had to be removed to make the room accessible to Cynthia.

Three witnesses heard Jackie's comments about the picnic: Tom Jones, Kathleen McDermott, and Diego Cameron. Tom and Diego both felt uncomfortable about Jackie singling out Cynthia; Kathleen didn't think Cynthia minded the jokes. All three confirmed that Jackie made jokes about Cynthia participating in games at the company picnic. See my notes from these interviews.

Martina Kowalski heard Jackie complain about the restroom. Martina said that Jackie complained that 20 women were inconvenienced just so Cynthia would be more comfortable. My notes from my interview with Martina are in the file.

I concluded that Jackie's treatment of Cynthia violated company policy. All of the witnesses confirmed the details of Cynthia's complaint. Jackie also confirmed the facts of the allegations. I gave Jackie a written warning on August 28, 200X. I explained to her that she had violated company policy, treated her employee disrespectfully, and used poor judgment. I warned her that she would be fired if her behavior did not improve immediately. I arranged for her to attend a diversity management seminar next month.

I met with Cynthia on August 28, 200X to tell her my conclusions. I also told her that Jackie had been disciplined and would be required to attend training on diversity in the workplace. I asked Cynthia if she felt comfortable continuing to report to Jackie. Cynthia said that she did. She said that Jackie treated her fairly in work assignments and evaluations. Cynthia said that she hoped the training would help Jackie understand workers with disabilities. I told Cynthia that the company was very sorry for what happened to her and that she should feel free to come to me with any concerns about her working relationship with Jackie in the future. I also told Cynthia that the company planned to move the company picnic to a location with paved walkways and ramps and to hold events and games in which every worker could participate.

2. Where to Keep Investigation Records

Now that you've written your investigation report, what should you do with it—and with your notes and other documents from the investigation? Create a separate investigation file to be kept with the company's other confidential records. The investigation file should be treated like an employee's medical records—it should be kept confidential and revealed only on a strict need-to-know basis. Don't put the investigation report in any employee's personnel file—in most states, employees have the right to inspect the contents of their personnel files.

If you took corrective action against an employee, that employee's personnel file should include a memo or other documentation of the discipline imposed. It should also indicate that a separate investigation file exists on the incident. That way, if another incident arises involving the same employee, the investigator will know to look in the confidential files for information on the previous problem.

 Don't toss documents without speaking to a lawyer.

Some investigators throw away their notes once they have written a final investigation report. However, this can be very risky. If the incident under investigation—or the investigation itself—turns into a lawsuit, you might be accused of destroying evidence. If you have a lot of extraneous paper you'd like to get rid of or you're concerned about a particular document, get some advice from a lawyer *before* you throw it away.

E. Follow Up

You've finished your investigation, taken action if you've found workplace wrongdoing, written your report, and filed it away. So now you can rest on your laurels, right? Wrong. There are still a few things you should do to make sure that you've really rooted out the underlying problem.

1. Meet With Employees

Check in periodically with the complaining employee, if there is one. Make sure that the misconduct has stopped, no retaliation has taken place, and the employee is comfortable in the workplace. If you learn of any problems during these conversations, take action right away.

In some cases, you may also want to follow up with the accused employee, if that employee is still with the company. Ask whether the employee has any concerns relating to the investigation, and whether things are getting back to normal.

2. Verify Corrective Actions

You'll want to make sure that any corrective actions you recommended were taken. Was the wrongdoer actually disciplined—for example, was a written warning placed in the personnel file, or did the employee actually serve a recommended suspension? If the wrongdoer was told to complete a training program, a rehabilitation program, or counseling (for example, on anger management), has it happened? If you recommended a change in reporting relationships, has that taken place?

3. Consider the Big Picture

Some investigations reveal company-wide problems that should be addressed. Did your investigation turn up significant confusion about company rules or appropriate workplace behavior? Are your managers in need of some advice about dealing with employees and employee problems? Did you discover that previous incidents had been swept under the rug or improperly documented? If you answer "yes" to any of these questions, you need to take some action. Your workers may need training on company policies, proper management practices, record keeping, or legal requirements. ■

PART **II**

Investigating Common Workplace Problems:

Discrimination

Harassment

Theft

Violence

CHAPTER

Investigating Discrimination

Investigating claims of discrimination can be complicated.

Because the essence of most discrimination claims is that the complaining employee was treated differently from other employees because of his or her protected characteristic (race, gender, religion, and so on), a thorough investigation will require you to look not only at how the complaining worker was treated but also at how other workers were treated, how the employee accused of discrimination has acted in the past, and whether the reasons the accused employee gives for the challenged decision or action are consistent and legitimate.

Because you will need to gather a lot of potentially sensitive information about a number of different employees, these investigations can easily mushroom. The trick to handling a discrimination investigation successfully lies in figuring out exactly what information you need and how you will get it. If you aren't thorough enough, the investigation might not hold up in court—or convince complaining employees that you've taken their concerns seriously. If you go overboard in your information gathering, however, you'll only delay solving the problem. (And in the meantime, you'll be creating endless grist for the employee rumor mill).

An investigation of discrimination is likely to trigger an emotional response, as well. Employees who feel they are being judged based on a protected characteristic rather than their skills and performance are likely to be angry—particularly if they are members of a group that has historically been mistreated in this country. An employee accused of discrimination will probably have a very strong reaction as well; being labeled as a bigot does not sit well with anyone.

This chapter will give you the information and strategies you need to conduct a thorough discrimination investigation that doesn't rage out of control. Section A explains the law of discrimination, including common types of discrimination claims. Section B covers the ten steps to a successful discrimination investigation.

A. What Is Discrimination?

It is illegal for an employer to make job decisions based on a person's race, religion, or other "protected characteristic" (see Section A1, below) rather than on that person's ability to do the job. This rules applies to every aspect of the employment relationship, from hiring to promotions, job assignments, pay raises, leaves of absence, working conditions, performance evaluations, demotions, discipline, and firing.

Discrimination is prohibited by federal, state, and some local laws. These laws are enforced by government agencies, including the Equal Employment Opportunity Commission (EEOC), which administers and enforces federal antidiscrimination laws, and state fair employment practices agencies, which handle violations of state law. You can find a list of EEOC offices and contact information for state fair employment practices agencies in Appendix C.

1. Protected Characteristics

Federal, state, and local laws determine which characteristics are protected and which are not. Under federal law, employers may not make job decisions based on an employee's race, color, national origin, religion, gender (including pregnancy), disability, citizenship status, or age (if the employee is at least 40 years old). Virtually every state and some localities also outlaw discrimination on these bases, and many protect employees from discrimination on bases that the feds left out, such as sexual orientation, marital status, or weight.

Which Antidiscrimination Laws Apply to Your Company

Not every antidiscrimination law applies to every employer. For the most part, whether you have to follow these laws depends on the size and location of your company. Federal antidiscrimination laws (listed below) apply only to employers with more than a minimum number of employees—and this minimum number is different for each law.

Name of Law	Discrimination Prohibited on the Basis of	Applies to
Title VII	Race, national origin, religion, sex	Employers with 15 or more employees
Age Discrimination in Employment Act	Age (against employees age 40 and over only)	Employers with 20 or more employees
Americans With Disabilities Act	Physical or mental disability	Employers with 15 or more employees
Equal Pay Act	Sex (applies only to wage discrimination)	All employers
Civil Rights Act of 1866	Race	All employers
Immigration Reform and Control Act	Citizenship status, national origin	Employers with 4 or more employees

States also have antidiscrimination laws; some of these laws apply to smaller employers, and many of them outlaw additional types of discrimination. You must follow all laws that apply to you, whether federal, state, or local. For example, if you have 30 employees and your state does not prohibit age discrimination, you still must comply with the federal Age Discrimination in Employment Act; if your state's law prohibits employers with more than ten employees from discriminating on the basis of sexual orientation, you must also follow that law, even though sexual orientation discrimination is not prohibited by federal law.

Finding out more about antidiscrimination laws.

To learn more about these federal antidiscrimination laws, see *Federal Employment Laws: A Desk Reference,* by Amy DelPo and Lisa Guerin (Nolo), which includes a chapter on each law. You can also find information on these laws at the website of the EEOC, at www.eeoc.gov. To find out what types of discrimination your state prohibits, check out the chart "State Laws Prohibiting Discrimination in Employment," in Appendix C. You can find out whether any local laws apply to you by getting in touch with your state fair employment agency (see Appendix C for contact information) or your local Chamber of Commerce.

a. Race and Color

Discrimination on the basis of an employee's race or color might include segregating employees of a particular race in certain jobs, making decisions based on stereotypes about race, treating an employee differently for associating with people of a particular race, making decisions based on conditions that correlate closely to race, or making distinctions based on skin color.

Here are some examples:

- A high-end department store chain routinely channels white employees to sales jobs, while Latino employees are placed mostly in restocking and warehouse positions.

- A delivery company refuses to hire Asian applicants for positions driving trucks; the hiring committee believes Asians are poor drivers and are more likely to get in accidents.

- A small consulting firm doesn't promote a white employee whose husband is Lebanese; the firm's principals often bring their spouses when they entertain important clients, and they are afraid their clients will feel uncomfortable around an Arab-American.

- A restaurant chain has hired many African-American employees; however, the chain routinely assigns lighter-skinned African-Americans to wait tables and seat customers, while African-Americans with darker skin get stuck washing dishes and bussing tables.

Discrimination Statistics

The Equal Employment Opportunity Commission (EEOC), the federal agency responsible for administering and enforcing laws that prohibit discrimination, collects statistics on how many discrimination charges are filed with the agency each year, and on what basis. In every year of the last decade, there have been more charges filed alleging race discrimination than any other type. Charges of sex discrimination run a close second, with age and disability discrimination not far behind. Although there have been more charges of discrimination based on national origin and religion filed in the last couple of years (in the wake of the World Trade Center attack of 9/11, many commentators believe), these charges still make up a very small portion of the EEOC's total docket.

b. National Origin

An employer discriminates based on national origin when it treats an employee differently because of ethnicity or country of ancestry, or because of traits closely linked to ethnicity (such as surname, accent, cultural identity, and so on).

Examples of national origin discrimination include:

- An airline doesn't allow anyone who appears to be from the Middle East to work in any position that involves dealing with passengers.
- A hardware and home supply store that serves a predominantly white neighborhood refuses to promote an employee who has adopted a traditional African style of dress.
- A Chinese restaurant only hires wait staff who have Asian features and surnames.
- An automotive supply store disciplines Latino employees more severely than white employees for showing up late or missing work without notifying their supervisors.

Employers can legitimately make job decisions based on an employee's accent, but only if the accent significantly interferes with the employee's ability to do the job. For example, a business might transfer an employee with a heavy Indian accent from a software help desk position to a job that doesn't require customer contact. Such a transfer would be legitimate if customers had complained that they could not understand his instructions; the same transfer would be illegal if the employee was transferred simply because he had an accent, not because the accent impaired his ability to do the job.

English-Only Rules

Some employers have adopted "English-only" rules, requiring employees to speak only English in the workplace. Sometimes, these rules are justified—for example, if a team of employees is working together and English is their only common language, or if safety or customer service requires it. An English-only rule will not be considered discriminatory as long as there is a legitimate business justification for the rule.

Example: An auto parts factory imposes an English-only rule for its line workers, who must work together using heavy machinery. Such a rule is probably justified by safety concerns. However, if the factory prohibited workers from speaking any other language even on their breaks and while making personal telephone calls, that would be a tougher sell. Similarly, if the company imposed a rule that prohibited workers from speaking only certain languages (such as a "no Spanish" or "no Farsi" rule), that would be discriminatory.

c. Gender

An employer discriminates based on gender when it makes decisions based on an employee's sex, stereotypes about men and women, or pregnancy. Here are some examples:

- A consulting business does not assign women to positions that require significant travel, believing that women have greater responsibilities at home and will be reluctant to leave their families.

- An employer refuses to promote a pregnant woman to a position for which she will need substantial training; the employer thinks, "I'll just spend all that money to get her up to speed, then she'll quit to stay home with her kids."

- A sporting goods store assigns only men to work in its golf section, on the assumption that its customers for golf equipment—who are mostly male—will be less inclined to listen to a woman's advice about clubs and shoes.

An employer must treat pregnant women just as it treats other workers who are temporarily disabled. For example, if a pregnant woman is medically restricted from lifting more than ten pounds during her pregnancy, the employer must treat her like it would any other worker who had such a temporary restriction. However, employers may not impose special rules only on pregnant women—for example, an employer may not prohibit a woman from working past a certain point in her pregnancy or require a woman to take a certain period of time off work after having a baby.

d. Age

It is illegal to base employment decisions on a worker's age—but only if the worker is at least 40 years old (this is the federal law—some states protect all workers, regardless of age, from age discrimination). Age discrimination includes excluding older workers from certain job opportunities, refusing to hire or promote older workers, making decisions based on stereotypes about age, or providing more expensive benefits to younger workers.

Here are some examples:

- A computer software company tends to hire mostly younger workers as programmers; although older workers apply, the hiring team assumes that they will have a harder time mastering the technology and staying on top of new developments.

- A company that provides human resources training has a team of trainers that are mostly in their 20s and 30s; the company wants a dynamic, energetic group of trainers, and so has screened out most of the older workers who have applied for training positions.

- A publishing company automatically stops paying for its workers' health insurance when they reach the age of 50—because older workers are more likely to use their health benefits and therefore more expensive to insure, the company simply cuts them off the plan.

 Benefits issues can be complicated.

The law recognizes that certain benefits become more expensive as workers age (and are more likely to take advantage of them). Although employers cannot discriminate against older workers by offering them less-expensive benefits, they can often give older workers a different benefit plan, as long as the employer spends the same amount on benefits for older and younger workers. However, the rules about age discrimination in benefits are fairly complex; if you need more information, take a look at *Federal Employment Laws: A Desk Reference*, by Amy DelPo and Lisa Guerin (Nolo)—it includes a chapter on the Older Workers Benefit Protection Act, the federal law that deals with this issue.

---

e. Disability

Disability discrimination occurs when an employer makes job decisions based on an employee's disability, the fact that an employee has had a disability in the past, or the employer's perception that the employee is disabled. A disability is a physical or mental impairment that substantially limits a major life activity (such as the ability to walk, talk, see, hear, breathe, work, or take care of oneself), despite any medications or other measures the employee is using (such as a prosthetic limb or hearing aid) to remedy the effects of the condition. Courts tend not to categorically characterize certain conditions as disabilities; instead, they consider the effect of the particular condition on the particular employee.

EXAMPLE 1: Gerard has suffered from depression. Before he started taking medication, he was often unable to get out of bed in the morning and could not take care of himself. Once he began treatment for his condition, Gerard improved to the point where he now has a fairly active schedule and enjoys his life again. Because Gerard is not currently limited in his major life activities, he is probably not disabled under the law. However, if his employer decided not to promote him because he has suffered from depression in the past, that would be illegal discrimination based on the fact that Gerard has a history of disability.

EXAMPLE 2: Jamal sometimes stutters when he talks. Although the stutter is noticeable, Jamal can easily be understood when he speaks. Jamal probably doesn't have a legally recognized disability. However, if his employer decided not to promote him to a position that involved dealing with customers because of his stutter, that could be discrimination. Although Jamal does not have a disability, his employer is treating him as though he is substantially limited in his ability to speak.

Although you may not discriminate based on an employee's disability, you are not legally required to hire or keep on employees who cannot do the job. If the employee cannot perform the job's basic functions, even with an accommodation, you are not required to hire or retain that employee.

EXAMPLE: Jean suffered a spinal cord injury in a car accident and is paralyzed from the waist down. She uses a wheelchair to get around. Because Jean is substantially limited in the major life activity of walking, she has a legally recognized disability. Jean applies to work as a secretary in a law firm. She can perform all of the job's essential elements—typing, transcribing, answering phones, and so on—but her wheelchair won't fit under the desk. Raising the height of the desk is a reasonable accommodation that will allow her to do the job. Because Jean is qualified and can do the job with an accommodation, she is protected from discrimination.

Now suppose Jean applies to oversee a private campground. The job responsibilities include traveling through the campground twice a day to collect fees and check on campers, providing emergency first aid treatment to campers as necessary, and helping campers with problems that may arise (for example, getting a car out of a ditch or helping to pitch a tent). Jean may not be qualified for this job—her wheelchair cannot travel over the forested and rocky campground trails, and her ability to assist campers will be limited. The employer could legally decide not to hire Jean because she cannot perform the job's essential functions.

Alcohol and Drugs

Scientists disagree over whether alcoholism and drug use are disabilities, diseases, habits, or something else entirely. As a legal matter, the issue is almost as murky. Here are the rules:

- **Alcohol.** Alcoholism is a legally recognized disability, which means that an employers cannot fire or discipline workers simply because they are alcoholics (for example, because they attend Alcoholics Anonymous meetings or take medication to help control the urge to drink). However, an employer can fire or discipline an alcoholic worker for failing to meet work-related performance and behavior standards, even if the worker fails to meet these standards because of drinking. For example, a worker who shows up at the job inebriated or is habitually late to work because of heavy drinking the night before can be disciplined or fired.

- **Drugs.** Employees who currently use illegal drugs are not considered disabled. However, a worker who no longer uses drugs and has successfully completed (or is currently participating in) a supervised drug rehabilitation program is considered a person with a disability—which means that an employer may not make employment decisions based on the fact that a worker is or has been in rehab.

f. Religion

An employer may not make job decisions based on an employee's religious beliefs or practices. (Employers also have to make reasonable accommodations for an employee's religious beliefs, in certain circumstances—see Section 2c, below.) Here are a few examples of religious discrimination:

- A group of friends who attend the same evangelical church go into business together; they refuse to hire anyone who does not share their faith.

- A company owner who is a self-proclaimed atheist tends not to promote religious employees to managerial positions; he believes that those who are religious have trouble exercising authority and thinking for themselves.

- A company that manufactures and distributes organic health supplies has a monthly company meeting, during which all employees must participate in a traditional Native American blessing ceremony.

g. Citizenship Status

An employer may not discriminate against employees based on their citizenship status, as long as they are legally authorized to work in the United States. This means an employer cannot make distinctions among employees based on the fact that they are or are not citizens of this country, as long as the worker is:

- a citizen or national of the United States

- an alien lawfully admitted for permanent or temporary residence

- an alien admitted as a refugee, or

- an alien granted asylum.

However, there are a couple of exceptions to this general rule. First, an employer may make job decisions based on an employee's citizenship status if federal law explicitly allows it (this exception generally applies only to government employers and some federal contractors). Second, an employer may give preference to a citizen or national of the United States over an equally qualified alien.

EXAMPLE: Khalid, a refugee from Afghanistan, and Judy, a citizen of the United States, apply for a position at a blood bank. If both are equally qualified, the blood bank may legitimately choose Judy over Khalid simply because she is a citizen. However, if Khalid has better qualifications, the bank may not hire Judy based on its preference for a U.S. citizen.

2. Legal Claims of Discrimination

The classic legal theory of discrimination: Sometimes called "disparate treatment"—is that an employer made a job decision based on a person's race, religion, or other protected characteristic. Most of the examples and the discussion in Section A1, above, focus on disparate treatment discrimination, because it is by far the most common type of discrimination claim employees might make. You'll find more information on disparate treatment claims in Subsection a, below.

However, there are two other types of legal claims that can be made under workplace discrimination laws:

- An employee who makes a "disparate impact" claim alleges that a company policy, practice, or requirement had the effect of discriminating against a protected group. For example, a woman might claim that an employer's failure to hire anyone who could not lift 60 pounds had the effect of discriminating against women. These claims are described in Subsection b, below.

- An employee who brings a "reasonable accommodation" claim argues that the employer failed to make reasonable changes in work rules, schedules, practices, equipment, or the physical layout of the workplace that would have allowed him to do his job. For example, an employee who is hard of hearing might claim that an employer's failure to purchase TTY communications equipment made it impossible for her to be promoted to a sales position. These claims, which only apply in cases of disability or religious discrimination, are explained in Section c, below.

It's important to learn the legal standards for each of these theories so you can recognize when an employee is complaining about something that might be illegal. Keep in mind, however, that you may want to take some corrective action even if your investigation reveals that an employee might not be able to prove discrimination in court. For example, if your investigation reveals that a manager accused of race discrimination is not making decisions based on race, but is favoring employees who are his friends outside of work over their co-workers, you will probably want to address that manager's behavior—even if it isn't discriminatory. See Sections B7 and B8, below, for more.

a. Disparate Treatment

Disparate treatment claims are the classic claims of discrimination: An employee claims to have been denied a job benefit because of a protected characteristic. Most disparate treatment claims involve firing, discipline, promotion, or inconsistent application of work rules.

The elements of a disparate treatment claim—what an employee must prove to win a lawsuit—depend on the employee's allegations. However, an employee usually has to start by showing that:

- he or she has a protected characteristic

- he or she was denied a job benefit or subjected to a negative job action (for example, did not receive a promotion, was not allowed to take time off, was disciplined more harshly than other employees, or was fired)

- he or she was qualified for the benefit (for example, the employee met the requirements for the promotion) or was undeserving of the negative job action (for example, the employee received a negative evaluation despite good performance), and

- employees who do not share the complaining employee's protected characteristic received the benefit or were not subjected to the negative job action (for example, male employees were not fired or a white person got the promotion).

Once the employee makes this showing, the employer must give a legitimate, nondiscriminatory reason for the decision the employee is challenging. To win the lawsuit, the employee must then show that the employer actually acted out of discriminatory motives (lawyers call this final showing "pretext," because the employee must show that the employer's stated reason is just an excuse or pretext for discrimination).

Most of the disputes in discrimination lawsuits are over this last issue—why the employee was treated differently. To show that the company was motivated by bias, an employee generally must come up with something more than the simple fact of different treatment. For example, it isn't enough to show that a woman didn't get a promotion that went to a man: The female candidate must also show some evidence that the decision was motivated by discrimination.

Often, this evidence takes the form of comments by decision makers—for example, the supervisor who says, "I'd like to bring in a more youthful, dynamic group of salespeople" before choosing a younger employee over an older employee, or the manager who makes frequent sexist jokes, then promotes only men to be in charge of accounts.

An employee can also try to prove discrimination by showing that the company's explanation for its employment decision doesn't hold water. For example, say that a company promotes a white employee to a managerial position, stating that he had more supervisory experience than the Chinese-American employee who was denied the promotion. If the Chinese-American employee can show that he actually had more years of supervisory experience and better qualifications for the job, the company's rationale starts to look a little suspect.

If the employer's rationale is really weak and the evidence of different treatment is strong enough, an employee can win a discrimination lawsuit, even without any direct proof (such as discriminatory statements) that the employer was motivated by bias.

EXAMPLE: Curtis, who is African-American, claims that he was disciplined more harshly for horseplay than white employees. Curtis says that white employees who engaged in the same behavior received a verbal warning, while he was fired. The company contends that Curtis's behavior merited harsher discipline because he damaged company equipment (he accidentally knocked a postage meter off of a table and broke it), while the white employees to whom he compared himself did not.

However, Curtis's clever lawyer reviews company records and discovers that each of the four employees who have been fired for horseplay are African-American—and that the company has relatively few (about 5%) African-American employees. The lawyer also discovers that ten white employees have been disciplined for horseplay, but none received any discipline harsher than a verbal reprimand. What's more, three of these white employees damaged company equipment—one pushed a forklift off the loading dock in a drunken rampage after the company holiday party! In this situation, Curtis might win a discrimination claim, even without any evidence that his supervisor is a racist or that the company has an explicit policy of only firing African-Americans. The company's explanation doesn't pass the blush test—and the numbers are pretty powerful evidence that something strange is going on.

b. Disparate Impact

An employer may commit illegal discrimination even if it didn't intend to make job decisions based on race, gender, or another protected characteristic. Under the theory of disparate impact, an employer discriminates if it adopts a neutral policy that has a disproportionate negative effect on a protected group. For example, an employer that requires all employees to have a college degree may exclude more employees of certain races. Similarly, an employer that imposes a height or strength requirement for some positions may screen out disproportionately large numbers of women.

Of course, these types of requirements may be perfectly legitimate—for example, a person who works loading and unloading heavy packages in a warehouse, felling trees, or rescuing people from burning building must have some strength to do the job. The law recognizes this dilemma and allows employers to defend against a disparate impact claim by showing that the rule or requirement in question is job-related and necessary to the business.

EXAMPLE 1: Delivery Co. delivers packages across the country for its customers. Delivery Co. requires all of its warehouse workers to be able to lift and carry 50 pound packages. Because the warehouse workers spend a large portion of their day carrying heavy packages, this requirement is job related and necessary to the business, even if it screens out disproportionate numbers of women.

EXAMPLE 2: Delivery Co. also delivers letters, contracts, and blueprints for business clients. Some warehouse workers deal exclusively with these documents, while others handle the packages. If Delivery Co. applied its "50-pound rule" to all warehouse workers, it could be subject to a sex discrimination claim. The document handlers don't have to lift heavy packages, so the rule is neither job-related nor necessary to the business as applied to them.

Disparate impact claims arise most often in the hiring context—for example, an employer that requires all applicants to take a written, standardized test might screen out disproportionate numbers of minority applicants, which could result in a disparate impact claim. Layoffs and other group firings could also result in a disparate impact claim if the employer uses firing criteria that result in a disproportionate number of protected workers losing their jobs. Generally, however, disparate impact claims are much less common than disparate treatment claims.

Age Discrimination Claims Based on Disparate Impact?

Courts disagree over whether employees can bring a disparate impact claim in an age discrimination case—in other words, that the employer's policy had the effect of discriminating against older workers.

This issue comes up most commonly during layoffs. For example, an employer trying to cut costs might lay off disproportionately large numbers of its highest-paid workers, in an effort to improve the bottom line. However, a company's highest-paid workers often tend to be its older workers, so the company's decision might result in older workers losing their jobs while younger workers are retained.

---

c. Reasonable Accommodation

In some situations, an employer may be required to take action based on an employee's protected characteristic in order to avoid discriminating. For example, in order to avoid discriminating against a disabled worker, an employer may need to install a handrail in the bathroom. This may sound counterintuitive—isn't it discriminatory to make decisions based on an employee's protected characteristic? Usually, the answer is yes. However, the law recognizes an exception to this general rule when an employee, because of religious beliefs or a disability, needs some changes to workplace rules or equipment in order to do the job.

Religion

Employers are legally required to reasonably accommodate an employee's religious practices, unless doing so would create an "undue hardship." These claims come up most often in regard to scheduling. For example, an employee whose religion prohibits her from working on the Sabbath might request a schedule change that will give her that day off. Religious accommodation claims might also involve dress codes—for example, an employee whose religion requires him to adopt a particular style of dress might ask the employer to make an exception from its usual rules about employee grooming and attire.

EXAMPLE: Alicia is a Seventh Day Adventist. She works as a hygienist in a large dental practice. Her employer has informed her that it plans to begin staying open on weekends in order to attract more clients. The employer says that every hygienist will be required to work either Saturday or Sunday each week. Alicia tells her employer that her religious beliefs prevent her from working on Saturdays. As an accommodation, the employer agrees that Alicia can work on Sundays and have Saturdays off every week.

An employer does not have to accommodate an employee if doing so would cause an undue hardship. Although the law isn't entirely clear about what constitutes an undue hardship, there are a few rules. If the accommodation would require more than ordinary administrative costs (for example, the cost of making a payroll or scheduling change), then the employer doesn't have to provide it. Similarly, an employer cannot be required to override a seniority system to accommodate an employee's religion—if granting the accommodation would deprive another employee of a transfer, shift preference, or other benefit, the employer doesn't have to provide it.

EXAMPLE 1: Rory, a Native American, works as a salesperson for an upscale furniture store. His employer institutes a dress code, requiring all employees to wear professional attire and requiring male employees to wear their hair no longer than their shirt collars. Rory's religious beliefs prohibit him from cutting his hair. As long as Rory is neat and clean, his employer can't claim that accommodating his request for an exception to the dress code is an undue burden. It won't cost the employer anything, and the employer will have a tough time proving that Rory's long hair will prevent him from presenting a professional image to customers.

EXAMPLE 2: Rachel works as a salesperson in a small antique store. During her shifts, she works with one other employee for most of the day; each works alone when the other takes a lunch break. She joins a religious group that believes in strict gender separation. The group's adherents are prohibited from interacting with persons of the opposite sex other than their spouse, their family, or clergy members. Rachel asks her employer to accommodate her religious beliefs by allowing her to serve only female customers. This accommodation would create an undue hardship: Her employer would have to either lose customers or hire another employee for the lunch hour, and Rachel's coworker would have to take on extra work.

Disability

Accommodating a disabled worker means providing assistance or making changes in the job or workplace that will enable the worker to do the job. For example, an employer might provide an accessible parking space, install ramps, or lower the height of desktops and other facilities to accommodate a worker in a wheelchair; provide a quiet, distraction-free workspace for a worker with Attention Deficit Disorder; or allow a worker who is fatigued from chemotherapy sessions to take more frequent breaks during the day.

It is the employee's responsibility to inform the employer of the disability and request a reasonable accommodation—the employer need not guess at what might help an employee do the job. Once an employee starts this conversation, however, the employer is legally required to brainstorm with the employee to figure out what kinds of accommodations might be effective and practical (the law calls this an employer's duty to engage in a "flexible interactive process"). Although an employer is not required to provide the precise accommodation a worker requests, you must work with your employees to try to come up with a reasonable solution.

However, you are not required to provide an accommodation if doing so would cause the business "undue hardship." The law imposes more responsibility on employers to accommodate disabilities than religious beliefs—while any cost beyond an administrative burden creates an undue hardship in a religious accommodation claim, an employer can be legally obligated to shell out some money to accommodate a worker with a disability. In determining whether a particular accommodation creates an undue burden, courts consider:

- the cost of the accommodation
- the size and financial resources of your business
- the structure of your business, and
- the effect the accommodation would have on your business.

If the cost of the accommodation is significant when compared to your business's resources, you probably don't have to provide it. Similarly, if providing an accommodation would impose significant changes on the way you do business, it isn't required.

EXAMPLE 1: Jon has Attention Deficit Disorder. He is easily distracted and unable to concentrate on a project if there is any background noise or activity. Jon works in the financing department of a large car dealership. He tells his employer of his disability and requests to be moved out of his cubicle near the showroom floor to an office with a door that closes, farther away from the wheeling and dealing. The company has some unused space upstairs and agrees to convert some of it into an office for Jon. This is a reasonable accommodation.

EXAMPLE 2: Gerrie works as a route supervisor for a company that sells and delivers bottled water. She arrives at work before anyone else, reviews the schedule for the day, and determines which driver will make each pick-up and delivery. She then creates a route assignment for each driver, which the drivers receive when they arrive at work. Gerrie tells her employer that she suffers from depression and that the medication she takes for her condition makes her groggy in the morning. She asks if she can change her schedule so that she comes in several hours later. Because the customers expect their water on time, and because the drivers cannot begin their deliveries until Gerrie gives them their route assignments, her requested accommodation probably poses an undue hardship. Allowing Gerrie to come in late would substantially disrupt the company's business.

B. Ten Steps to an Effective Discrimination Investigation

In discrimination cases, your investigation will almost always begin with an employee complaint. Unlike harassment or employee theft, discrimination cannot really be anonymous—and it always has a victim. You are most likely to hear about discrimination directly from the employee who feels mistreated. If that employee doesn't come forward, you may hear a complaint from another employee—for example, a coworker or supervisor who feels that an unfair decision was made.

Read Part I first.

This section explains how to apply the basic investigation steps covered in Part I of this book to a discrimination investigation. If you haven't read Part I, you should do so before getting into this more specific material—the discussion that follows assumes that you are already familiar with basic investigation procedures.

Here are some of the ways you may learn of a discrimination claim:

- **Formal complaint.** An employee may use your complaint policy (see Appendix A) to complain of discrimination.

- **Performance evaluation.** An employee may raise a discrimination issue during a performance review. For example, the employee might believe that the evaluation itself is discriminatory ("I got rated poorly because my project was three days late, but my white coworker turned in his project three weeks late, and he was rated higher than me"). Or the employee might use the performance evaluation as a forum to raise discrimination concerns ("I'm wondering why I always seem to get the projects that don't involve client contact—and I'm concerned that it might have something to do with the fact that I'm older than the other account managers").

- **Exit interview.** An employee leaving the company may be more willing to be frank about problems within the company. The employee might say that he is leaving because he believes he is discriminated against. Or, he may raise a more systemic issue—for example, an African-American employee might say, "I finally decided to take another job offer because I noticed that only white employees are promoted to management positions, no matter how many employees of color apply. I felt that I would never move up the ladder here."

- **Administrative charge.** Before an employee can bring a lawsuit alleging discrimination, he or she must file charges with the EEOC or a similar state fair employment practices agency. If an employee (or former employee) files an administrative charge, you will be notified and receive a copy of the charge. In most cases, you will also be asked to respond to the charge—to give your side of the story. This means you'll have to investigate, so you'll know what to tell the agency.

The Government May Investigate, Too

If an employee files a charge of discrimination with a government agency, that agency may perform its own investigation. The agency will almost always ask you to respond to the charge. However, the agency may also ask you to hand over personnel files, performance evaluations, and other documents; to allow the agency investigator to visit your workplace; and to make employees available for interviews with the agency investigator. If you find yourself embroiled in an agency investigation—especially one that involves more than one complaining employee—you should consider consulting with an attorney. The statements you make and actions you take during this investigation should be carefully choreographed, to avoid giving the complaining employee fodder for a lawsuit.

To learn more about agency investigations, check out the EEOC's factsheet, "EEOC Investigations—What an Employer Should Know." You can find it—as well as many other helpful resources on discrimination and harassment—on the EEOC's website, www.eeoc.gov. From the home page, click "Quick Start—Employers" on the navigation bar to see a list of available resources.

- **Letter from an attorney.** This is possibly the least popular way to find out about a discrimination claim. If an employee asks a lawyer for help in dealing with potential discrimination, your first notice of the problem may come in an envelope with an "Esquire" in the return address. Many lawyers will recount the facts as their clients have related them, then ask you to respond within a certain period of time. If you are the unfortunate recipient of one of these letters, investigating is a must; you should also consider hiring your own attorney to help you decide how to respond.

Once you are aware of a claim of workplace discrimination, you are ready to use the ten basic investigation steps, as described below.

I. Decide Whether to Investigate

When dealing with discrimination claims, an employer should generally err on the side of investigating. The Supreme Court has held, in the case of *Kolstad v. American Dental Association*, 527 U.S. 526 (1999), that employers may not be liable for punitive damages for discrimination by managers and supervisors, as long as they make good-faith efforts to prevent discrimination. (Punitive damages are damages intended to punish the employer for especially egregious conduct, to deter future discrimination—they often make up the largest part of a damages award in a discrimination case, sometimes totaling two, three, or ten times the amount of other damages awarded in a case.)

The Court didn't specify exactly what constitutes good-faith efforts, but it suggested that having an antidiscrimination policy and responding appropriately to complaints of discrimination—by performing an investigation and taking disciplinary action against wrongdoers—could protect an employer from these types of damages. In light of this decision, it makes sense to investigate most claims of discrimination.

Discrimination or Harassment?

Sometimes, it can be hard to tell whether an employee is complaining of discrimination or harassment. As a legal matter, harassment is a form of discrimination. Like discrimination, harassment is mistreatment based on a person's protected characteristic. While discrimination most often results in a negative job action (such as losing a promotion, getting fired, or being denied a job benefit), harassment can consist solely of demeaning behavior—for example, racist jokes, sexual innuendo, or repeated negative comments about an employee's disability or ethnicity.

In some harassment cases, however, an employee complains that the harassment resulted in a negative job action. This happens most often in sexual harassment cases, in which an employee may allege that she was denied a promotion or fired because she refused to submit to sexual demands.

If you get confused about whether an employee is complaining about discrimination or harassment, take heart: The way you classify the claim is not as important as what you do about it. In either situation, you will be looking at whether an employee was mistreated because of a protected characteristic. And in either case, your job will be to figure out what happened, document your findings, and take action to make sure that the mistreatment stops.

However, not every claim of discrimination is a claim of *illegal* discrimination. Discrimination is only illegal if it is based on a protected characteristic, as explained in Section A, above. Discrimination on other bases—for example, because of an employee's hair color, fashion sense, or sense of humor—is not illegal.

EXAMPLE: Yvonne claims that she didn't receive a promotion to a customer service position because she favors outlandish outfits in loud colors. She says this is unfair, because the way she dresses has nothing to do with her ability to serve customers. Yvonne may be right and she may be wrong, but she has not been discriminated against. No law prohibits an employer from making decisions based on an employee's clothing style, per se.

However, if Yvonne claims that she didn't receive the promotion because she wears a hijab (a body covering or head scarf worn by some Muslims), she could have a discrimination claim. Although the employer's decision was based on her clothing, that clothing is strongly associated with a particular religion and ethnicity. Therefore, the employer's decision could be discriminatory.

 Remember state laws.

Many states prohibit discrimination on bases that are not covered by federal law—such as sexual orientation, marital status, or weight. Check the chart in Appendix C—and contact your state fair employment practices agency—to find out your state's rules.

 Even if it isn't illegal discrimination, it might bear a closer look.

If you decide that an employee has not alleged illegal discrimination, you still might want to investigate. For example, say that an employee alleges that his manager allows workers who play or cheer for the company's softball team to leave early once a week to attend games, while everyone else has to be at their desks until 5 o'clock. Discrimination on the basis of softball? Well, probably not, but it may be a poor management practice—one you'll want to look into and possibly stop.

---

2. Take Immediate Action, If Necessary

Before you start your inquiry, you will have to decide whether some immediate action is necessary to prevent further incidents and to protect the integrity of your investigation. You should consider taking action before the investigation if:

- The accused employee continues to make managerial decisions. For example, if the vice president who approves promotions is accused of discriminating against older workers, you might not want the VP to fill any new vacancies until the investigation is complete.

- Tension between the accused employee and the complaining employee has reached a fever pitch. For example, if an employee accuses his supervisor of applying the rules more strictly to him because he is Chinese, you may have to change this reporting relationship until you sort things out.

- The alleged victim and/or witnesses appear to be intimidated by the accused employee. This might be the case, for example, if the complaining employee says that her supervisor threatened retaliation if she complained.

Whatever course you take, you must be very careful to avoid retaliation (or the appearance of retaliation). For example, if you separate the employees by moving the worker who complained to another shift or a different work area, you could be accused of retaliating.

What About Time Off for the Complaining Employee?

If an employee who complains of discrimination asks to take some time off, find out why the employee wants out of the workplace. If the employee has been threatened with retaliation or is being shunned by coworkers for making a complaint, these are facts you'll need to know. Also, make sure the employee doesn't feel forced to take time off—explain that retaliation is prohibited and that you will investigate as quickly as possible.

If an employee simply wants to take some time to catch his or her breath, you can arrange for a brief period of paid leave. However, make sure that the employee will be available to participate in the investigation.

Your safest strategy in these circumstances is to move the accused employee
or suspend him or her with pay until you complete the investigation. When
you tell the accused employee about the change, emphasize that it's a temporary situation, that no conclusions have been made about the truth or falsity of
the allegations, and that the company does not view the transfer or suspension
as punitive. If you must take an immediate action like this, complete the investigation as quickly as possible to minimize workplace disruption.

 Don't suspend workers without pay.

From a legal standpoint, you generally can't suspend exempt, salaried employees—those who are not entitled to overtime if they work extra hours—without
pay. And even though you can suspend hourly, nonexempt workers without
pay, it's not a good idea. A suspension without pay is punitive: It improperly
signals that you have made up your mind about the allegations before you've
even begun to investigate. A worker who is suspended without pay will probably be angry about it—and if the allegations are false, that anger may well
provide the fuel for a lawsuit. And unpaid suspensions can be an administrative
hassle, as they require you to interrupt your usual payroll system. The wages
you shell out to a temporarily suspended employee will be a small price to pay
to avoid these problems.

---

3. Choose the Investigator

You can find tips on choosing the right investigator in Chapter 2, Section D.
However, there are a couple of additional things to consider when choosing an
investigator for a discrimination claim.

a. Impartiality

An employee who alleges discrimination believes that she was treated unfairly—
that other workers received benefits she was denied, for illegitimate reasons. It
follows, therefore, that the person who investigates such a claim must be objective and impartial—and be perceived in the workplace as objective and impartial.

Of course, this is an important consideration in any investigation, but it is especially crucial when investigating discrimination. Make sure your chosen investigator doesn't have any connection to the complaining employee or the accused employee, doesn't have any involvement in the alleged discriminatory acts, and doesn't have any history of problems or controversy on issues of race, gender, and so on.

EXAMPLE: Fiona alleges that her employer does not promote women to higher levels of management; she says this "glass ceiling" has kept her from getting several promotions. The company is considering asking Brian to investigate Fiona's claims. Brian has no connection to Fiona or to the promoting supervisors, and he doesn't participate in promotion decisions. However, Brian belongs to an all-male country club and he has vociferously opposed allowing women to become members. Even if Brian could investigate Fiona's claims impartially, he is the wrong choice as an investigator. Fiona and other women he interviews could reasonably question his ability to look fairly at a sex discrimination claim, and he wouldn't have much credibility if he had to defend the investigation in a lawsuit.

b. When to Use an Outside Investigator

In some situations, it makes sense to bring in an outside investigator. Consider hiring a professional in these situations:

- Widespread discrimination is alleged—for example, that the company never promotes women, fires disproportionate numbers of older workers, or bends the rules only for white workers.

- Discrimination by a high-ranking company official (such as the CEO, president, or chairman) is alleged.

- An employee challenges a company practice or policy as having a disparate impact on a particular group (see Section A2, above)—these cases require an investigator to review statistics and information about lots of workers and potentially affect a large number of people.

- The charges have been publicized in the community and/or media.

- An employee has filed a charge of discrimination with the EEOC or a similar state fair employment practices agency.

- An employee has hired a lawyer or filed a lawsuit.

4. Plan the Investigation

Because discrimination investigations almost always begin with an employee complaint, you'll have a natural starting point for your investigation planning. And because discrimination complaints will almost always require an investigator to dig deeply into personnel files and other written records, you should spend some time gathering the documents you will need to make your decisions.

a. Examine the Allegations

Your first planning step is to carefully review the complaint. Whether an employee used your complaint policy to file a complaint or alleged discrimination during an exit interview, performance evaluation or other discussion with management, you will have some basic information to help you start thinking about the shape of the investigation. Consider these issues as you review the allegations:

- Who complained? What is the employee's protected characteristic? Did the employee allege that other employees were also discriminated against?

- The nature of the complaint. What type of discrimination is alleged? Does the employee claim that he or she alone was discriminated against, or is the employee challenging a company policy or practice that affects a group of employees? Did the employee request a reasonable accommodation for a disability or a religious practice? If so, what was the accommodation?

- Who is accused of discrimination? Is it a high-ranking company official? Does the employee accuse this person of making bigoted comments and holding biased views, or is the employee complaining of a single personnel action? Is the employee accusing one person of discrimination, or is the charge leveled at a group of people or the entire company?

- The employment decision at issue. Is the employee alleging a failure to promote, improper firing, unfair application of workplace rules and procedures, or failure to accommodate a disability or religious practice? Who is responsible for making the decision complained of?

- Has the employee named any witnesses?

    Based on your answers to these questions, you can begin to structure your investigation and determine what documents and other evidence to gather, whom to interview, and what questions to ask.

Courts caution employers to cast a wide net in discrimination investigations.

Some courts—and juries—have penalized employers for inadequate investigations of discrimination. The flaw in these investigations is often the employer's failure to look at the big picture: how the company treats employees who share the complaining employee's characteristic, as compared to how it treats other employees. If an employee alleges that Latinos are not promoted, or that women are denied work benefits (such as time off or flexible schedules) that are granted to men, for example, you will have to look beyond the complaining employee and the accused wrongdoer to examine company-wide practices. In these examples, your work might include examining which employees were promoted and which were not, or how many requests for time off were made in the last year, how many were granted, and to whom.

b. Documents and Other Evidence

Discrimination investigations often rely heavily on documents. To adequately examine an employee's allegation that an unfair decision was made, you'll need to find out the basis for the decision and what information the decision maker relied on. Generally, this means you'll spend some time looking at personnel files, performance evaluations, employee qualifications, and other paperwork. Particularly if an employee alleges that another worker was unfairly selected for promotion, you will have to closely examine evaluations, recommendations, work samples, and other evidence of performance to figure out whether there was a legitimate, business-related reason for choosing one employee over the other.

In most situations, you will also want to look at similar employment decisions made by the accused employee in the past, to see if you can find a pattern (or lack of one). For example, if an employee alleges that he wasn't promoted because of his age, you should look at previous promotion decisions made by the same supervisor. Has the supervisor consistently promoted younger workers, or have older workers been promoted in the past?

Here are some of the documents that might be relevant in a discrimination investigation:

- Company policies, including policies on discrimination and policies on the specific job action in question. For example, if an employee alleges that he was unfairly denied a promotion, you'll want to examine any company policies or other written materials that describe how promotion decisions should be made. If an employee claims that she was disciplined unfairly, you'll want to look at company discipline procedures.

- Personnel files, including the files of the complaining employee and the accused employee. If the employee complains of being denied a benefit, you also may want to examine the personnel file of any employee who received the benefit, to figure out whether the decision was justified.

- Performance records, if the decision was (or should have been) based on employee performance. For example, in a promotion case, you'll need to examine the work records of the employee who was denied the promotion and the employee who received it.

- Attendance records or sign-in sheets from antidiscrimination training.

- Any other records related to the employment decision at issue. For example, if an employee complains that he was disciplined more harshly for unexcused absences than other employees, you will want to examine attendance records to find out how many times each employee was absent.

5. Interviews

Once you've finished your investigation planning, you'll have some ideas about which employees you should interview. Start by interviewing the employee who complained. Next, move on to the employee (often a supervisor or manager) accused of discrimination. Then, interview any witnesses, others who were involved in the contested decision, other employees who received the benefit the complaining employee was denied, and/or other employees who share the complaining employee's protected characteristic and report to the same supervisor (to find out whether they feel that they've been treated fairly).

Start every interview with some opening remarks to set the employee at ease, explain the process, and answer any questions the employee may have. Next, proceed to your specific questions, remembering to follow up on any new information raised by the witness's responses. Close the interview by letting the witness know what will happen next and inviting the witness to come to you with any concerns or additional information. And conduct follow-up interviews if any new information comes to light.

a. Getting Started

Some of your opening comments will be the same, no matter whom you're interviewing. Some of them will be geared more specifically towards a complaining employee, an accused employee, or a witness. The opening statement you make to every person you interview should cover these points:

- **The purpose of the meeting.** The information you give here will depend on whom you're interviewing. You can tell the complaining employee that the company will be investigating the complaint and that the purpose of the meeting is to gather as much information as possible Tell the accused employee that a complaint has been made, that you're investigating, and that your role is to gather as much information as possible. A witness can simply be told that you're investigating a workplace problem and you believe the witness might have some relevant information.

- **The investigation process.** Explain that the company will be investigating the problem and interviewing other employees and will take appropriate steps if it finds that misconduct occurred.

- **Confidentiality.** Emphasize that you expect the employee to keep the investigation confidential and that talking about the investigation to other employees could be grounds for discipline. Explain that you will maintain confidentiality to the extent possible, although it will be necessary to reveal certain details in order to conduct thorough interviews and reach a decision.

- **Retaliation.** Explain that retaliation is prohibited and that the company will take immediate steps to discipline anyone who retaliates based on the complaint or investigation. Ask the employee to come to you with any concerns about retaliation.

- **Questions or concerns.** Ask whether the employee has any questions or concerns about the process.

When you interview the accused employee, emphasize that the company has not reached any decisions about what happened. Explain that you are interested in hearing what everyone has to say before making a decision or taking any action. Because you will probably have to reveal the name of the complaining employee (see Subsection b, below), spend some extra time discussing retaliation: what it is, that the company prohibits it, and that employees who engage in retaliation will be subject to discipline. Although the accused employee will probably want to know the allegations right away, you are better off postponing this discussion until later in the interview, after you have had a chance to gather some important background information. Explain that the accused employee will have the opportunity to hear and respond to the allegations before the interview is over.

For witnesses, your opening remarks can be brief. The witness doesn't need to know who complained, who is accused, or what the specific allegations are. Once you have explained that you are investigating a workplace problem and talked about confidentiality and retaliation, you can begin asking your questions.

b. Sample Questions

The specific questions you ask will depend on the nature of the problem and on whom you are interviewing.

Questions for the Complaining Employee

The questions you ask the complaining employee should focus on getting all of the details about the job action or decision at issue, as well as the employee's reasons for believing that the action was discriminatory. Your questions should be geared towards the specific employment decision in question. Here are some sample questions to consider when investigating a complaint that the employee was passed over for some job benefit, a complaint that the employee was fired or otherwise disciplined, and a reasonable accommodation complaint.

Employee Did Not Receive Benefit

- What benefit were you denied [for example, a promotion, a job transfer or schedule change, time off work, a raise]?

- Did you have to apply for the benefit? If so, when and how did you do so? If not, did you make it known that you wanted the benefit? How, when, and to whom?

- Do you know who made the decision to deny you this benefit? Do you report to this person? If so, when did you begin reporting to this person? Describe your work relationship to this person.

- How did you find out that you were denied the benefit? Who told you, if anyone? What did that person say? How did you respond? When did this happen?

- Do you know of other employees who have received this benefit, either now or in the past? Did any employees receive this benefit instead of you [this might be the case if the employee is challenging a failure to promote]? What are the names of these employees?

- [if the employee is alleging that another employee improperly received the benefit] Do you believe that you should have received the benefit instead of [employee X]? Why?

- Why do you believe that this decision was based on your [protected characteristic] rather than your qualifications?

- Aside from this decision, is there anything else that leads you to believe you were discriminated against? Have you heard anyone make comments about [employee's protected characteristic]? If so, who made them, when, and what did they say?

- How has not receiving this benefit affected you? Have you had to spend any money, or lost potential income, because you did not receive the benefit? How would you like to see this situation resolved?

- Do you know of anyone who might have information about this decision?

- Do you know of any documents relating to your complaint?

Employee Was Disciplined or Fired

- When were you fired or disciplined?

- Who told you about the firing or discipline? What reasons did that person give for the firing or discipline? What did you say in response, if anything? Do you know of any documents relating to this discussion?

- Do you know who made the decision to discipline or fire you? Is that person your supervisor? If so, for how long have you reported to that person? Describe your work relationship with that person.

- Do you know of anyone else who was involved in the decision to discipline or fire you? Describe your work relationship with that person.

- Were you told that you were fired or disciplined because of misconduct, performance problems, or other work-related reasons? Describe any incidents that were given as the basis for your firing or discipline. Are these allegations accurate? If not, why do you believe you were accused of these things?

- Do you know of others who were not fired or disciplined for the same misconduct or behavior? What are their names? When did these incidents occur?

- Why do you believe the decision to discipline or fire you was based on your [protected characteristic]?

- Aside from this decision, is there anything else that leads you to believe you were discriminated against? Have you heard anyone make comments about [employee's protected characteristic]? If so, who made them, when, and what did they say?

- How has being disciplined or fired affected you? Have you had to spend any money, or lost potential income, as a result? How would you like to see this situation resolved?

- Do you know of anyone who might have information about this decision?

- Do you know of any documents relating to this decision?

Employee Was Denied an Accommodation

- Did you request an accommodation? If so, what did you request, when, and of whom? If not, did you make your need for an accommodation known in some other way? How, when, and to whom?

- Why did you request an accommodation? How would the accommodation you requested have assisted you?

- [if employee is disabled] What is your disability? How does your disability affect your everyday activities? Describe the essential functions of your job. Are you able to perform these essential functions? How would the accommodation have helped you in this regard?

- [if employee requested an accommodation for religious reasons] What is your religion? What are the religious beliefs or practices that require a modification to our usual work rules or practices? How would the accommodation have helped you in this regard?

- How did you find out that your request for an accommodation was denied? Did you receive written notice? If you were told in person, who told you? What did that person say? Do you report to this person? If so, for how long? Describe your work relationship to this person.

- Do you believe your requested accommodation was reasonable? What do you think the company would have had to do to provide the accommodation? If you know, approximately what would the accommodation have cost?

- How has the denial of your request affected you? Have you had to spend any money, or lost potential income, because you did not receive the accommodation? How would you like to see this situation resolved?

- Do you know of anyone who might have information about this decision?

- Do you know of any documents relating to this decision?

Questions for the Accused Employee

The questions you ask the accused employee should focus on the reasons for the challenged decision. Because discrimination complaints usually challenge a job decision or action, the accused employee is almost always a supervisor or manager (in other words, someone with the authority to make those decisions or take those actions). You will want to explore the accused employee's work history, treatment of other workers, and similar decisions or actions taken in the past. Here are some sample questions geared towards the type of discrimination alleged.

Employee Did Not Receive a Benefit

- Do you supervise any employees? What are their names? For how long have you been a supervisor/manager? Have you had any managerial training? If so, when, for what, and who conducted the training?

- Do your responsibilities include deciding who gets [the benefit at issue—for example, promotions, raises, time off]? How do you make these decisions? Are there company guidelines or policies on the topic? What criteria do you consider? How often do you decide whether to [promote someone, give someone a raise, grant a request for time off]?

- Do you supervise [the complaining employee]? For how long have you worked together, and in what positions? Describe your work relationship.

- Did you decide [the action at issue—for example, not to give the complaining employee a raise, who would be promoted to account manager, not to give the complaining employee time off]? If not, who made this decision? If you made the decision, did anyone else have input? Who?

- Explain the basis for your decision. What did you consider? Are there any documents that you looked at? Did you create any documents, notes, or memos in the process of making the decision?

- [if the complaining employee alleges failure to promote] Who received the promotion? Why? Why did you decide not to promote [the complaining employee]?

- [if the complaining employee alleges denial of another benefit] Have you given other employees this benefit [for example, time off, raises, or shift changes]? If so, what are their names, and why did they receive the benefit? Why did you deny [the complaining employee] the benefit? How is [the complaining employee]'s situation different from that of the employee(s) who received the benefit?

- Describe the qualifications for the position or the criteria for receiving the benefit. Did [the complaining employee] meet those criteria or qualifications? If not, in what ways?

- Who told [the complaining employee] of your decision? If it was you, what did you say? How did [the complaining employee] respond? If someone else relayed your decision, who? Do you know what that person said? Why didn't you tell [the complaining employee] yourself?

- [The complaining employee] thinks [he or she] should have received the benefit because [state the complaining employee's reasons]. Did you consider that when making your decision? If so, why did [the complaining employee] not receive the benefit? If not, why not?

- [The complaining employee] thinks that your decision was based, at least in part, on [complaining employee's protected characteristic]. What is your response to that? Can you think of any reason why [the complaining employee] might think that?

You must allow the accused employee to respond to the allegations.
Some investigators are so eager to keep the interview civil—or to protect the complaining employee's privacy—that they never actually get around to confronting the accuser with the allegations. This is a big mistake, one that could undermine the legitimacy of the entire investigation. Courts have held that accused employees who never learns precisely what they are accused of haven't had a fair opportunity to tell their side of the story, to offer the names of relevant witnesses, or to explain why the complaining employee might have made the accusation. You don't necessarily have to say who complained, but you should say whom the employee is accused of discriminatng against. And don't worry about privacy concerns—you have a very compelling business reason for revealing this information.

- Do you know of anyone who might have information about this decision?
- Do you know of any documents relating to this decision?

Employee Was Disciplined or Fired

- Do you supervise any employees? What are their names? For how long have you been a supervisor/manager? Have you had any managerial training? If so, when, for what, and who conducted the training?
- Do your responsibilities include deciding whom to discipline and fire? How do you make these decisions? Are there company guidelines or policies on the topic? What criteria do you consider?
- [If the complaint is about a termination] How many employees have you fired in the past few years? What are their names? Why were they fired? Were there other employees that you considered firing? If so, what are their names, and why did you decide not to fire them?
- [If the complaint is about discipline] How many employees have you disciplined in the past few years? What are their names, and for what were they disciplined? Were there other employees that you considered disciplining? If so, what are their names, and why did you decide not to discipline them?

- Do you supervise [the complaining employee]? For how long have you worked together, and in what positions? Describe your work relationship.

- Who decided to fire or discipline [the complaining employee]? If it was your decision, did anyone else have input?

- Why did you fire or discipline [the complaining employee]? Tell me every factor you considered in reaching this decision. Did you rely on any documents in making your decision? Did you prepare any documents about the decision?

- Have you fired or disciplined other employees for similar conduct? Who, when, and for what reasons? Are there any documents relating to these decisions? What is the [complaining employee's protected characteristic—for example, race, age, or religion] of each of these employees?

- Did you tell [the complaining employee] that s/he would be disciplined or fired? If not, who did? Do you know what that person told [the complaining employee]? Why didn't you tell [the complaining employee] yourself? If so, what did you say? How did [the complaining employee] respond?

- Was the employee fired or disciplined for misconduct, poor performance, or other workplace problems? Does the employee have a history of these kinds of problems? Are these problems reflected in the employee's performance evaluations? Have you ever disciplined this employee before for the same problem? If so, when, what did you say, and how did the employee respond?

- [if the employee was fired] Has the employee been replaced? By whom? What is this person's [complaining employee's protected characteristic—for example, race or national origin]?

- [The complaining employee] believes [he or she] should not have been disciplined or fired because [give the complaining employee's reasons]. Did you consider that in reaching your decision? Why or why not?

- [The complaining employee] believes that [complaining employee's protected characteristic] played a role in your decision. What is your response to that? Can you think of any reason why [the complaining employee] might think that?

- Do you know of anyone who might have information about this decision?

- Do you know of any documents relating to this decision?

Employee Was Denied an Accommodation

- Do you supervise any employees? What are their names? For how long have you been a supervisor/manager? Have you had any managerial training? If so, when, for what, and who conducted the training?

- Do your responsibilities include deciding whether to change work rules, schedules, or other workplace issues to accommodate an employee's disability or religious practices? How do you make these decisions? Are there company guidelines or policies on the topic? What criteria do you consider? How often do you decide whether to [promote someone, give someone a raise, grant a request for time off]?

- Do you supervise [the complaining employee]? For how long have you worked together, and in what positions? Describe your work relationship.

- Did [the complaining employee] ever ask you to make a workplace change to accommodate a disability or religious practice? If so, what did the employee request? How did you respond? If not, has [the complaining employee] ever spoken to you about a disability or religious practice? What did [the complaining employee] say, and how did you respond? Has [the complaining employee] ever asked you to make a workplace change for any reason? What was the change? How did you respond?

- If a request for accommodation was made, did you deny the request? What did you consider in making your decision? What would the company have had to do in order to fulfill the request? What would the request have cost the company? Did you discuss the request with anyone else? Did you get input from anyone else in making your decision?

- Did you tell the employee that the request was denied? If so, what did you say, and how did the employee respond? If not, who told the employee? What did that person say, and how did the employee respond, if you know? Why didn't you tell the employee yourself?

- Did you offer the employee an alternative accommodation? If so, what did you offer, and how did the employee respond? What would the company have had to do in order to provide the alternative accommodation? What would the request have cost the company? If not, can you think of any other accommodations that would meet the employee's needs?

- Do you know of anyone who might have information about this decision?

- Do you know of any documents relating to this decision?

Questions for Witnesses

When questioning witnesses, your goal is to gather information without giving too much away. To plan your questions, consider who suggested the witness and why. Did the witness play a role in the employment decision at issue? Did the witness see or hear allegedly discriminatory conduct or statements? Did the witness receive a benefit that was denied the complaining employee, or was the witness otherwise treated differently than the complaining employee? Is the witness another possible victim of discrimination?

Start by explaining, in very general terms, why the witness is being interviewed—that you are investigating a workplace problem, and you believe the witness might have information that will help you figure out what happened. Then, move into questions that will help you figure out how the witness fits into the picture (if at all). Finally, find out what the witness knows. Start with general questions like these:

- How long have you worked at the company? What positions have you held? What is your current position? What are your job responsibilities? To whom do you report? Who reports to you?

- Do you work with [the complaining employee or the accused employee]? How would you describe their work relationship with each other?

Your next questions will depend on what the witness said, did, or knows. Here are some examples.

For a witness who played a role in the decision:

- Are you responsible for deciding or participating in decisions about [the decision at issue—for example, who gets promoted, who gets fired, whether the company will grant an employee's request for an accommodation]? How many such decisions do you make or participate in each year? What is the process for making these decisions? What do you consider in making these decisions?

- Were you involved in the decision to [fire, promote, deny time off to] [the complaining employee]? What was your role? What did you consider in making this decision? Whom did you talk to about the decision? Did you consider any documents in reaching this decision? Did you create any documents?

- Have you been involved in any previous decisions to [deny time off, promote, fire] an employee at the company? What are the names of these employees? What did you decide? Why?
- What role did [the accused employee] play in this decision?
- [The complaining employee] believes that [protected characteristic, such as race or age] played a role in this decision. How do you respond to that? Can you think of any reason why [the complaining employee] might think that?
- [The complaining employee] believes the decision was unfair because [give reason, such as he had more seniority than the employee who was promoted, or she was told she would receive a raise by February]. Did you consider that in making your decision? Why or why not?

For a witness who may have seen or heard something:

- Describe your typical workday.
- Has [the complaining employee] ever spoken to you about [the accused employee]? Has [the accused employee] ever spoken to you about [the complaining employee]?
- Have you seen any interactions between [the complaining employee] and [the accused employee] that made you uncomfortable? Describe them to me.
- If the witness may have seen or heard the incident, ask questions to figure out whether the witness was there and what happened.
- Have you ever heard [the accused employee] make any comment about [the complaining employee's protected characteristic, such as national origin or disability]? If so, what did the accused employee say?

For a witness who received the benefit:

- Did you recently [apply for a promotion, receive a raise]? When? Who made the decision? Did you have to apply for the benefit? If so, what materials did you submit?
- Do you know of any other employees who applied for the benefit?
- When did you learn that you would receive the benefit? Who told you? What did that person say? How did you respond?

- Do you know what the qualifications or other criteria are for receiving this benefit? Do you meet those qualifications or criteria?

No matter what your reason for interviewing the witness, make sure to ask whether the witness knows of anyone else who might have information about the complaint or knows of any documents or other evidence relating to the complaint.

c. Closing the Interview

Once you have finished your questions, review your notes with the person you interviewed. Make sure you got everything right and that your notes include all of the important details. Ask the employee not to discuss the complaint or the investigation with any coworkers. Remind the employee (especially the accused employee) that retaliation is prohibited. And ask the employee to come to you immediately with any new information.

This is all you have to tell witnesses. When you close an interview with the complaining or accused employee, let them know what will happen next. Tell them that you'll interview them again if any important new information comes up.

d. Follow-Up Interviews

If any new information comes up during your investigation, you should conduct follow-up interviews with the complaining or accused employee. Both employees should have the opportunity to respond to new allegations or defenses, to make sure that you have a complete understanding of the facts when you make your decision and to give you the opportunity to gauge credibility. It is especially important to let the accused employee know of any additional allegations that come up during the investigation. If you don't, the accused employee may claim, in court, that he or she was denied the opportunity to respond— and, therefore, that the investigation was not thorough or fair.

EXAMPLE: Roy claims that Anna unfairly denied him a promotion because of his race and national origin (Asian). You interview Roy and Anna, focusing primarily on the promotion decision. You also interview Rachel, a witness whom Roy suggests because she has told him that she believes Anna is biased against Asians. Rachel tells you that she and Anna used to be friends outside of work until one night when Anna, after a few drinks, made a number of racist comments about Asians and Asian-Americans, including Roy and other

Asians who report to her. One of the comments, according to Rachel, was "Asians think they're better than everyone else—well, they're not going to get any positions of power in this company while I've got anything to say about it." Before you wrap up the investigation, you should go back to Anna to confront her with these allegations and allow her to respond.

6. Gather Documents and Other Evidence

Most discrimination claims allege that the employer made an unfair job decision—that is, a decision that was based on the employee's characteristic, rather than appropriate work considerations (such as performance, ability, skills, and so on). Your job as an investigator is to find out the real reason for the allegedly discriminatory decision, and this will require you to carefully review employment-related records to see whether they support—or contradict—the accused employee's stated rationale.

You should always start by gathering up any relevant policies (such as an antidiscrimination policy, or a policy relating to the job decision in question) and the personnel files of the complaining employee and the accused employee. These records should yield quite a bit of information, including:

- Whether company policies clearly spelled out a procedure for making the decision in question. For example, if an employee complains that she was unfairly denied an annual raise, examine workplace policies on raises (if there are any). Are employees promised an annual raise? Does the policy list the criteria for awarding or denying raises?

- The complaining employee's work history at your company. Has the employee had a history of performance problems? Has the employee been promoted repeatedly, received raises, or otherwise been rewarded? For how long has the employee reported to the accused employee? Examine the employee's evaluations and other work records during that time—are they generally consistent with the employee's work history, or do the records reveal a change in treatment? Has the employee complained of discrimination before? If so, how were those incidents handled?

- The accused employee's work history at your company. Has anyone else ever accused this person of discrimination? If so, how were those situations resolved? What are the accused employee's qualifications as a supervisor? Has the employee ever received training or coaching in that area? Who else reports to the accused employee? What similar decisions has the accused employee made in the past—for example, who else has been promoted, or who else has received or been denied a raise?

Once you have examined these records, you will want to look at documents relating to the employment decision in question. For example, if an employee complains that she was not promoted because of her gender, you should gather up any documents relating to the promotion decision—these might include the applications of everyone who applied for the position, any other written materials (such as performance evaluations, work samples, or written tests) the supervisor considered in deciding whom to promote, and any written notes the supervisor took when interviewing candidates.

After you've reviewed documents relating to the decision that is the subject of the complaint, you'll want to widen your net to look at similar decisions made by the same decision maker in the past. Using the same example, if a supervisor is accused of sex discrimination for failing to promote a woman, you'll want to look at other promotions by the same supervisor. If the supervisor has never promoted a woman even though plenty of qualified women have applied, you'll want to follow up on that. Similarly, if the supervisor has a history of promoting women, that might lead you to believe that the explanation lies in something other than the complaining employee's gender.

7. Evaluate the Evidence

In many discrimination cases, everyone agrees on what happened. Unlike a sexual harassment case, for example, in which the complaining employee and the accused employee may tell very different stories about what each said and did, a discrimination case is often based on some undisputed facts. An employee did not receive a promotion, was not granted time off work, was disciplined, was demoted, or was fired. The dispute in discrimination cases is often over the reasons for these actions—that is, everyone may agree on *what* happened, but they disagree about *why*.

In these situations, it can be tough to get to the bottom of things. Motivation—why a person does something—can be very difficult to gauge. You'll have to rely on outward indications of intent, including plausibility, corroboration, and consistency.

- **Plausibility.** Whose story makes the most sense? Does the employee's version of events ring true? What about the decision maker—has that person given a commonsense, nondiscriminatory reason for the challenged decision?

- **Corroboration.** If the complaining employee alleges that the decision maker made biased comments, did anyone else witness them? Do personnel files, performance evaluations, and other documents support the decision maker's rationale? Or do they support the complaint?

- **Consistency.** This is probably the most important factor to consider in many discrimination claims. A discrimination claim is, at its core, an allegation of inconsistent treatment based on a protected characteristic. Does the evidence support the decision maker's stated reason for action? Has the decision maker been consistent in applying the rules? Has the decision maker used the same objective criteria to judge all employees? Have these criteria been used consistently over time?

EXAMPLE: Manuel requested a week off to attend his mother's funeral in Mexico and help his siblings wrap up her personal affairs. He complained that his request was denied because of his race and national origin; he tells you that white employees have been allowed to take time off for family matters. Manuel's supervisor agrees that he denied Manuel's request but claims that he was only following company policy, which requires employees to have worked for the company for at least one year before taking time off. After examining the attendance records of the other employees who report to this supervisor, you discover that two employees, both white, have taken time off during their first year of employment. When you ask the supervisor why they were allowed to take time off, he responds that they both had serious personal emergencies: One had to stay home to care for her child for a week while her nanny was in the hospital, and the other had a fire in his home, which required him to miss work for a week while he moved his family's belongings out and met with contractors and insurance adjusters.

Has this supervisor acted consistently? Not really. He has bent the rules and made exceptions. Does he have a principled reason for distinguishing between Manuel's situation and that of the other two employees? Again, not really. A mother's death is a serious personal problem; although Manuel could miss her funeral, the employee with child care problems could have hired a temporary babysitter and the employee with the fire could have moved his family after work hours. The long and the short of it is that this supervisor has not acted consistently, in a manner that—intentionally or not—has favored white employees. Whether or not Manuel could win a discrimination lawsuit, he has brought an important problem to light, which the company should deal with right away.

Of course, some discrimination cases involved disputed facts. If a supervisor is accused of making racist or sexist comments, the supervisor may deny the statements altogether or claim to have said something different. For example, if an employee claims that her supervisor told her that she should stop working after having her baby, the supervisor might respond, "That's not true. What I said was that many women decide to quit their jobs after having babies, and that I understood why they made that decision." In these situations, you'll have to decide which version of the facts makes the most sense—review the guidelines in Chapter 4 for help in sorting things out.

As you evaluate the evidence, remember that you can find that conduct was improper even if it's not clear that illegal discrimination took place. In the example involving Manuel, above, a court may not find in Manuel's favor—at least, not without some other evidence that the supervisor's decisions may have been based on race or national origin (such as racist comments or a long history of denying Mexican-Americans' requests for time off). However, the supervisor's explanation is unsatisfactory and begs the question of why these other workers got to take time off when Manuel did not—which means that one of your supervisors is making decisions that are unpredictable and confusing to your employees and have led at least one person to suspect that bias is at work. This is a situation you'll want to deal with as improper managerial conduct, whether or not it amounts to illegal discrimination.

8. Take Action

If you find that discrimination occurred—or that improper management decisions were made, even if you aren't completely convinced that they were intentionally discriminatory—then you should take corrective action. Your two goals in taking action are:

- to end the discrimination or other questionable management behavior, and

- to put the victim where he would have been had decisions been made appropriately.

a. Ending the Discrimination

It can be very tough to decide what to do about a discrimination claim. If you face a really cut-and-dried case, in which a supervisor made bigoted comments and made employment decisions based on his biased views, firing is clearly appropriate. However, cases like this are rare. A more likely scenario is this: A supervisor makes employment decisions that aren't entirely consistent and objective but also aren't clearly discriminatory. What you decide to do in these situations will depend, in part, on the supervisor's explanation for the actions, willingness to consider that the actions were inappropriate, and attitude about the future.

EXAMPLE: Toby is a regional manager for a large company. In the last year, he has promoted three employees to be site supervisors, all of them men. One of the women who applied for this position complained of sex discrimination. Your investigation reveals that thirty employees applied for these three positions, 20 male and 10 female. Toby claims that he promoted the best-qualified candidates; however, the woman who complained had more experience and better performance evaluations than one of the men Toby chose. When you asked Toby about this, he says that the woman "seemed pretty reserved and timid in the interview; she didn't strike me as someone who could supervise a hectic job site."

What do you do now? Well, Toby had a reason for failing to promote the woman. The problem is, that reason is kind of subjective—and it's not clear that he judged all of the candidates by the same standards. Your decision will probably depend partially on Toby's attitude. If Toby expresses remorse about the trouble his decision caused and is willing to consider that he made a mistake, you might settle for a written warning, along with some management training. On the other hand, if Toby says, "I have the right to promote whomever I see fit, and she'll just have to get used to it," or if he reveals that bias played a role in his decisions ("Very few women are going to have what it takes to supervise one of these sites"), a harsher punishment is probably in order.

The action you take must stop the discrimination. However, if you are too severe in your response, you might be facing a lawsuit from the employee accused of discrimination. The only way to walk this fine line is to make the punishment fit the crime. Consider:

- the severity of the discrimination
- how many total incidents of discrimination took place
- the harm to the victim
- whether the law was violated
- whether workplace policies were violated
- whether the accused employee holds a position of authority in the company, such as officer, manager, or supervisor (discrimination by a higher-level employee is more serious and requires a heightened response)
- how the company has treated similar incidents in the past
- the accused employee's attitude towards the incident, and
- the accused employee's history at the company—does the employee have a record of similar problems, or is this a one-time lapse from an otherwise stellar worker?

b. Restoring the Victim

If you find that improper conduct occurred, you should take steps to right the wrong. If the complaining employee suffered some negative job action (as is often the case), it may be appropriate to undo the damage. Here are some actions you might consider:

- Remove negative performance evaluations or disciplinary warnings from an employee's file, if doubt has been cast on the fairness of those documents.
- If an employee has been suspended without pay, pay the employee for that time.
- If an employee has been unfairly denied a transfer, promotion, raise, or other job benefit, grant the benefit retroactively.
- If an employee has been demoted or fired, reinstate the employee, with pay retroactive to the date of the decision.

Sometimes, you may have to work with an employee to figure out how to deal with a problem in the past. Remember Manuel, who was denied time off to attend his mother's funeral? There's no obvious way to undo this damage, but the company may be able to give Manuel a related benefit instead. For example, the company might give Manuel a week of paid leave to use whenever he wishes or make a small donation to a charity in his mother's name.

In some situations, you may not know whether discrimination occurred—but you do know that the employment decision was not made properly. In these cases, it may not be appropriate to just give the complaining employee the denied benefit (such as a promotion or job transfer), because that wouldn't really be fair to others. At the same time, however, you should take some action to rectify the situation. The solution might be to make the decision again, this time using fair, job-related criteria.

EXAMPLE: Jim has worked for a law firm for a couple of months as a file clerk. Jim has extensive experience and training as a paralegal, but the law firm had no paralegal positions open when he applied. When a paralegal position became vacant, Jim applied. Tom, who supervises the paralegals, hired someone from outside the firm. Jim alleges that this decision was based on his age (he is 62 years old, and the person Tom hired is 28). Tom responds that he assumed Jim didn't have the right experience for the position, because he was working as a file clerk. Tom admits that he didn't even look at Jim's application. The firm hires paralegals regularly—on average, a paralegal is hired every several months. Tom has hired dozens of paralegals for the firm in the past; many of them have been over the age of 40.

What do you do now? Clearly, Tom's decision was flawed. However, there's no clear indication that it was based on Jim's age. And, now, you've got someone else in the picture—the new employee who got the paralegal job. In this situation, your best move might be to promise that Jim will be considered for the next available position. Because the firm hires so frequently, Jim won't have to wait long to be considered. And you won't have to displace a worker who has already been hired.

9. Document the Investigation

Document your discrimination investigation, following the guidelines in Chapter 4. Remember, if an employee files a lawsuit based on the investigation (or the alleged discrimination you investigated), your documentation could well end up in the hands of a judge or jury. Make sure to write a report that's complete and professional and fully supports the conclusions you reached.

 Don't create evidence that can be used against your company.

If you investigate a really egregious situation in which you believe rank discrimination took place, you might want to state this conclusion in your report. This is a temptation you should resist, however. Remember, if the affected employee decides to file a lawsuit, your company will generally be liable for discrimination by supervisors and managers. If you state, in your report, that discrimination occurred, you will be tying your company's hands in the courtroom. The employee's lawyer will tell the jury, "The company's own investigator admitted that my client was discriminated against"—and you can imagine how the argument goes from there. The better strategy is simply to state that company policies were violated and that the manager or supervisor acted inappropriately or unprofessionally, and leave it at that.

---

10. Follow Up

Once the investigation is complete, it's a good time to think about what the company could do differently to prevent future problems. For example, did your investigation reveal racial insensitivity, ignorance about the needs and contributions of disabled workers, or a general lack of understanding among different groups of employees? If so, some diversity training may be in order. You might also consider training for your supervisors, if you discover that they were making inconsistent or haphazard managerial decisions, or if they simply weren't clear about their obligations under the antidiscrimination laws.

This is also a good time to examine any company practices that the investigation has called into question. For example, do all of your supervisors understand the company's criteria for promotions? For discipline and termination? Are these criteria fair, objective, and job-related?

You should also follow up with the employees involved in the complaint. Retaliation can be a problem if the accused employee continues to work for the company—especially if you determined that the complaint was unfounded. An employee who was accused of discrimination and ultimately vindicated is likely to be angry—and may feel justified in taking out some of that anger on the complaining employee. To guard against this problem, meet with the complaining employee a few times after the investigation to make sure everything is going smoothly and no retaliation is taking place. You should also meet with the accused employee to make sure that things are getting back to normal.

If an employee raised any reasonable accommodation issues, you may need to follow up on that as well. If the employee and the company were able to come up with an accommodation, check in with everyone involved to make sure that the accommodation is working. If the employee's suggested accommodation ultimately created an undue burden on the company, you may need to spend some time with the employee (and perhaps the employee's manager), trying to come up with an alternative accommodation that will be effective. ∎

CHAPTER

Investigating Harassment

You've probably heard about the multimillion dollar verdicts some employees have won in harassment lawsuits. Maybe you've even seen news reports about huge companies facing class action claims and government investigations for mistreating women, people of color, or disabled workers. These stories demonstrate that claims of workplace harassment can do some serious damage to a business, in bad publicity and in dollars and cents. It's no wonder why most employers feel some anxiety when they get a complaint of harassment.

Harassment claims can also be uncomfortable to investigate. If you're looking into a complaint of sexual harassment, for example, you may need to pry into personal relationships, sexual misconduct, graphic language, and more. For other types of harassment claims—such as racial harassment or harassment based on disability—you may hear disturbing accounts of bigotry and insensitivity. And no matter what type of harassment you're investigating, you can be sure of one thing: The people involved will have very strong feelings about the situation and about how the company decides to handle it. This can put a lot of pressure on you to maintain your objectivity, stay focused on the facts, and make the right decision.

That's the bad news. The good news is that investigating these complaints properly can help you avoid legal liability for harassment. And you'll have plenty of guidance on what you need to do to stay out of trouble: The Supreme Court has decided several recent cases explaining an employer's obligation to investigate harassment complaints. And the Equal Employment Opportunity Commission—the federal government agency that enforces laws prohibiting discrimination and harassment—has issued some written guidelines for employers on how to investigate harassment. Although harassment investigations can be challenging, the information in this chapter will help you do the job right—and stay out of legal trouble.

Section A explains the law of harassment: what it is, what it isn't, and what employers are obligated to do about it. This section covers both sexual harassment and other types of workplace harassment. Section B describes ten steps to a successful harassment investigation.

A. What Is Harassment?

Some workers are quick to cry "Harassment!" whenever they feel that a supervisor is being tough on them or they're being treated unfairly:

- "These deadlines are too tight. Forcing all of us to meet them is just harassment!"

- "Making us smoke outside the building when it's this cold out is ridiculous. I feel like we're being harassed."

- "Just because I forgot to call in sick, my supervisor called me to find out where I was. She shouldn't be calling me at home, regardless of the reason—this is harassment."

These kinds of gripes generally don't meet the legal definition of harassment. Harassment is an offshoot of the laws that prohibit discrimination—which means that harassment is illegal only if it is based on a person's race, gender, age, disability, or other protected characteristic. (For more on antidiscrimination laws, see Chapter 5, Section A.) General complaints about working conditions don't meet this standard unless the employee is being subjected to tougher supervision or more onerous rules because of, for example, race or gender.

EXAMPLE: Carla wants to leave work early two days a week to get a graduate degree. She works for a department store that does not offer flexible scheduling. Her supervisor tells her that she can't take the time off, because company policy prohibits it and because it would be difficult to find someone to work her station for just a few hours a week. Her supervisor offers to let her take those days off entirely, but she would have to work on the weekend. Although this is unfortunate for Carla, it isn't harassment.

Now suppose Carla's employer has usually accommodated employees' requests to take time off for personal pursuits. In fact, Carla had spoken to her supervisor before she signed up for school, and her supervisor assured her that he would rearrange her schedule. However, when Carla told her supervisor that she would be attending divinity school to become a minister, his attitude changed. He was not as friendly towards her and seemed to avoid her at work. When she asked to meet with him to work out the scheduling details, he told her that he wasn't willing to lose an employee for several hours each week just so she could "go to Bible school." Carla may have a valid claim of religious harassment—she was subjected to different rules because of her religious beliefs.

The general rules that apply to all kinds of harassment are discussed in Section 1, below. There are a couple of additional issues that are more likely to come up in sexual harassment cases; these are covered in Section 2, below.

1. Harassment: The Basics

Legally speaking, harassment is offensive, unwelcome conduct (whether words, actions, gestures, or visual displays) that is so severe or pervasive that it affects the terms and conditions of the victim's employment. Sometimes, harassment directly affects the victim's job opportunities—for example, when a supervisor tells an employee, "I'm not going to give you that promotion unless you agree to go on a date with me" or subjects an employee to harsher rules because of her protected status (like Carla in the example above). Other times, harassment doesn't result in discipline or lost opportunities but does make it difficult for the victim to do her job because of constant ridicule, belittling comments, teasing, or sexual come-ons. This second type of harassment is referred to as "hostile environment" harassment.

a. Harassing Conduct

As noted above, workplace mistreatment can be construed as harassment only if it is based on a protected characteristic. Under federal law, protected characteristics include race, color, national origin, sex, disability, age, and religion. Many states expand this list to include sexual orientation, marital status, and other categories. And some municipalities prohibit additional types of discrimination—on the basis of appearance, weight, or transgender status, for example. (See Chapter 5, Section A1 for more information on protected categories—and how to find out the laws of your state and local government.)

What kinds of conduct constitute harassment? Anything from derogatory jokes based on ethnicity or age to name-calling and slurs to threats and outright physical violence. Harassment may take the form of actual comments about an employee's protected characteristic or it may be more subtle—for example, an employer may treat workers of a certain ethnicity better than other workers. Here are some examples:

- A Jewish office worker is subjected to jokes about the Holocaust and is assigned to a bookkeeping position because "Jews know how to handle money."

- An African-American salesman works at a car dealership. His coworkers make racist comments about nonwhite customers; after he tells them that he finds their comments offensive, they start referring to themselves jokingly as "the KKK."
- A clerical worker with cerebral palsy is mimicked by her supervisor, who ridicules her speech and the way she walks, blames her for errors she did not commit, and tells her coworkers that she is incompetent "but we can't fire her because she's disabled."

b. Unwelcome Conduct

To constitute illegal harassment, conduct or statements must be unwelcome to the victim. In most types of harassment cases, this isn't really an issue. Someone who is referred to in offensive or derogatory terms, made fun of because of age or disability, or threatened with racial violence generally finds the conduct unwelcome. However, this sometimes is a disputed issue in sexual harassment cases, because some sexual advances, comments, or jokes might not offend their target. (See Section A2, below, for more information.)

There may be a legitimate question of welcomeness in some cases that don't involve sexual harassment. For example, if an older worker frequently refers to himself as "gramps" or "the old-timer" and makes jokes about his "senior moments," other employees may feel that he doesn't mind being teased about his age. Similarly, workers who share a protected characteristic (such as the same ethnic background or sexual orientation) may feel comfortable exchanging jokes about it but quite uncomfortable hearing the same kinds of comments from someone else.

c. Severe or Pervasive

Harassment is illegal only if it is severe or pervasive. Generally, this means that there must be a pattern of harassment or a series of harassing incidents over time. One teasing comment, request for a date, or use of a bigoted epithet probably does not constitute harassment by itself. On the other hand, courts have found that a single act can be harassment if the act is truly extreme—such as rape or a racially motivated physical assault.

There's no clear line or "magic number" of incidents when name-calling, teasing, and such cross the line to become harassment. Courts will look at the totality of the circumstances in deciding whether harassment has occurred. This means that the court will consider all of the incidents in context. The more egregious each incident is, the fewer will be necessary for an employer to be held liable.

 It may be inappropriate even if it isn't illegal.

This section explains how the law defines harassment. However, you shouldn't base your decision to investigate solely on whether the conduct alleged meets these legal standards. For one thing, you can't predict with utter certainty how a judge or jury will decide a particular harassment claim. More important, behavior doesn't have to be illegal to violate your company's standards on proper workplace behavior. A few isolated sexual jokes or bigoted comments can quickly escalate into a full-blown harassment claim—and even if they don't, they will certainly create an uncomfortable atmosphere for at least some of your workers. If you investigate, you can put a stop to this type of unprofessional behavior right away, before legal trouble develops.

---

d. Terms and Conditions of Employment

In order for a court to determine that harassment occurred, the conduct must affect the terms and conditions of the victim's employment. There are several ways this might happen. If the harasser is a supervisor or someone else who has the right and authority to make job decisions, harassment might take the form of a negative job action, such as firing, failure to promote, demotion, discipline, a pay cut (or refusal to grant a pay raise), or an undesirable transfer, reassignment, or change in job duties or title.

However, harassment can occur even if the victim is not subjected to a negative job action like this. The victim can make a hostile environment claim if he or she reasonably finds the workplace to be abusive or hostile as a result of the harassment. The key word here is "reasonable." It is not enough that the victim believes the workplace is hostile; the circumstances must be such that a reasonable worker in the victim's position would also find the workplace hostile. This rule ensures that employers won't be liable to hypersensitive employees who see harassment behind every smile and gesture.

Who's a Reasonable Worker?

The "reasonable person" test for harassment can be tough to figure out. After all, reasonable people can differ on what constitutes harassment or whether a particular situation has crossed the line from sophomoric to abusive.

The law says that employers (and juries, if it comes to that) must consider the situation from the viewpoint of a reasonable worker *in the victim's position*. This means that the typical sexual harassment claim must be considered from the perspective of a reasonable woman, and a case of racial harassment against an African-American employee must be looked at from the vantage point of a reasonable African-American. This rule is an effort to acknowledge the fact that different groups in our society may react differently to particular actions, words, and comments.

2. Sexual Harassment

Sexual harassment is defined in essentially the same way as other types of harassment: It's offensive, unwelcome sexual conduct that is so severe or pervasive that it affects the terms and conditions of the victim's employment—either because the victim's submission or failure to submit to the behavior is the basis for job-related decisions (like firing or demotion) or because the victim reasonably finds the workplace abusive or hostile as a result of the harassment. However, sexual harassment cases sometimes place more emphasis on the issue of welcomeness, to recognize the fact that not all sexual or romantic behavior in the workplace is offensive to the recipient.

It's safe to say that harassment based on race, disability, and so on is rarely a misguided effort to establish a closer relationship with the victim. Although such harassment is sometimes meant in fun, its victims tend not to find it very amusing. In contrast, behavior that could be construed as sexual harassment under certain circumstances might not bother the recipient at all. After all, some requests for dates are accepted happily—and lead to mutually satisfying relationships. While one person might find sexually explicit comments and jokes offensive, another might find them flattering and flirtatious. In an era when everyone spends so much time on the job—and, according to some surveys, a majority of us have had a relationship with someone we met at work—the law can't presume that every sexual advance or provocative comment is offensive.

At the same time, of course, it is very disturbing to be subjected to unwanted sexual attention, to be told that you have to submit to sexual advances in order to get ahead, or to work in an environment where X-rated comments and jokes that you find offensive are the order of the day.

a. Unwelcome Harassment

Sexual harassment is unwelcome when the victim finds it offensive rather than flattering or innocent. Notice the focus on the victim—unlike the reasonableness standard discussed above, unwelcomeness is in the eye of the beholder. It's a subjective determination—which means that when you are investigating a sexual harassment claim, you will want to ask the victim how he or she felt about the alleged harassment and what impact it had on him or her.

Who's Harassing Whom?

The majority of sexual harassment claims involve a male harasser and a female victim. However, courts have recognized harassment claims by male victims of female harassers, male victims of male harassers, and female victims of female harassers. And the Equal Employment Opportunity Commission, or EEOC (the federal government agency that enforces antidiscrimination and harassment laws), reports that harassment claims by men have been steadily increasing—last year, such claims made up almost 15% of all sexual harassment charges filed under federal law (these statistics don't indicate the gender of the harasser).

Regardless of the gender of the victim or harasser, the same standards apply: The victim must be subjected to offensive sexual conduct that is severe or pervasive, affects the terms and conditions of employment, and is unwelcome.

Keep in mind that what may be welcome to one employee could be unwelcome to others. For example, a group of men enjoy teasing and making sexual jokes with the office receptionist, an attractive young woman. The receptionist finds the jokes amusing and harmless, and sometimes tells one herself. This isn't illegal harassment, because the conduct is welcome. However, a female secretary who shares space with the receptionist finds these comments offensive and disruptive. Although none of the jokes are directed at her, she finds them unwelcome and must put up with them to do her job. She may be a victim of sexual harassment.

Claims of Sexual Favoritism

If a worker is required to submit to sexual advances in order to get some type of job benefit (such as a promotion or desired assignment), that worker has a pretty good sexual harassment claim. But what about the other workers, those who weren't put under sexual pressure but also didn't get the job benefit? According to the EEOC, these workers may also have a legal claim against the company for harassment. Even though they weren't directly subjected to harassment, their job opportunities suffered because of sexual harassment against another employee.

However, these claims are allowed only if the employee who gets the benefit has been harassed. If the supervisor is engaged in a consensual relationship with an employee and gives that employee preferential treatment based on the relationship, other employees don't have a viable harassment claim. The benefits were not conferred because of harassment, but because of a personal relationship. Although this is clearly a poor management practice—and one that many workers will resent—it isn't harassment.

b. Prior Relationships

Remember all of those consensual relationships that began at work? Well, common sense tell us that many of them are bound to end at some point—which means that all of the drama, hurt feelings, and denial that can accompany a relationship's demise might find their way into the workplace.

Unfortunately, it also means that sexual harassment claims might not be far behind. Some sexual harassment claims are brought by a victim who used to be in a consensual relationship with the harasser. This is a particular danger when one member of the former couple supervises the other or holds a position that gives him the right to make decisions about the other's future at the company. The subordinate employee might claim that she is being punished for ending the relationship or that she is being subjected to advances that are now unwanted. In extreme cases, one employee might even make a false claim of harassment against the other, out of spite or anger over the breakup.

If you learn, during the course of your investigation, that the alleged harasser and victim used to be romantically involved, you'll probably have to ask some questions about that relationship so you can figure out how it plays into the harassment allegations. This can be a sticky situation for investigators, as it requires you to get into some issues that the parties might think of as private. (See Section B5, below, for tips on handling this type of problem.)

c. Sex-Based Harassment

Some courts have recognized claims of sex-based harassment—that is, harassment that is based on sex but is not sexual in nature. In these cases, the harasser is not interested in having a sexual relationship with his victim(s) or otherwise "sexualizing" the workplace with jokes and stories but instead wants to intentionally create a hostile environment for workers of a particular gender (almost always women). Often, these claims are made by women working in traditionally male professions.

Although women in these cases have clearly been subjected to a hostile work environment because of their sex, there are none of the traditional signs of sexual harassment—requests for dates, dirty jokes, sexualized comments about women's bodies, and so on. Instead, harassing conduct in these cases might include sabotaging the tools, vehicles, or work of women employees; soiling or defacing women's workspaces, lockers, or restroom facilities; subjecting women to dangerous work conditions; displaying cartoons or telling jokes that depict violence towards women; and making comments about women's inability to do the job.

Some states have not yet recognized these claims. Whether or not the courts in your state treat this kind of behavior as sexual harassment, you will obviously want to investigate and put a stop to it. When your employees are spending part of their workdays engaging in, or being subjected to, cruel or dangerous conduct, you are losing productivity and morale. You also may be at risk for workers' compensation claims or personal injury lawsuits if an employee is harmed by this kind of behavior. And you won't be able to hold on to your female employees for long, if they have to put up with daily abuse on the job.

3. Legal Liability for Harassment

In 1998, the Supreme Court decided two cases that spell out when an employer will be legally responsible for harassment. In these cases, the Court held that employers who have an antiharassment policy and investigate harassment complaints quickly and fairly can avoid liability in certain kinds of cases—even if the employee proves that she was harassed.

Generally, you have a legal duty to take effective action to stop harassment as soon as you learn of it, whether the harasser is a supervisor or a coworker of the victim. But in some cases, you will also be held responsible for harassment committed by one of your managers or supervisors, even if you didn't know what was going on. The Supreme Court and the Equal Employment Opportunity Commission (EEOC), the government agency charged with handling complaints of discrimination and harassment, have come up with the following rules for employer responsibility for harassment.

An employer is generally responsible for harassment by a manager or supervisor if the harassment results in a "tangible employment action"—an action that significantly changes the harassed employee's job status, like getting fired, demoted, or reassigned—even if the employee never complained and the employer had no idea what was going on. The logic behind this liability is that when managers and supervisors make these types of decisions, they are acting for the company. Therefore, if their decisions are influenced by discrimination, the company is responsible.

Who's a Supervisor?

These rules—which make employers liable for harassment that results in a negative job action, even if the employer isn't aware of it—apply only to harassment by supervisors. So which employees qualify as supervisors? According to the EEOC, a supervisor is someone who either has the authority to make or recommend decisions affecting the employee or has the authority to direct the employee's daily work activities.

However, certain employees may occupy such a lofty position on the corporate ladder that they are something more than supervisors. These employees—which might include corporate officers, the president, the CEO, an owner, or a partner, depending on how the company is organized—generally have the authority to act on the company's behalf in all matters. Therefore, if they harass employees, the law will presume that the company knows about it, even if the harassment doesn't result in a negative job action. In these situations, employers can't rely on the defense described in this section: The company will always be liable for harassment by these high-ranking employees.

However, an employer is not necessarily responsible for harassment by a manager or supervisor that doesn't have any of these repercussions—for example, a manager who tells racist jokes or repeatedly asks an employee out on dates. In these cases, an employer can defend itself by showing that:

- the employer exercised reasonable care to prevent and promptly correct any harassment, and

- the employee unreasonably failed to take advantage of opportunities the employer offered to prevent or correct the harassment—for example, by failing to make a complaint.

The first step requires employers to make efforts to create a harassment-free work environment—for example, by training employees and managers to recognize and report harassment, by adopting a nonharassment policy and a complaint procedure that encourages employees to come forward, and by investigating harassment complaints quickly and fairly. If the employer takes these precautions and a harassed worker delays in making a complaint or fails to complain at all, the employer will not be responsible for harassment that occurred prior to the complaint.

 Need an antiharassment policy?

A sample antiharassment policy, which you can modify to fit the needs of your workplace, is included in Appendix A.

The policy behind this defense is pretty simple: If an employer has an antiharassment and investigation policy that it follows faithfully, the employee has to use it if he or she wants the problem to stop. If an employee fails to make a complaint, you have no notice of the problem and, therefore, no reason to investigate or take action. But in order to take advantage of this protection, you must make it clear to your employees that you will investigate their complaints fully and fairly. The only way to drive this point home is to investigate every harassment complaint. This way, no employee can argue that she didn't report harassment because she didn't think you would do anything about it. Remember that once you learn of this second kind of harassment—through a complaint or in any other way—you are responsible for any harassment that continues after you find out. This gives you an incentive to investigate and take action quickly.

EXAMPLE 1: Sheila's boss, Roger, has asked her out several times. She has turned him down each time, explaining that she has no romantic interest in him and would prefer to keep their relationship professional. Roger refuses to approve Sheila's scheduled raise, because she will not go out with him. Roger's employer will be legally responsible for Roger's harassment, even if Sheila never complains about it, because she has been subjected to a negative job action.

EXAMPLE 2: Katherine works on the production line in an auto plant. Her coworkers and supervisor, mostly men, constantly tell sexual jokes and refer to women in crude terms. The top executives in the company visit the plant. Although the men are on their best behavior during the official tour, several executives remain in the building afterwards to review paperwork and overhear the men's crude remarks. The company will be liable for any harassment Katherine suffers after the visit. Although she has not made a complaint or suffered a negative job action, the company now knows about the harassment and has a duty to take action.

EXAMPLE 3: Same as Example 2, except the executives never visit the plant. If Katherine wants to hold the company responsible for her harassment, she will have to make a complaint to put the company on notice of the problem. If Katherine fails to make a complaint, she can hold the company responsible only if she can show that (1) the company had no policy against harassment, or (2) the company did not take complaints seriously, failed to investigate, or failed to act on reported problems. For example, if Katherine can show that several women from her plant had complained in the past few years and nothing had been done about the problem, the employer will be liable despite her failure to complain.

 Need more information on liability for harassment?

For more information on employer liability for harassment by supervisors and managers, check out the EEOC's guidelines, "EEOC Enforcement Guidance: Vicarious Employer Liability for Unlawful Harassment by Supervisors" (June, 1999), available from the EEOC's website at www.eeoc.gov/docs/harassment.html.

Check your state's laws.

Although many states have adopted the rules explained in this section and most others are likely to adopt them, there may be a few states that buck the trend. States that have stronger antiharassment laws—and therefore are more likely to hold employers responsible for harassment—might not follow the Supreme Court's lead. An employment lawyer can help you figure out whether you need to take additional steps to protect your company.

B. Ten Steps to a Successful Harassment Investigation

This section explains how to apply the basic investigation steps covered in Part I of this book to a harassment investigation. If you haven't read Part I, you should do so before getting into this more specific material—the discussion that follows assumes that you are already familiar with basic investigation procedures.

1. Decide Whether to Investigate

When you're dealing with possible harassment, it's best to err on the side of investigating, even if the allegations don't seem that serious. As explained in Section A3, above, failing to investigate harassment claims can have serious consequences—not just for the claim you decide not to investigate, but for future claims of harassment that might be made against your company.

But this doesn't mean you have to jump into investigative high gear every time an employee utters the "h" word. First, figure out whether the employee is complaining about conduct based on a protected characteristic—race, gender, disability, and so on. (See Section A, above.) If not, you may still want to look into the incident further, depending on the allegations, or refer them to an appropriate person in management for further consideration.

EXAMPLE: Roland goes to the Human Resources department to complain about his supervisor, Marie. Marie was recently hired to improve the performance of the sales department. Roland complains that Marie has imposed deadlines on the department that are difficult to meet and has required everyone to attend mandatory sales training, even if they have years of experience. She has arranged a standing meeting with every employee once a week to review their sales figures and talk about ways they could improve their numbers. Roland claims this is harassment: "She's working all of us like dogs. She's always there, looking over someone's shoulder, telling them what they're doing is wrong. Our group is really demoralized—it feels like she doesn't respect our experience and opinions."

Even though Roland used the term "harassment," he isn't complaining about illegal harassment based on a protected characteristic. Although Marie's management style isn't winning her any friends, she is applying it equally to all, regardless of race, gender, and so on. This isn't a complaint that demands an investigation. However, it is a legitimate concern that should be communicated to Marie and her supervisors. The company may decide that Marie is doing exactly what it hired her to do and urge her to keep up the good work. Or it may decide to tell Marie to back off a bit and try using some management techniques that are a bit more successful at motivating her employees.

Even if the conduct appears to be based on a protected characteristic, the situation may not call for a full-blown investigation. There may be cases in which the alleged conduct is minor, everyone agrees on what happened, and a simple discussion with both parties (carefully documented, of course) will put the matter to rest.

EXAMPLE: Mark asks Georgia, his coworker, to have dinner with him one night after work. Georgia declines, telling Mark that she has a boyfriend. Mark says, "Well, he's a very lucky man." Nothing further happens between them, but Georgia tells her supervisor about the incident and confides that it made her a bit uncomfortable to know that Mark finds her attractive. You interview Georgia, who confirms what she told her supervisor and says that Mark has never asked her out again or acted inappropriately towards her. Mark tells you that Georgia's statement is accurate. He says that he won't approach her socially again—"I don't want to make her uncomfortable. In fact, I feel kind of bad for asking her out in the first place."

Is this a situation in which you'll have to interview witnesses, comb through files, and carefully weigh the evidence? Nope. Once you've talked to the two employees involved, made sure that Mark understands that he shouldn't bother Georgia, (or retaliate against her for complaining), explained the outcome to Georgia, and documented your conversations, you're done. Of course, a few different facts could lead to a different conclusion. For example, if Mark's response was "I can't believe my bad luck—she's the third person in my department I asked out this month, and they all turned me down" or Georgia said, "I think Mark felt comfortable asking me out because our supervisor is always joking and making comments about the supposedly wild sex lives I and the other women in our department have," then you've got a more serious problem on your hands that will require a more extensive investigation.

 When there is no complaint.

Remember, you have an obligation to investigate harassment, no matter how you find out about it. Although you may learn of harassment through an employee complaint, there are lots of other ways harassment might come to your attention. For example, a supervisor might notice racist graffiti on the walls of the employee locker room, overhear an X-rated joke, or notice that employees are picking on a disabled coworker. An employee might make an anonymous complaint of harassment or raise the issue in an exit interview. Your duty to investigate kicks in as soon as you know of the allegations, regardless of how they surface. (See Chapter 2, Section A, for more on how incidents warranting an investigation might come to your attention.)

---

2. Take Immediate Action, If Necessary

Before you begin your investigation, you will have to decide whether some immediate changes are necessary in the workplace, to prevent further harm and to ensure that the investigation won't be disrupted. You should consider taking steps to separate the alleged harasser from the alleged victims when:

- very serious allegations—for example, unwanted sexual touching, sexual assault, violence, threats, or extremely abusive verbal harassment (such as the use of offensive racist epithets)—have been made
- ongoing harassment is alleged, or
- the alleged victim(s) and/or witnesses appear to be intimidated by the alleged harasser.

You must be very careful to avoid retaliation (or the appearance of retaliation) when you decide what to do. If you separate the employees by moving the worker who complained to another shift or a different work area, you could be accused of retaliating: "As soon as I complained, they moved me to the night shift, while the person who harassed me got to continue working his usual shift, just like nothing happened."

What About Time Off for the Complaining Employee?

Sometimes, an employee who complains of harassment asks to take some time off. If you face a request like this, find out exactly why the employee wants out of the workplace. If the employee has been threatened with retaliation or her coworkers are shunning her because she made a complaint, these are facts you'll need to know. Explain that retaliation is prohibited and that you will investigate as quickly as possible.

If an employee simply wants to take some time to catch her breath, you can arrange for a brief period of paid leave. However, make sure that the employee will be available to participate in the investigation.

The best way to avoid these types of charges is to move the harasser or suspend him with pay while you investigate. When you tell the alleged harasser about the change, emphasize that it's a temporary situation, that no conclusions have been made about the truth or falsity of the allegations, and that the harasser shouldn't view the transfer or suspension as punitive. If you must take an immediate action like this, make extra efforts to complete the investigation quickly, to minimize workplace disruption.

Don't suspend workers without pay.

From a legal standpoint, you generally can't suspend exempt, salaried employees—those who are not entitled to overtime if they work extra hours—without pay. And even though you can suspend hourly, nonexempt workers without pay, it's not a good idea. A suspension without pay is punitive: It improperly signals that you have made up your mind about the allegations before you've even begun to investigate. A worker who is suspended without pay will probably be angry about it—and if the allegations against her are false, that anger may well provide the fuel for a lawsuit. And unpaid suspensions can be an administrative hassle, as they require you to interrupt your usual payroll system. The wages you shell out to a temporarily suspended employee will be a small price to pay to avoid these problems.

3. Choose the Investigator

Chapter 2, Section D, explains the qualities that make an investigator particular effective—such as professionalism, experience, and impartiality. Those considerations always apply, no matter what type of problem you're investigating. However, there are a few special issues to consider when you're choosing an investigator for a harassment complaint.

a. Your Chances in Court Depend on Your Investigator

Because the Supreme Court has held that a prompt, complete, and impartial investigation could shield you from liability for certain types of harassment (see Section A3, above), your ability to defend yourself in a harassment case could well depend on your investigator. Will your investigator handle the job carefully and quickly, without letting personal feelings get in the way? Will your investigator be able to testify professionally and accurately in court, in a manner that a jury will believe?

Watch out for claims of bias.

Some courts have disregarded a company's efforts to investigate—and the conclusions of the investigation—if any of the employees involved in a harassment claim perceived the investigator as biased. This means you must be especially careful to choose an investigator who is beyond reproach, and to confirm with the complaining employee and the accused employee that they are comfortable with the investigator. The investigator should not be someone who directly supervises or has a personal relationship (or a history of negative encounters) with either worker. For more on choosing an unbiased investigator, see Chapter 2, Section D.

Of course, these are important questions to ask yourself when choosing an investigator for *any* type of workplace problem. But they are particularly important in cases of harassment, because the Supreme Court's decisions have virtually guaranteed that the quality of the investigation will be on trial, if you are faced with a lawsuit.

b. Sensitivity

Harassment claims can be particularly uncomfortable, for alleged harassers and alleged victims alike. In a sexual harassment case, for example, the investigator may have to ask about prior relationships, sexual comments, flirtations, and more. To investigate a case of racial harassment, the investigator might have to ask the victim to repeat racial slurs and offensive statements that are deeply disturbing. Many of us are reluctant to reveal or talk in detail about these kinds of incidents, which means the investigator must be especially skilled at drawing people out and encouraging them to speak openly.

Some experts recommend choosing an investigator who shares the victim's protected characteristics (to the extent possible), to encourage the victim to open up. And this is often sound advice—for example, many women would feel more comfortable (and less embarrassed) discussing sexual harassment with another woman. And a victim of racial harassment might feel that an investigator of the same race is more likely to understand how offensive certain statements or actions were.

However, you won't always be able to follow this advice, particularly if you run a small business. It probably won't be too difficult to make a female investigator available, but what if a disabled Puerto Rican lesbian complains of harassment? No company will have the wherewithal to come up with a "demographically correct" investigator for every claim—and that's okay. Your main concern should be to find an investigator who can listen attentively and carefully to all the parties and who won't come to the investigation with preconceived notions about what happened.

c. When to Use an Outside Investigator

As explained in Chapter 2, it makes sense to consider hiring an outside investigator in certain circumstances. You may want to bring in a professional investigator if:

- an employee has raised allegations of sexual assault, rape, or violence motivated by bias

- several employees have complained about the same problem—for example, a group of African-American employees complain of widespread racial harassment

- the accused harasser is a high-ranking company official (in this situation, employees might not believe that an investigator who works for the company can be impartial)

- an employee has filed a lawsuit or an administrative charge (with the Equal Employment Opportunity Commission or a state antidiscrimination agency) based on the harassment

- an employee has hired a lawyer because of the harassment, or

- the allegations have been publicized in the media.

 For tips on hiring an outside investigator, see Chapter 2, Section D.

---

4. Plan the Investigation

Although you might become aware of harassment in any number of ways (see Chapter 2), you will often be dealing with an employee complaint of inappropriate behavior. This gives you a leg up on the investigation—you'll have some basic information before you begin your interviews, and you'll be able to plan your investigation accordingly.

You won't always have a complaint to work from, however. If one of our managers happens to notice X-rated cartoons or racist graffiti on the walls, for example, or if you receive an anonymous complaint of harassment, you'll have to begin your complaint without knowing who may have committed wrongdoing or who may have been harmed by it.

a. When Someone Has Complained

If an employee has complained of harassment, that complaint is your natural starting point for planning your investigation. Using the complaint as your guide, these questions will help you define the scope of your inquiries:

- Who complained? Is there more than one complaining employee? If not, does the complaining employee allege that other employees were also harassed?

- What misconduct is alleged? Is the victim alleging harassment based on a protected characteristic? Is the victim alleging that she suffered a tangible job action—such as demotion, failure to get a raise or promotion, or a change in job duties—or is she alleging a hostile work environment?

- Who is the alleged wrongdoer? Are there more than one alleged harassers? What position does the alleged harasser hold?

- How many incidents of harassment does the victim allege?

- Has the victim named any potential witnesses?

- Where did the alleged incidents take place? Is the alleged misconduct limited to one work group, one shift, or one area of the workplace, or is it more widespread? If the incidents took place as the victim says they did, are there any employees who may have witnessed them?

The answers to these questions will help you decide whom to interview, what documents or other evidence may be available to shed some light on the allegations, and what kinds of questions you'll need to ask. Of course, you may not know the answers to all of these questions right now—if the victim made a barebones complaint, for example, you might not find out any details until you actually begin to investigate. In this situation, simply keep these questions in mind as you conduct your initial interview with the complaining employee.

b. When There's No Complaint

Where should you start when there's no complaining employee? As always, start with what you know. How did the alleged harassment come to your attention? Did a manager or another employee report it? If so, what did that person notice? If you received a report of interpersonal harassment—that is, one employee harassing another—consider starting with the alleged victim. Even though that person hasn't come forward, he is probably in the best position to tell you exactly what happened.

You might learn of possible harassment that isn't focused on a particular victim (for example, that particular employees frequently use foul language or refer to others in racist or ageist terms, that sexually explicit images or jokes have been posted on an employee bulletin board or electronic mail message board, or that disabled employees have been the victims of anonymous practical jokes). In cases like these, you may wish to start by talking to someone who manages the work group where the problem arose to find out which employees may be involved, what schedules they work, how the employees seem to get along, and so forth.

If the information you begin with isn't sufficient to identify the alleged harasser(s), remember that anyone you interview to gather background information could be involved in the wrongdoing—and plan your questions accordingly.

c. Documents and Other Physical Evidence

No matter how you learn of the harassment, part of your investigation planning should include gathering relevant documents. For example, these types of documents may help you figure out who to interview and what questions to ask:

- the company's harassment policy
- the personnel files of the alleged harasser and the complaining employee or victim (if there is one)
- any allegedly harassing documents, including emails, correspondence, cartoons, postings on company property, or notes
- performance evaluations and other documents reflecting personnel decisions, if the complaining employee claims to have suffered a negative job action as a result of the harassment, and
- attendance records for any company trainings on harassment.

You should also consider whether any physical evidence other than documents might exist. If someone has reported sexist graffiti in the locker room, for example, you will want to photograph the graffiti and record exactly what it says. Other types of evidence that may be relevant in a harassment investigation include:

- objects given to or left for the victim—including gifts, suggestive clothing, sexual toys, offensive items (like a noose or Ku Klux Klan imagery), or pictures

- photographs from company events where harassment allegedly took place (such as a company holiday party or other social event), and

- work-related items connected with the alleged harassment. For example, if the victim alleges that her toolbox was tampered with, his briefcase or computer was defaced, or his equipment was sabotaged, you will want to collect those items (or at least photograph them and take careful notes of the apparent damage).

5. Interviews

Once you've finished your investigation planning, you'll have some ideas about which employees you should interview. If an employee has made a complaint, you should generally start by interviewing that person. If no employee has complained, you can start by interviewing whomever noticed the problem, a manager in the work group where the problem exists, or any known victims. (See Section B4, above.)

No matter who you're interviewing, you should start the interview with some opening remarks to set the employee at ease and explain the process. Next, proceed to your specific questions, remembering to follow up on any new information raised by the witness's responses. Close the interview by letting the witness know what will happen next and inviting him to come to you with any concerns or additional information. And conduct follow-up interviews if any new information comes to light.

a. Getting Started

Some of your opening comments will be the same, no matter whom you're interviewing. Some of them will be geared more specifically towards a complaining employee, an accused employee, or a witness. The opening statement you make to every person you interview should cover these points:

- **The purpose of the meeting.** The information you give here will depend on whom you're interviewing. You can tell the complaining employee that the company will be investigating the complaint and that the purpose of the meeting is to gather as much information as possible. The accused employee will need to be told that a complaint has been made, that you're investigating, and that your role is to gather as much information as possible. A witness can simply be told that you're investigating a workplace problem and you believe the witness might have some relevant information.

- **The investigation process.** Explain that the company will be investigating the problem and interviewing other employees and will take appropriate steps if it finds that misconduct occurred.

- **Confidentiality.** Emphasize that you expect the employee to keep the investigation confidential and that talking about the investigation to other employees could be grounds for discipline. Explain that you will maintain confidentiality to the extent possible, although it will be necessary to reveal certain details in order to conduct thorough interviews and reach a decision.

- **Retaliation.** Explain that retaliation is prohibited and that the company will take immediate steps to discipline anyone who retaliates based on the complaint or investigation. Ask the employee to come to you with any concerns about retaliation.

- **Questions or concerns.** Ask whether the employee has any questions or concerns about the process.

When you interview the accused employee, emphasize that the company has not reached any decisions about what happened. Explain that you are interested in hearing what everyone involved has to say before making a decision or taking any action. Because you will probably have to reveal the name of the complaining employee (see Subsection b, below), spend some extra time discussing retaliation: what it is, that the company prohibits it, and that employees who engage in retaliation will be subject to discipline. Although the accused employee will probably want to know the allegations right away, you are better off postponing this discussion until later in the interview, after you have had a chance to gather some important background information. Assure the accused employee that he will have the opportunity to hear and respond to the allegations before the interview is over.

For witnesses, your opening remarks can be brief. The witness doesn't need to know who complained, who is accused, or what the specific allegations are. Once you have explained that you are investigating a workplace problem and talked about confidentiality and retaliation, you can begin asking your questions.

b. Sample Questions

The specific questions you ask will depend on the nature of the problem and on whom you are interviewing.

Questions for the Complaining Employee or Victim

Harassment is usually a pattern of incidents rather than one single event. Because the complaining employee will probably be describing several separate occurrences, you need to be especially careful to ask precise questions and take clear notes—otherwise, you could easily get confused about the details. Experienced investigators advise discussing each incident separately. First, ask the complaining employee about every incident she can recall. Then, go through the list and ask for the details of each, starting with the most recent problem and working backwards.

 Act like a reporter.

When interviewing the complaining employee, follow the universal rule of journalists everywhere: Ask who, what, where, when, and how (and sometimes why). By sticking to these open-ended questions, you'll elicit as much information as possible while keeping the witness focused on the facts.

Here are some sample questions you can tailor to the facts of your investigation:

- What happened? How many incidents have there been?
- Who was involved? What did that person say or do?
- How did you react? Did you say anything to [the accused employee]? What did you say? Did you react physically [for example, by leaving the room, slamming a door, crying, or blushing]?
- Prior to these incidents, what was your relationship like with [the accused employee]? Did you work together frequently? Did you have any problems working together? Did you socialize outside of work?

Asking About a Prior Relationship in a Sexual Harassment Investigation

If the complaining employee and the alleged harasser used to be romantically involved with each other, you will have to ask some questions about that relationship. What each party says about the relationship, why it ended, and how it affected their dealings with each other at work will help you figure out whose story is more credible—and help you get to the bottom of the complaint.

But proceed with caution: Once you start asking about personal matters—and we can all agree that our romantic relationships fall into this category—you risk invading an employee's privacy. The best way to avoid this problem is to limit your questions to issues related to work and the complaint. In most cases, you could safely ask about when the relationship started, when it ended, who ended it and why, how the parties have gotten along at work since the breakup, and what relevance each party thinks the prior relationship has on the current situation. (For example, does the complaining employee think that she's being harassed because she ended the relationship, or does the accused harasser think his former paramour has made a false complaint out of jealousy or anger?) Once you start interrogating employees about where they went on their weekend getaways or how many nights they spent together each week, you've probably wandered into dangerous territory.

In some situations, you might find yourself asking more intimate questions, based on the information that comes out in your interviews.

Example: Rosalie complains that Xavier, her coworker and former boyfriend, is harassing her. She says that he frequently follows her to her car after work, hangs around her desk all of the time, and asks her a lot of questions about her personal life. She says she has told him to stop, but he persists in asking her out and asking whether she's dating anyone else. She decided to complain when she found a sexual aid on her desk. She says, with some embarrassment, that she and Xavier had used a similar toy when having sex, and that finding it on her desk convinced her that Xavier was not going to stop bothering her unless she agreed to date him again.

When you interview Xavier, are you going to ask him about the sexual aid? Ordinarily, you should stay very far away from any questions about sexual practices. In this case, however, you need to find out who left the item on Rosalie's desk—and the evidence so far points to Xavier. Because this particular sexual device is relevant to the complaint, you will have to ask about it. Just make sure to limit your questions to what you need to know to resolve the complaint. (In other words, you can ask whether Xavier put the item on her desk, but not why the couple used it or "How the heck does this thing work?")

- When did each incident take place? How often did they occur? When did they begin?

- Where did each incident take place?

- Was anyone else present? Could anyone else have witnessed the incident(s)?

- Did you tell anyone about the incidents? Who did you tell? What did you tell them?

- Do you know of any similar incidents involving other people?

- Have you been affected by the incidents? How? Did you take any time off as a result of the incidents? Did you seek medical treatment or counseling?

- Are there any documents or other kinds of evidence relating to the incidents? Did you take notes or keep a journal recording these incidents?

- When did you first complain about these incidents? [if the employee says she complained earlier and nothing was done] Whom did you complain to? What did you say? What did the person you complained to say? [if the employee only complained after a delay] Why did you decide to come forward now?

- How would you like to see this problem resolved?

- Is there anyone who might have information about these incidents that you'd like me to interview?

Questions for the Accused Employee

Your interview with the accused employee is likely to be a tense affair. If the employee committed misconduct, he may try to evade your questions or lie about what happened. If the employee has been wrongly accused, he is likely to be upset—at both the complaining employee and the company, for taking the allegations seriously. Either way, you may be facing a defensive and combative interview.

One way to defuse the tension is to emphasize that the company has a legal obligation to investigate the allegations and that you haven't reached any conclusions yet. Explain that the purpose of the investigation is to figure out what really happened. Assure the employee that you are eager to hear what he has to say and that you will be interviewing witnesses and examining documents to help you get to the truth.

You work for the company.

It can be tough to interview an angry witness, particularly one who blames the company—or even you, personally—for the investigation. You may hear things like "I can't believe you think I did this," "I won't sit here and be accused of this nonsense," or "I'm outraged that anyone would take these allegations seriously." To avoid taking these kinds of statements personally, just remember that you are playing a very important role for the company. Your job is to find out what happened and resolve the situation—and you should explain this to the accused employee.

Because the accused employee is likely to be defensive—and may have something to hide—you'll have to plan the order of your questions carefully. Start with easy, basic questions about the employee's work. This will allow both of you to ease into the interview and will give you the opportunity to gather potentially important facts while the employee's guard is down.

EXAMPLE: Ricardo, a Mexican-American supervisor at a company that manufactures food products, complains that another supervisor, Jessica, has harassed him based on his national origin. He says that Jessica constantly teases him about his accent and the foods he likes to eat and tells jokes about Ricardo being an illegal alien. Ricardo is responsible for giving biweekly safety presentations to the line workers. As a fellow supervisor, Jessica is neither required nor expected to attend these meetings, but Ricardo says she has attended the last five meetings and made comments about his accent.

If you start your interview with Jessica by saying, "Ricardo claims that you've been attending his safety meetings and making inappropriate comments about his accent. Is this true?," Jessica now thinks to herself, "Aha! They're saying I did something wrong at these safety meetings." This could give her a reason to lie or make up an innocent explanation for her attendance.

If you start your interview instead by asking, "Tell me about your job responsibilities," then following up with questions about who she supervises, what she does in a typical workday and workweek, and whether she is required to attend or run any regular meetings with other workers, Jessica may not know what you're fishing for, and won't have a chance to shape her answers to put herself in the best possible light. This means you'll have a better chance of getting an honest answer.

Once you are done with the background questions, tell the accused employee what the allegations are and ask for his response. As you did with the complaining employee, go through each allegation chronologically, asking whether the accused employee was present at the time and place alleged, who else was present, what happened, and how everyone reacted. Give the accused employee the opportunity to offer any explanations, denials, alibis, and witnesses for each alleged incident.

Here are some sample questions to consider:

- What is your typical workday or workweek like? What time do you arrive? What time do you leave? What are your job responsibilities?

- Do you supervise any employees? What are their names and positions?

- How would you characterize your working relationship with your direct reports? Your coworkers?

- [Tell the accused employee what misconduct is alleged or suspected.] What is your response to these allegations?

 You must allow the accused employee to respond to the allegations.

Some investigators are so eager to keep the interview civil—or to protect the complaining employee's privacy—that they never actually get around to confronting the accuser with the allegations against him. This is a big mistake, one that could undermine the legitimacy of the entire investigation. Courts have held that an accused employee who never learns precisely what he is accused of hasn't had a fair opportunity to tell his side of the story, to offer the names of relevant witnesses, or to explain why the complaining employee might have made the accusation. You don't necessarily have to say who complained, but you should say whom the employee is accused of harassing. And don't worry about privacy concerns—you have a very compelling business reason for revealing this information.

- Did these things happen? [if the accused employee does not completely deny the allegations] What did happen? When and where?
- How did [the alleged victim] respond? Did she indicate that your statements or actions bothered her?
- Did anyone witness these incidents?
- Have you told anyone about these incidents?
- Have you kept any notes or a journal about these incidents?
- What is your work relationship like with [the alleged victim]
- [if the accused employee denies the allegations] Could another person have misunderstood your actions or statements? Do you think someone made up these incidents? Why?
- Have you ever used foul language in the workplace?
- Have you ever used racial epithets in the workplace? [Ask about other biases as appropriate, based on the allegations.]
- [for sexual harassment complaints] Have you ever seen [the alleged victim] outside of work? Have you ever had a social relationship with each other? A romantic relationship? Have you ever asked [the alleged victim] out on a date? What was her response?
- Have you ever been accused of harassment before? How was the issue resolved?
- Have you had any training on workplace harassment issues?
- Are you aware of the company's antiharassment policy?
- Do you know of anyone who might have information about these incidents?
- Do you know of any documents or other evidence relating to these allegations?

Questions for Witnesses

When questioning witnesses, your goal is to gather information without giving too much away. To plan your questions, consider who suggested the witness and why. Did the witness see or hear the misconduct? Was the witness told of the misconduct? Is the witness privy to some details of the relationship between the complaining employee and the accused?

Start by explaining, in very general terms, why the witness is being interviewed—that you are investigating a workplace problem and you believe the witness might have information that will help you figure out what happened. Then, move into questions that will help you figure out if the witness could have seen or heard the alleged incidents. Finally, find out what the witness knows. Here are some sample questions to consider:

- Describe your typical workday or workweek. Who is your supervisor? Where is your workstation? What time do you typically arrive at work each day? What time do you leave?

- Do you work with [the alleged victim or the accused employee]? How would you describe their work relationship?

- Has [the alleged victim] ever spoken to you about [the accused employee]? Has [the accused employee] ever spoken to you about [the alleged victim]?

- Have you seen any interactions between [the alleged victim] and [the accused employee] that made you uncomfortable? Describe them to me.

- If the witness may have seen or heard the incident, ask questions to figure out whether the witness was there and what happened.

EXAMPLE: If the complaining employee says that the witness was present when her supervisor told a racist joke, you might ask: Did you attend a meeting to discuss sales techniques last Monday? What time was the meeting? Were you present for the whole meeting, or did you leave the room at any time? Who else was at the meeting? Do you remember any comments Tom made at the meeting?

If these questions don't get you the information you need, you'll have to ask more specific questions, like: Did Tom tell any jokes at the meeting? Do you remember him making any comments about Native Americans? What did he say?

- Have you heard these issues discussed in the workplace? When, where, and by whom?

- Have you ever had any problems working with [the alleged victim or the accused employee]?

- Do you know of anyone else who might have information about these incidents? Are there any documents or other evidence that you know of relating to these incidents?

c. Closing the Interview

Once you have finished your questions, review your notes with the person you interviewed. Make sure that your notes include all of the important details. Ask the employee not to discuss the complaint or the investigation with any co-workers. Remind the employee about retaliation, especially the accused employee. And ask the employee to come to you immediately with any new information.

This is all you have to tell witnesses. When you close an interview with the complaining or accused employee, let them know what will happen next. Tell them that you'll interview them again if any important new information comes up.

d. Follow-Up Interviews

If any new information comes up during your investigation, you should conduct follow-up interviews with the complaining or accused employee. Both employees should have the opportunity to respond to new allegations or defenses, to make sure that you have a complete understanding of the facts when you make your decision and to give you the opportunity to gauge credibility. It is especially important to let the accused employee know of any additional allegations that come up during the investigation. If you don't, you may be accused of unfairness for refusing to give him an opportunity to give his side of the story.

EXAMPLE 1: Siri complains that her supervisor, Jeff, is sexually harassing her. She says that he has persistently asked her out and has recently told her that he will not recommend her for promotion unless she agrees to go on a weekend trip with him. When you interview Jeff, he says that he has never asked Siri out or invited her away for the weekend, but that he has told her that he cannot recommend her for promotion because her performance has been slipping in recent months. He also says that Siri responded that she would get the promotion, regardless of his recommendation. In this case, you should definitely re-interview Siri and find out how she responds to Jeff's comments.

EXAMPLE 2: Emily complains that a coworker, Gabe, has harassed her because she is a member of Jews for Jesus. She says that Gabe frequently taunts her because of her religion, making comments like "If the Jews really liked Jesus, they wouldn't have killed him." You interview Gretchen, who works with both Emily and Gabe. Gretchen tells you that Gabe has made offensive anti-Semitic comments to her on several occasions, including calling Emily a "kike" and saying that Hitler had the right idea. Before you wrap up the investigation, you should go back to Gabe and confront him with these new allegations.

6. Gather Documents and Other Evidence

Unless harassment has escalated to physical touching or violence, it is primarily accomplished through communication. Racist epithets, pornographic images, demeaning jokes, slurs, or cartoons only become harassment when they are conveyed to another person who finds them offensive. Sometimes this communication is carried out in writing, at least in part. In a harassment investigation, part of your job is to gather any written communications relating to the problem—which could include email messages, letter, notes, and items posted in cubicles, on company bulletin boards, or in shared company spaces (such as locker rooms, restrooms, or the mail room).

If the victim alleges that harassment resulted in a negative job action—for example, that she was denied a promotion, raise, or desired transfer or that she was demoted or punished in some way—there should be a paper trail. Consider whether performance evaluations, payroll records, or other personnel documents will shed some light on what happened.

Official company documents might also corroborate or raise doubts about one person's story. For example, an employee complains that her supervisor harassed her, most recently by pressuring her to accompany him on a business trip as his "companion." The supervisor denies the harassment and contends that he wasn't even in the office on the date of the alleged incident—he had already left for his trip. In this situation, you could take a look at attendance records and the supervisor's expense reports to find out the truth.

Finally, physical evidence (other than documents) may play an important role in the investigation. If the complaining employee claims that the alleged harasser gave her gifts or left offensive objects for her (such as some racy lingerie, a photo of a mass murderer, or a noose), try to track down those items. Ask about photographs of offensive items, if they aren't still available. For example, several female employees complain that a cake baked in the shape of a naked woman was served at an office function. Obviously, the cake is long gone—but someone may have taken a picture of it (or you might be able to find out which bakery supplied the creation).

7. Evaluate the Evidence

Sometimes, there are many witnesses to harassment. For example, an entire work group may hear a supervisor's racist jokes or sexual come-ons. If the victim is complaining of a hostile work environment, other workers may have seen or heard something. More often, however, harassment occurs behind closed doors, and only the harasser and harassee really know what happened. If you're facing this type of investigation and you've received conflicting stories, your credibility determinations will be especially important.

Review the factors listed in Chapter 4 as you try to figure out where the truth lies. Two factors can be especially relevant in harassment cases: corroboration and motive.

- **Corroboration.** Even if no one else was in the room when the alleged harassment took place, you can still try to corroborate other details of each person's story. For example, a secretary complains that her boss called her into his office several times a day and pulled up pornographic websites on his computer. Although no one else saw the images, you might find other corroborating evidence. Did anyone see her entering or leaving his office? If so, did she appear to be upset? Did she tell anyone about the incidents? Have other employees seen him viewing pornographic material? Does his computer show that he has visited pornographic sites or downloaded pornographic material in the past?

- **Motive.** Does either party have a motive to lie? Has either party told any other employees that he or she might make a false claim or false denial? Does the alleged harasser have any reason to act—or not to act—as the victim has claimed? Especially in sexual harassment cases where the parties have a prior relationship, it's important to consider any reasons either person might have for their actions and statements.

8. Take Action

If you find that some form of harassment occurred, you have a legal obligation to take prompt corrective action, reasonably calculated to end the harassment. The right corrective action is one that

- stops the harassment
- prevents harassment from recurring, and

- restores the victim to the position she would have held absent the harassment

Employers face some tough decisions when considering how to deal with harassment. On the one hand, an employer will be legally liable for any harassment that occurs following a complaint. In other words, the action you take must be effective at stopping the harassment—if it isn't, you'll be on the hook for any further incidents. On the other hand, if you punish an employee too severely, he might have a separate legal claim against you for breach of contract, discrimination, or defamation, depending on the circumstances.

If the Harassment Stops, You Made the Right Call

When courts have to decide whether an employer took appropriate corrective action, they will focus on whether the harassment stopped. The ultimate test of whether an action was appropriate is effectiveness: Actions short of serious disciplinary measures can pass this test as long as they work.

Example: Hattie, a housekeeper at a Veterans Medical Center, complained that her coworker, Oliver, had grabbed her and put his arms around her twice during a work shift in September of 1996. Hattie reported the incidents to her supervisor, who investigated, confronted Oliver and told him the allegations were serious, and warned him to stay away from Hattie. Hattie told her supervisor that she was afraid of Oliver, although he hadn't done anything else to her since the incidents. A month later, Hattie filed a charge of sexual harassment; in response, Oliver was switched to a different shift, which overlapped Hattie's shift by an hour and a half.

Hattie sued for sexual harassment, complaining that her employer was required to "discipline" Oliver and that telling him to stay away from her and changing his shift didn't constitute discipline. The court disagreed. Because the employer took action that was effective in ending the harassment, the court found that it had met its obligation to take prompt remedial action. *Star v. West*, 237 F.3d 1036 (9th Cir. 2001).

If the harassment continues, however, the same corrective action might be insufficient. In the case of *Grego v. Meijer* (239 F.Supp.2d 676, W.D. Ky, 2002), an employer told the harasser that his comments were inappropriate and told him to leave the plaintiff alone. However, the court found these actions insufficient, because the victim had twice reported the harassment, the employer was aware that other women were being harassed by the same man, and the harassment continued after the reports.

The only way to walk this fine line is to make the punishment fit the crime. Consider:

- the severity of the incidents
- how often they occurred
- how many total incidents took place
- the harm to the victim
- whether the law was violated
- whether workplace policies were violated
- whether the harasser holds a position of authority in the company, such as officer, manager, or supervisor (harassment by a higher-level employee is more serious and requires a heightened response)
- how the company has treated similar incidents in the past, and
- the harasser's history at the company—does the employee have a record of similar problems, or is this a one-time lapse from an otherwise stellar worker?

(For more information on choosing an appropriate response to wrongdoing—and on what to do if your investigation is inconclusive or reveals that no wrongdoing took place—see Chapter 4, Section B.)

Finally, don't forget the victim. You have a legal obligation to undo any harm the victim suffered as a result of the harassment. This could include:

- reinstating a victim who was fired for refusing to acquiesce to harassment
- restoring any job benefits or promotions a victim lost as a result of the harassment
- removing negative evaluations or critical comments in the victim's personnel file, if they arose from the harassment, and
- crediting the victim with any paid leave taken as a result of the harassment.

9. Document the Investigation

Document your harassment investigation just as you would any other workplace investigation. (See Chapter 4 for details.) Because of the Supreme Court's decisions creating a potential defense for employers who promptly investigate claims and take other steps to prevent harassment, you can expect that your investigation report will end up in the hands of a jury if an employee files a lawsuit based on the underlying incidents. Make sure to write a report that's complete and professional and fully supports the conclusions you reached.

10. Follow Up

Once the investigation is over, take some time to consider what you discovered. If you concluded that harassment—or even inappropriate behavior short of harassment—occurred, think about whether your workplace policies against harassment and misconduct could use some revamping. Do employees understand what types of conduct violate company policy? Is there some confusion over whether particular types of behavior—joking around, teasing, flirtatious comments, or references to an employee's race or religion—are appropriate in the workplace? You may need to update your company policies against harassment to ensure that everyone understands what's allowed and what's prohibited.

This is also a good time to consider harassment training. Many companies and workplace consultants offer harassment training, often in separate sessions for managers and employees. If your employees don't seem to get the difference between an innocent compliment and an offensive come-on, training can help make these distinctions clear.

You should also follow up directly with the employees involved in the incident, particularly if an employee complained of harassment. Retaliation can be a problem if the alleged harasser remains in the workplace—and some experts say that it's especially likely if the accused employee was cleared of wrongdoing. That employee probably feels pretty upset about the allegations and the investigation, and his anger may naturally focus on the employee who complained. He may feel that he has every right to take his frustration out on the complaining employee, because the company found that he was in the right (or at least, not in the wrong).

To guard against this risk, meet with the complaining employee regularly after the investigation ends. You might hold these meetings every couple of weeks for a month or so, then check in once a month for a few months to make sure that no retaliation is taking place. You should also meet with the accused employee a few times to make sure that things are getting back to normal and that there have been no repercussions as a result of the investigation. ■

CHAPTER 7

Investigating Workplace Theft

Some readers might be tempted to skip this chapter, thinking to themselves, "Our company has never had a theft problem—our employees wouldn't steal from us." Well, guess again. According to the U.S. Department of Commerce, businesses lose more than $50 billion a year to employee theft. Employee theft costs retailers in this country more than $21 billion per year—in fact, retailers lose more to their own employees than to shoplifters, according to a 2002 survey by Ernst & Young. And experts estimate that up to one-third of small business closures and bankruptcies are due to employee theft.

Perhaps the most surprising statistics are not about the dollars lost to employee theft, but about employees' willingness to steal. According to a 1998 survey by The Security Group of Cahner's Business Information, 66% of employees would steal if they saw others getting away with it—and that's on top of the 13% who will steal regardless. These statistics show that an employer's response to theft can make a huge impact. An employer who investigates and punishes thieves shows other employees that they shouldn't expect to get away with anything. Given these facts, it's imperative for companies to investigate every internal theft, no matter how large or small.

Theft investigations differ from investigation of workplace violence, harassment, or discrimination in several ways:

- **The company is usually the victim.** This means that you probably won't have to anticipate a potential lawsuit from an employee who was harmed by theft, so proving that you took appropriate action to stop the misconduct won't be your foremost concern (as it often is in other types of investigations). It also means that you won't have a complaint or an interview with a victimized employee to fill in the basic facts, which is why documents are the backbone of many theft investigations.

- **Theft is unlikely to be reported.** Most employees are not highly motivated to rat out their coworkers, especially if they are stealing from the company rather than from a particular individual. So, unlike other investigations, the real trick in a theft investigation is learning about the problem in the first place. Section A, below, describes some of the warning signs of various types of theft, so you'll know what types of situations warrant a closer look.

- **Theft investigations are whodunits.** Unlike a harassment or discrimination investigation, in which you sort out conflicting stories to determine whether something improper occurred, a theft investigation is usually about one thing: catching a thief. This means that you'll want to gather all of your evidence—and conduct all of your other interviews—before you confront your suspect. (See Section B, below).

- **Employers want payback.** In addition to stopping the flow of stolen money or property, you'll also want to get your cash or goods back, if possible. There are several ways to do this—see Section B10, below, for more information.

Because theft investigations are unique, this chapter differs slightly from others in this book. Section A describes some common types of scams, rip-offs, and embezzlement that can occur in the workplace. This information will help you figure out if you have a theft problem that requires investigation.

As in the other chapters in Part II, Section B of this chapter provides ten steps to an effective investigation. But you will notice that the order of the steps is slightly different—here, you'll look at documents before you conduct your interviews. You can't confront or interview a workplace suspect until you have examined all of the evidence that supports your position; this will help you elicit a confession, if possible. Section B also addresses other unique features of a theft investigation, including tips for minimizing theft and dealing with insurers.

A. How Employees Steal

Did you know that most employee theft is *never discovered*? In most cases, employees get away with theft—the money is never returned and the employers never figure out that profits are trickling out through the back door. That's why the real trick in a theft investigation is figuring out that theft has occurred in the first place.

The bad news is that the methods and means of employee thieves are unlimited—thieves invent new way to bilk employers every day. The good news is that a handful of schemes and patterns come up again and again and account for much of the theft most employers are likely to face. By familiarizing yourself with these methods—and the telltale signs of workplace thievery—you'll know when you might have an employee theft problem on your hands, which in turn will help you figure out when you need to investigate.

Follow the Money

No matter how an employee steals from an employer, the net result is the same: The employee has more money, while the company has less. The employee's found money is one key to discovering employee fraud. An employee who suddenly has several fancy cars, a new summer home, and expensive clothing and jewelry (and no good explanation of how it all came about) is probably someone you'll want to talk to if you uncover a theft problem. Tread carefully when making inquiries, however, because snooping into an employee's personal finances can leave you open to an invasion of privacy claim. See Section B4, below, for more on this type of digging.

Employee theft can be broken down into four basic categories:

- schemes for stealing money
- schemes for stealing property
- false disbursements—schemes that trick the company into paying money to the employee, and
- conflicts of interest, in which the employee uses his or her position in the company to favor particular vendors, suppliers, or other third parties.

Why Do Employees Steal?

The most basic reason employees steal is because they *can*. In other words, the opportunity is there, and the employees believe they won't get caught or suffer any consequences. (Your company can nip this kind of theft in the bud by making it difficult to steal and by disciplining those who do steal.)

In addition to plain old opportunism, experts say that some other common reasons for workplace theft are:

- financial need (sometimes caused by problems like gambling or substance abuse)
- revenge for perceived mistreatment by the employer, and
- excitement—some employees report stealing to see if they can get away with it, or because they are bored.

There are nearly endless numbers of employee theft schemes, and more are discovered all the time.

For more information on these schemes—and ways to prevent theft in the first place—check out the following books and resources:

Fraud Examination & Prevention, by W. Steven Albrecht and Chad Albrecht (Thomson, 2004)

Corporate Crime Investigation, by Jack Bologna and Paul Shaw (Butterworth-Heinemann, 1997)

The website of the American Institute of Certified Public Accountants, www.aicpa.org. Click "Online Journal of Accountancy" to view back issues of the Institute's magazine, particularly the monthly "Fraud Beat" column. Written by Joseph Wells, a recognized expert in the field of organizational fraud (including employee theft), these columns are full of useful information and tips.

The website of the School of Criminal Justice at Rutgers University, http://crimeprevention.rutgers.edu/crimes.htm. Click "Employee Theft" for a variety of articles and tips on theft schemes (and how to thwart them).

1. Stealing Money

Employees can steal money in a variety of ways, from simply pocketing cash rather than putting it in the register to developing elaborate schemes for diverting funds (and covering their tracks). Here are some of the most common ways employees rip off money—and a few of the warning signs of a money theft problem.

a. Skimming

In a skimming scheme, an employee steals money before it is entered into the company's records. Any employee who is responsible for recording payments to the company can skim—this includes employees who run a register, record customer payments, do the company's books, or otherwise act as an intake point for money coming in to the company. Skimming can be tough to detect because it doesn't "unbalance" the company's books. Because the money is taken before it is entered into the records, the thief doesn't have to make up a reason why the money disappeared or make false entries in the company's accounting system.

EXAMPLES OF SKIMMING:

- **Failing to ring up or record sales.** The employee charges the customer and pockets the money, and the company never knows the sale was made. The skim can be accomplished at a cash register or anywhere else money comes in—for example, at customer's homes, for an outside salesperson.

- **Diverting checks.** The employee endorses the incoming check on behalf of the company, then on his or her own behalf. The employee then cashes the check or deposits it in a personal account.

- **Under-ringing sales.** The employee records the sale for a particular amount, charges the customer more, and then pockets the difference.

WARNING SIGNS

Skimming

Most types of skimming work by the following equation: The customer is receiving goods or services, but the employee—rather than the company—is getting paid for them. Therefore, most of the warning signs of skimming involve discrepancies between how much work your company is doing (or how much product it is moving) and how much money you are taking in.

Red flags for skimming include:

- Lower revenues than expected.

- Increased inventory shrinkage (that is, goods are disappearing in numbers that are not accounted for in sales).

- Declining cash sales as a percentage of total sales (because most employees want to pocket cash, these are the sales that don't get recorded).

- Customer complaints. (A customer who notices an overcharge is likely to complain, but some customers will also tell you if they notice an employee who fails to ring up a sale, or if they receive a cancelled check endorsed to someone other than the company.)

---

b. Lapping

Lapping is a more complex method of theft that resembles a pyramid scheme. The employee steals some money as it comes into the company, then uses subsequent incoming payments to make up the difference. As long as the employee keeps up the scheme, the shortfall won't be noticed.

EXAMPLE: Sam is the bookkeeper at a small company that supplies uniforms to institutional customers. All of the payments from customers go through Sam, who enters them in the company's books and deposits them into the company's bank account. Sam receives a payment for $100 from one customer, which he diverts to his own bank account and does not enter into the company's records. The next day, Sam receives a payment for $300 from a second customer. He credits $100 to the first customer's account, then waits for another payment to make up the shortfall to the second customer—and so on, and so on.

Fraud experts say that most lapping schemes eventually collapse under their own weight. The employee won't be able to resist the temptation to take more and more money, which creates a larger and larger discrepancy to be hidden. At some point, there won't be enough money coming in to make up the shortfall. By the time this happens, however, you might be out many thousands of dollars.

WARNING SIGNS

Lapping

Lapping is a pretty complicated affair, which requires the employee to keep careful track of precisely which Peter was robbed to pay which Paul, and by how much. Here are some of the red flags of lapping:

- A money-handling employee who never takes a day off work—if the lapper isn't in the office to apply incoming payments to shortchanged accounts (and to handle any queries about whether and when certain payments were made), the whole system will fall apart.
- Delays in posting customer payments.
- A slowdown in incoming payments and/or an increase in late accounts.
- Customer complaints.

c. Void/Refund Schemes

Anyone who has ever worked a register knows about the void function—it zeroes out a sale that has already been entered. Voiding is legitimately used when the cashier enters an incorrect amount or a customer decides not to buy the item after all. However, it can also be used to back money out of the system, which the employee can then steal.

Refund schemes are similar: The employee enters a false refund, then pockets the "refunded" money. Employees can also use an employer's promotional refunds or discounts to steal money. For example, an employee who can lay hands on a stack of cards offering "$10 off any purchase of $50 or more" can apply the cards to sales (unbeknownst to the customer), then pocket the $10 discount on each transaction. Similarly, a waiter can use "buy one entrée, get one free" promotional ads to get some quick cash by applying the discount to tables that paid in full.

Either method can be used at cash registers or at any other point where money comes into the company.

EXAMPLE: Joanna is a cashier in a drug store. The store offers customer refunds on items that have not been used and are returned in their original packaging within 30 days of purchase. The cashiers are responsible for checking the condition of the item and making sure the customer shows a receipt; the cashier is supposed to cross the returned item off of the receipt, return it to the customer, then tender the refund, using the "refund" key on the register to record the money paid out. Joanna gets a lot of use out of that refund key— she records at least a refund a day, to the tune of several hundred dollars a week, then pockets the money at the end of her shift.

WARNING SIGNS
Void/Refund Schemes

In void and refund schemes, the company pays out money (to the employee) for returned or "unsold" items, but those items never find their way back to the shelves. Therefore, as in a skimming scenario, these schemes result in depleted inventory and shrinking cash. Here are some of the red flags of void and refund frauds:

- Increased refund and void transactions.
- Cash sales declining as a percentage of total sales (again, because the employee wants to "be paid" in cash).
- Irregularities in refund paperwork (missing documents, illegible customer names, duplicates).
- One employee getting particularly high numbers of customers taking advantage of a promotional offer.
- Voids or refunds issued at the end of a shift.

d. Ripping Off Customers

Schemes to steal from customers (rather than from the company) are especially troubling for business owners. Although you aren't losing money directly off your bottom line, you are ripping off the very people you most want to please. However, because this kind of theft depends on customer ignorance, it doesn't always work. All it takes is a customer complaint or two, and you'll uncover the whole scheme—as long as you are vigilant.

WARNING SIGNS

Stealing From Other Employees

Some workplace thieves target their coworkers. For example, you may face a rash of missing wallets or personal items stolen from employee offices. This type of theft is less common than stealing from an employer, for two reasons: (1) while employees may perceive stealing from the company as a "victimless crime," stealing from coworkers directly harms a particular person, which makes it harder for the thief to justify; and (2) very few employees would hesitate to turn in a thief who was stealing from them, while many employees would be reluctant to turn in a coworker who was ripping off the company.

The warning signs of a thief who is ripping off coworkers are pretty straightforward: Employees will notice money or items missing. In addition, watch out for employees who spend time in another employee's workspace when that employee isn't there—or in a common area, such as a locker room or changing room, without a good reason. Some employees try to avoid detection by committing theft when they know other employees won't be in their usual places—before work hours, after work hours, during lunch, or during times when all employees are supposed to be elsewhere, such as during a fire drill, company-wide event, or mandatory training.

The most common way employees steal from customers is simple overcharging. For example, a waiter might charge a diner for something the diner didn't order or receive, or a cashier might ring up an item twice or charge more than the store does for an item. If the customer doesn't notice, then the employee takes the money attributable to the overcharge. These schemes can get more elaborate—and more costly as well. An employee might steal customer credit card numbers to use for personal purchases, for example.

WARNING SIGNS
Stealing From Customers

When employees steal from customers, the customers themselves are your early warning system. Here are some red flags of this type of theft:

- Customer complaints, especially when most of them point to the same employee.
- Frequent "errors" and voids attributable to the same employee—these are the signs that the customer caught on to the overcharge, and the employee had to correct the bill.
- Increased contacts from credit card issuers. Customers have the option of protesting an overcharge or unauthorized use of their credit card to their credit card issuer, which must then investigate the situation. If you start hearing about a number of questionable charges by your company, you know you have a problem on your hands.

e. Larceny

An employee commits larceny by taking money *after* it has been entered into the company's records. These are the least imaginative—and easiest to detect—theft schemes, because the losses will show up in your company's books eventually.

EXAMPLES OF LARCENY:

- A cashier takes $20 or $30 from the register during each shift.
- An employee responsible for making bank deposits takes cash out of the deposit bag, then alters the deposit slip to show the lower amount.
- An employee steals money from the petty cash drawer.
- An employee writes company checks payable to "cash" or to him- or herself.

WARNING SIGNS

Larceny

An employee who commits larceny makes either no efforts or halfhearted efforts to cover up the crime. Therefore, the red flags of larceny are all about discrepancies between how much money you should have and how much money you do have, including:

- cash register drawers that are always short
- bank deposits that don't match total sales, as shown by receipts, register tapes, and so on
- cash missing from anywhere the company keeps it (the petty cash account, a safe, the area where the company keeps change for registers)
- company checks that are missing or out of sequence
- company checks made out to "cash" or to an employee, or excessive numbers of checks that are recorded as void.

2. Stealing Property

Although most workplace thieves are after money, some will go after other things, too—merchandise, raw materials, equipment, trade secrets, and so on. It's easy to understand why employees steal money: They can use it immediately, to purchase whatever they want. But stealing property is a different game. Unless the employee wants the item for personal use (as might be the case with a computer or jewelry), the employee will have to convert the item into cash or some other compensation. This means that those who steal goods are often working with an outsider, such as a fence or a competitor, who wants to buy.

a. Theft of Goods

If you take a look around your business, you'll probably find that there are lots of things an enterprising thief could take. If you manufacture, your raw materials and finished product could be stolen. If you are in retail, your merchandise is up for grabs. And virtually every business uses some equipment, from computers and adding machines to tools, building supplies, and heavy machinery.

Common shipping and receiving theft schemes include undercounting goods received—or shorting customers on goods shipped—and keeping the extra stuff, categorizing received items as damaged, or fudging paperwork to make it look like more goods are legitimately leaving the warehouse than customers are actually ordering.

EXAMPLE: Roger works in the warehouse of a computer store. When he receives shipments from suppliers, he sometimes sets aside equipment like modems or speakers, which he steals at the end of his shift. To keep his theft from showing up when inventory is taken, Roger sets aside the invoice, alters the numbers, and submits a color photocopy of the doctored document.

Employees who steal merchandise often act just like shoplifters—they take your products and slip them into purses or bags, stuff them into coat pockets, or spirit them off to their cars during a break or after work hours.

Equipment thieves sometimes concoct stories to explain away the missing property. For example, an employee who has a company-issued laptop computer might falsely claim that it was stolen from the employee's car or home.

⚑ WARNING SIGNS
Theft of Goods

An employee who steals goods needs some way to get them out of your business and sometimes needs a third party to sell them to. Here are a few red flags:

- Employees who are in the wrong place at the wrong time, take frequent breaks, or carry bags or wear bulky clothing on the floor.
- Employees who meet with outsiders on or near company property.
- Employees who leave work with large packages.
- Shipping and receiving paperwork that has been altered or is missing.
- Inventory numbers that don't add up.

b. Intellectual Property Theft

The real value of many businesses lies not in their equipment or their merchandise, but in their intellectual property (IP)—the trade secrets, customer lists, formulae, recipes, business methods, and other intangible information that makes the company a success. An employee who steals these assets can wreak enormous damage on a company—usually because these assets are what gives the company an edge over competitors. Once the information is out, the competitive edge is gone.

Some IP thieves sell business secrets to competing companies, while others use the secrets to start their own competitive business, publicize the information as an act of revence, or give the secrets to a subsequent employer.

EXAMPLE: Harold works for a sports food company that manufactures energy bars, drinks, and gels. The company recently developed a new line of energy bars that are salty rather than sweet—the end result is a bar that tastes like potato chips or pretzels rather than cookies or candy. The bars have proven enormously popular with athletes, and competitors are trying desperately to reverse engineer the product. (Reverse engineering is a legitimate way of obtaining another company's secrets.) Harold downloads the company's recipes on to a floppy disk and sells them to a competitor, who then claims to have successfully cracked the code.

IP Theft

Unfortunately, employers often learn of IP theft only after the horses have left the barn. Here are some red flags:

- Employees leaving to start a competing business.
- Competitors suddenly developing products that are similar to yours or calling on your customers.
- Unusual attempts to access physical areas of your company or portions of your computer system where trade secrets are kept. Employees who are in the wrong place at the wrong time—in the workplace or in cyberspace—bear a closer look.
- Increasing computer password violations, indicating that someone is trying to get into sensitive files.

Stealing isn't stealing if you don't protect your secrets.

To convince a court that an employee stole secrets from your company, you will have to prove that you treated the information as a secret. If you routinely left your "secrets" where everyone can see them, or you published important formulas or customer lists on a website that is accessible to the public, you will have a tough time proving that this information constituted a trade secret. For more information on trade secrecy standards, see *Nondisclosure Agreements: Protect Your Trade Secrets & More*, by Richard Stim and Stephen Fishman (Nolo).

3. Fake Disbursements

In a fake disbursement scheme, an employee gets the company to pay money to the employee on false pretenses. Rather than simply stealing the money, the employee submits phony invoices, expense reimbursements, or other paperwork so that the company will disburse money to the employee. In effect, the employee submits illegitimate requests through legitimate company channels to commit the crime. Here are a few of the most common types of fake disbursements.

a. Phony Vendor/Supplier and Other Billing Schemes

Many an employer has paid money to a nonexistent vendor—a company or account set up by an employee, who then submits fake invoices or other requests for payment to the company. An employee might also set up a false vendor in order to overcharge the company for goods. For example, an employee might establish a company to purchase raw materials the employer uses to make its products, then sell the materials to the employer at a steep mark-up.

EXAMPLE 1: George is in charge of buying materials for a clothing manufacturer. The company buys buttons in huge quantities from a variety of suppliers. George sets up his own company and purchases buttons from some of his employer's biggest suppliers. Then, in his role as buyer for the clothing company, he purchases buttons from his own company, at a sweet 100% mark-up.

EXAMPLE 2: Hannah is a bookkeeper for a company that provides human resources training to businesses across the nation. The company has some on-staff trainers, but it also uses consultants to provide training in distant locations. These consultants submit invoices for payment. Hannah starts drafting her own invoices and slipping them in with the consultants' requests for payment. The invoices are submitted in the name of "HHH Training," a name she also uses to open a bank account. When the checks are cut, she simply deposits the HHH Training check in her new bank account.

An employee can also set up a phony billing scheme using the company's existing vendors. For example, an employee might copy a legitimate invoice and submit it twice: The first check goes to the vendor, and the second goes to the employee. A more elaborate version of this scheme involves refunds. The employee submits the invoice twice and actually pays the vendor twice. When the vendor realizes the error and refunds the second payment, the employee keeps the money.

WARNING SIGNS
Phony Vendor Schemes

In a phony vendor scheme—as in other fake disbursement scenarios—an employee covers the theft with false paperwork. This means that your first clue to the problem will often be a document that doesn't look quite right.

Here are some red flags to phony vendor schemes:

- New vendors who are unknown to you.
- Invoices that lack the usual information, such as a taxpayer ID number, address, or phone number, or are not printed on letterhead.
- Duplicate invoices or invoices that appear to have been altered.
- Invoices that don't contain the usual billing detail, or that request nice round numbers. For example, if most of your consulting invoices list hours expended on various types of tasks and an hourly rate, you should question an invoice that requests a flat $5,000 without explanation.
- Vendors who have the same name (or initials), address, or telephone number as one of your employees.
- Cancelled vendor or supplier checks that have been endorsed by one of your employees.
- Increased costs for vendors, suppliers, or materials.

b. Expense Schemes

If your employees are entitled to claim expense reimbursements, you are at risk of paying out money for expenses that were never incurred. For example, an employee might claim false expenses, claim that personal expenses were incurred for business purposes, or make unauthorized charges on a company credit card.

EXAMPLE: Marvin takes a three-day business trip for his employer. He submits an expense reimbursement form claiming that he spent $150 a night on a hotel room, about $50 each day on food, $50 on cab fare to get from the hotel to customer locations, and $300 taking a client and her husband to a fancy restaurant for dinner. In fact, Marvin stayed with his brother-in-law, ate fast food, took public transportation, and had dinner at the client's home. Less money spent on bus fare and hamburgers, Marvin can clear almost $1,000 in phony reimbursements from a single trip.

WARNING SIGNS
Phony Expenses

The most vulnerable moment for a false expense scheme is when the employee reports the expenses to be reimbursed. Here are some red flags:

- Failure to submit receipts for claimed expenses.
- Receipts that have been doctored or photocopied, do not clearly show the merchant and amount of sale, are not dated, or appear to claim duplicate expenses (for example, two receipts for dinner on the same day).
- Expense claims for personal items.
- Expense claims that are higher than they should be (for example, an especially high rate for a hotel room or meal).
- Expense claims that are just below the limit for an internal audit. Some companies routinely approve expense claims up to a certain amount but will look more closely at a claim that exceeds the limit. If an employee's expenses always approach the audit limit without crossing the line, that person might be gaming the system.

4. Conflicts of Interest

In a conflict of interest scheme, an employee uses company resources or a company position to create illegitimate moneymaking opportunities. These schemes often involve hiring preferred vendors or suppliers, either in exchange for a bribe or kickback or because the vendor has some financial connection to the employee.

a. Bribes and Kickbacks

An employee who takes money to help an outsider get business with the company is participating in a bribe or kickback scheme. A bribe is a simple payment up front for the privilege of getting work; a kickback is a payment of a percentage or portion of the money the outsider makes from the company.

EXAMPLE: Ron is the office manager for a large medical practice. His responsibilities include making sure that the vending machines are stocked and that coffee, snacks, and other amenities are available to the staff. A new vendor that is trying to break into the field offers Ron a 5% kickback to get the contract for coffee service at his company. Ron agrees and soon begins collecting a monthly payment from the vendor.

WARNING SIGNS
Bribes and Kickbacks

Bribe and kickback schemes involve third parties: not only the company that is paying the employee, but also the companies that are left out in the cold because they are *not* paying the employee. Here are some red flags:

- Vendor complaints. If your usual vendors suddenly find themselves out of a contract, they might complain. And if your employee-thief tries to hit up an unwilling company for a bribe, you might hear about it.
- New and unknown vendors.
- Increased costs—a vendor who has to pay a bribe or kickback is going to have to charge more to cover that cost. And an employee who is receiving a kickback wants the vendor to earn as much as possible from your company.
- Increasing inventory or services (because the employee wants your company to buy as much as possible from the crooked vendor).
- A high percentage of business going to one vendor or supplier (the one who's paying off your employee).

b. Self-Dealing Schemes

In a self-dealing scenario, an employee uses his or her position in the company to improperly favor outsiders that are connected with the employee—family members, friends, or the employee's own side business, for example. An employee might hire her husband's law firm to provide legal services, contract to purchase computer training from a friend, or arrange to sell your company's products—at a discount—to her own company, for quick mark up and resale.

EXAMPLE: Shawna runs her own crafts business, making scented candles and bath salts. Her boyfriend, Tom, works for a chain of gift shops that lease space in upscale hotels. Tom arranges for the company to purchase Shawna's products at a hefty mark-up, even though it already sells several similar items.

WARNING SIGNS
Self-Dealing

The whole point of self-dealing is to favor certain vendors and suppliers over others. This favoritism sometimes leads to discovery. Here are some red flags:

- New or unknown vendors.
- Vendors who have the same name, address, or telephone number as an employee.
- Complaints from vendors who are *not* receiving special treatment or who were frozen out so the employee could favor a relative or friend.
- Higher than usual costs for products or services.
- A high percentage of business going to one vendor.

B. Ten Steps to a Successful Theft Investigation

This section explains how to apply the basic investigation steps covered in Part I of this book to an investigation of employee theft. If you haven't read Part I, you should do so before getting into this more specific material—the discussion that follows assumes that you are already familiar with basic investigation procedures and will not repeat all of the information covered in Part I.

How Employers Learn of Theft

According to the Association of Certified Fraud Examiners, employers find out about workplace fraud—including theft by employees and managers—in a variety of ways. The most common way is a tip from another employee. Somewhat less encouraging is the second most common method employers learn of workplace fraud: by accident. Here are some others:

- internal audits or internal controls
- external audits
- tips from vendors or customers
- anonymous tips, and
- notification by law enforcement personnel.

I. Decide Whether to Investigate

Once you learn about employee theft, you should always investigate, regardless of how much is missing. Studies have shown that workplace thieves tend to start small, then expand their operations. They take small amounts of money or items that aren't very valuable, then wait to see what happens. If nobody catches on, pretty soon the sky's the limit. What this means for the savvy employer is that investigating a $50 register shortage or slight increase in inventory shrinkage today could save you from falling victim to a much more expensive theft scheme tomorrow.

Your investigation will also serve as a deterrent to others. If other employees see a coworker getting away with stealing from the company, they are more likely to start taking a five-finger discount as well.

Investigating will also shield you from legal hassles down the road. If you want to take action against an employee who you believe is stealing from the company, you will want some solid evidence to back up your decision. Otherwise, you could be looking at a potential defamation claim.

EXAMPLE: Maurice is a sales clerk at a clothing store. Another clerk, Rhonda, tells you that she saw Maurice putting several expensive leather jackets into a bag and taking it out to his car. You immediately fire Maurice. If Maurice actually stole the jackets, then you have nothing to worry about—because truth is a defense to a defamation claim, treating Maurice as a thief doesn't constitute defamation if he actually is a thief. But if Maurice didn't steal the jackets—if Rhonda made the whole story up to cover her own theft, for example—then you have a major problem. Not only did you falsely treat Maurice as a thief, but you also didn't even bother to look into the allegations. Now you're facing a potential lawsuit *and* you still have a thief on your payroll.

Also, if the thief stole from someone outside of the company—for example, a customer, client, or vendor—then you could be liable for any future losses that person suffers if you fail to take reasonable precautions to stop the theft. And reasonable precautions include investigating to find and stop the culprit.

Employee Theft and the Sarbanes-Oxley Act

In the wake of Enron and other corporate accounting scandals, Congress passed the Sarbanes-Oxley Act of 2002. This law is intended to increase the accountability of publicly traded companies for their reported financial results, thereby making sure that investors have accurate information on which to base their decisions. Among the law's many requirements is a mandate that all publicly traded companies must establish procedures by which employees can anonymously and confidentially submit concerns about questionable accounting and auditing matters. Certain kinds of employee theft might fall within this category, particularly if it results in doctored financial records. The Act also imposes a number of obligations on public companies that discover errors or falsifications in their financial reports.

Because Sarbanes-Oxley is a relatively new law, its requirements are still being fleshed out. If yours is a publicly traded company, get some legal advice about implementing the law's provisions, including those applicable to employee theft.

2. Take Immediate Action, If Necessary

If you suspect employee theft (or you know that someone is stealing, but you don't know who), there are a few actions you can take right away, before you start investigating. Of course, the options available to you will depend on what you know, what type of theft you suspect, and who might be responsible.

a. Enhance Security and Safeguards

If you can isolate the theft to one area of your operations, you can take some steps to make stealing more difficult. A great way to do this is to simply add more people to any process where money might be disappearing. Because most workplace theft is committed by employees acting alone, increasing the number of people who have to be involved in any transaction will foil opportunities for theft. Fraud experts call this "segregation" of job duties—if you make sure that no one employee is responsible for every step of a transaction, you will make it much more difficult for any employee to use the transaction as a vehicle for theft.

For example, if you know that there is something fishy in the bookkeeping department, you could require a second signature (of the company president or other high-ranking official) on all outgoing checks, or have someone outside the department open all incoming mail and log any payments received. If you have a problem in the receiving department, require two employees to check the items received against the purchase order, invoice, and/or packing slip.

There are other ways you can increase workplace controls against theft. Requiring additional paperwork—particularly paperwork that involves other people—is another good way to cut down on theft. For example, if you suspect that one of your cashiers is giving false refunds, you could require all cashiers to fill in a form with the name, address, and phone number of every customer who received a refund. Let your workers know that you will follow up with the customers—then do it. Or, if you are concerned about inflated expense reports, require your employees to submit a dated, itemized receipt for all claimed expenses.

 Consider making your safeguards permanent once the investigation is over.

The same procedures that will help you draw the brakes on theft while you conduct your investigation will help you prevent theft in the future. See Section B10, below, for more information on preventing theft.

Another way to deter employee theft (at least temporarily) is to tell your employees that the company will be conducting a routine audit for the next couple of weeks (this will also give you a good cover for your investigation). Of course, you can't do this forever, but most workplace thieves will put their schemes on hold if they know that scrutiny will be especially high.

b. Suspend the Suspected Wrongdoer

If you have a pretty good idea where your problem lies, you might consider suspending that employee while you conduct the investigation. One benefit of this approach—other than immediately stopping the theft—is that the employee won't have time to destroy workplace evidence. On the other hand, by tipping your hand at the outset, you lose any chance you might have to catch the employee in the act. You'll have to weigh the company's risk of further losses against your need for this kind of evidence of the theft.

EXAMPLE: Rick is the night manager of a department store's warehouse. In the past several months, the warehouse has had some serious "shrinkage" problems, particularly in big screen televisions. The store owner suspects Rick, because the thefts are taking place at night and Rick is the only worker who has a key to the loading dock area—the only place where the televisions could be removed without attracting suspicion. If he suspended Rick right away, the owner could stop the theft problem, but he might never get proof that Rick is behind the robberies. Instead, the owner decides to hang around outside the loading dock for a few nights after the store receives a large shipment of television sets. When he sees Rick and a couple of his friends making off with a few TVs, the owner has all the proof he needs.

Suspending an employee before you conduct an investigation also poses some legal risks. If your hunch proves wrong, the company could be liable for damaging the suspended employee's reputation. For this reason, you should only suspend an employee if you have strong, objective evidence of wrongdoing—and you should not publicize the suspension in the workplace. You should also make special efforts to wrap up your investigation quickly.

Don't suspend workers without pay.

From a legal standpoint, you generally can't suspend exempt, salaried employees—those who are not entitled to overtime if they work extra hours—without pay. And even though you can suspend hourly, nonexempt workers without pay, it's not a good idea. A suspension without pay is punitive: It improperly signals that you have made up your mind about the allegations before you've even begun to investigate. A worker who is suspended without pay will probably be angry about it—and if the allegations later prove false, that anger may well provide the fuel for a lawsuit. And unpaid suspensions can be an administrative hassle, as they require you to interrupt your usual payroll system. The wages you shell out to a temporarily suspended employee will be a small price to pay to avoid these problems.

c. Contact Your Insurance Company

Most businesses carry insurance for a variety of potential mishaps. Believe it or not, you can insure against employee theft—and it's possible your business already has such coverage. If your company has a fidelity bond or a crime loss or employee dishonesty policy, contact your insurance agent right away to find out how to file a claim. If an employee theft is covered under one of these policies, you will ordinarily have a short period of time after you discover the loss to notify the insurance company. Your agent or business lawyer should be able to tell you what documents and information you need to file a claim.

 If theft may be covered by your insurance, contact a lawyer before you investigate—and before you report the loss.

When you buy an insurance policy, you give the insurance company the right of "subrogation." This means that the insurance company has the legal authority to proceed against anyone who causes you a covered loss in order to get back the money it had to fork over to you. If you take any action that compromises the insurance company's subrogation right, you may not be entitled to collect on your policy. If your insurance covers employee theft, talk to a lawyer right away to get some advice on conducting an investigation that won't run afoul of the insurance company's rights. Otherwise, the insurance company may refuse to make good on your claim.

3. Choose the Investigator

You'll find general information on choosing an investigator—including the importance of impartiality, experience, and professionalism—in Chapter 2, Section D. While those qualities are important when investigating any kind of workplace problem, investigating employee theft often requires some additional qualifications, including subject matter expertise and interview skills.

a. Subject Matter Expertise

As you can see from Section A, above, unraveling an employee theft scheme sometimes requires a good deal of technical knowledge. Depending on the type of theft you are facing, you may need some special expertise to complete the investigation. For example, investigating the theft of intellectual property might require a background in computer technology or science. Investigating a complex vendor fraud or lapping scheme might require accounting or auditing skills.

If you're facing a large-scale or highly sophisticated theft problem, you should consider using an outside investigator who has the necessary expertise. Another option is to team up an in-house investigator with an expert who can provide the necessary information. You can use an internal expert (for example, the head of your technology services division or your chief financial officer) or bring in an expert from the outside. If you decide to bring in an outside expert to assist with the investigation, remember that your company will ultimately be responsible for any actions the expert takes. This means that someone on your company's payroll should be overseeing the expert's work. In addition, if the theft is related to confidential company information, you should have the expert sign a nondisclosure agreement.

 Don't use an internal expert unless you're sure that person isn't involved in the theft.

If you need a particular type of expertise to ferret out a theft, chances are good that your thief also has some experience in that area. This means that your in-house expert could also be your prime suspect—and ultimately, your thief. When considering internal experts, make very certain that person could not have committed the theft. If you aren't sure, bring someone in from the outside.

Here are some examples of experts who might be valuable in an employee theft investigation:

- **Forensic accountants.** These experts review a company's financial documents for signs of fraud. They comb through the books, looking for missing paperwork, financial improprieties, unexplained transactions, and other red flags of theft. (Although their title might make them sound like crime scene specialists, "forensic" refers to work that is done in possible preparation for legal proceedings.)

- **Certified fraud examiners.** These specialists—who come from many different professional backgrounds, including criminology, accounting, and law—are trained in the prevention and detection of fraud. Like forensic accountants, they can help uncover signs of fraud in your company's books.

- **Document examiners.** These experts examine disputed or suspect documents and determine how old they are, whether they are copies or originals, whether they have been altered or supplemented, and whether handwriting and signatures are genuine, among other things. If you are facing a document-intensive investigation—particularly if there is a question about whether documents have been altered—these experts may be useful.

- **Computer specialists.** Sometimes, you just need a techie to help you sort things out. A computer specialist can help you figure out whether certain files or documents were accessed, altered, deleted, or copied. They can also track who has been where in your computer system—valuable information for uncovering bookkeeping fraud or intellectual property theft.

- **Experts in your company's field.** If you are trying to figure out whether your company's intellectual property has been copied, taken, or handed off to others, an expert who is familiar with the type of work your company does can help.

Bringing in the Police

Should you call the cops to investigate your workplace theft? It depends on the situation. Once you bring in the police, the investigation will be out of your hands—and you'll have the law in your workplace. This can lead to all kinds of problems, from discovery of things that you wish they hadn't found to serious morale problems in your workforce. On the other hand, the police can use investigative tools that are pretty much off limits to private employers—and they are very experienced at conducting interrogations and getting suspects to confess.

Ultimately, it probably isn't worth bringing in the police unless you have a very serious problem that you can't handle on your own—such as an employee who has stolen controlled substances or weapons. Investigating these types of situations yourself could lead to greater problems, such as liability for personal injuries that result from use of the dangerous items or from your investigation. In situations that are less urgent, you might lose more than you gain by calling the cops. And unless your problem is fairly sizable, the police may not be willing to spend many resources going after your workplace thief.

If you do bring in the police, make sure that the information you give them is accurate and fair. Employees who are ultimately exonerated can sue for malicious prosecution if there was no good cause for the prosecution and you maliciously gave the police false or misleading information. The likelihood of being sued for malicious prosecution is quite low, but you should still consult with an attorney if you are considering going to the police.

b. Interviewing Skills

An investigation of employee theft has a slightly different focus than many other types of workplace investigation. Unlike a harassment or discrimination case, in which your ultimate goal is to find out what happened, your goal in a theft investigation is to gather the proof you need and then get a particular employee to admit committing the theft.

This means your investigator will have to be skilled not only at gathering information, but also at eliciting confessions. Some techniques for interviewing a suspected employee are described in Section B6, below. However, if you don't have anyone on your staff who has some experience in these types of interviews—including how to press for admissions without crossing any legal lines—it might be a good idea to hire an outside investigator or certified fraud examiner to help out.

4. Plan the Investigation

In a theft investigation, you have several goals. First and foremost, you have to figure out whether theft occurred, or whether there's some other explanation for the problem. If you conclude that you are dealing with theft, you will want to find the thief, extract a confession if you can, and get back as much of the stolen property as possible. This means that you'll want to gather as much information as you can up front, before you interview the suspect, so you'll have lots of ammunition and evidence to encourage a confession. The point of your investigation planning is either to come up with a suspect or list of suspects or to figure out what evidence of theft might exist that exonerates or implicates your suspect. So your planning will depend on whether or not you have a suspect at the outset.

As always, you should start your investigation preparations by reviewing what you know. If you learned of the theft through a complaint, anonymous or otherwise, you can begin with those allegations. If theft is suspected because of anomalies in paperwork, problems in bank balances, or inventory shortages, you can start there.

a. Starting Without a Suspect

If there is no immediate suspect, start by figuring out what you know. Did someone make a complaint about theft? If so, review the allegations. What was stolen? When and where? Some complaints are quite detailed; others are more enigmatic ("Your employees are robbing you blind!"). In either situation, catalogue the information from the complaint carefully.

EXAMPLE: The XYZ Corporation supplies canned and preserved food products to hospitals, schools, and other institutions. The food is shipped to XYZ's warehouses, where it is stored until it is packaged and loaded in response to customer orders. XYZ receives an anonymous complaint, dropped in a company suggestion box, that says only this: "Wonder why the Seattle warehouse is missing so much inventory? You might want to check out what the night shift is up to."

Pretty sparse complaint, right? Well, yes and no. The complaint doesn't indicate exactly what is happening and who is responsible. But it does indicate that there is some kind of inventory theft going on during the night shift at the Seattle warehouse. Based on this complaint, you might immediately pull inventory records for all of the company's warehouses, get an employee roster of the night shift workers in Seattle, and plan to visit the Seattle warehouse at night, unannounced, to see what's going on.

Whether you start from a complaint or simply some management suspicions or "funny numbers," you'll want to figure out two things: what's missing and who had access to it. Often, this will require you to review financial records and other documents. (See Section B5, below, on documents that might be helpful to a theft investigation.) Before you actually begin interviewing anyone, you'll want to have the best possible handle on what has been stolen, how, when, and where. This information will help you narrow down your list of suspects.

As you review what you know, start piecing together the information you need to figure out who's behind the theft. Depending on the circumstances, you may need to find out who makes bank deposits; who works each cash register and when; what the inventory, sales, and bookkeeping records show; or who has access to altered records or missing cash. Gather any information you can behind the scenes, before you start your interviews.

b. Starting With a Suspect

If you are beginning your investigation with a suspect in mind, your first steps will depend on why this person has come under suspicion. Do you know what the alleged theft is? If so, consider what documents, witnesses, or other evidence will help you figure out what (if anything) is missing and how it was taken.

If you have only a name and little other information to go on (as might be the case if you receive a vague, anonymous complaint, such as "John is crooked" or "Kathy is a thief"), consider what types of assets the suspect has access to. Then, think about documents, witnesses, or other evidence that might help you figure out whether anything was taken, and how.

 The theft you know about may be just the tip of the iceberg.

Experts warn that many thieves just aren't satisfied with one type of scam. Like the murderer who is discovered by police after being pulled over for a traffic violation, a workplace thief may be caught for a relatively small offense but be guilty of much more. For example, you might catch a manager for submitting reimbursement forms for expenses he never incurred but never discover that he is also accepting bribes from clients. Once you have evidence of a particular theft, don't stop there. Examine everything the employee had access to and every financial transaction the employee was involved in to make sure you know all of the bad news.

---

c. Privacy Issues

This section offers some basic tips that will help you plan an investigation that won't violate your employee's privacy rights. Generally, however, the best strategy to avoid privacy problems is to gather only the information you need to know, through the least intrusive means possible—usually through interviewing employees and reviewing company documents, rather than through searches, surveillance, or lie detector tests.

 For an overview of privacy issues, see Chapter 1, Section B.

This section focuses on a couple of issues that are of particular concern in a theft investigation: workplace searches and polygraph testing.

Workplace Searches

Workplace thieves have to put the money and property they steal somewhere. And an employee who is running a complicated bookkeeping scam (such as a lapping scheme) probably keeps an extra set of books nearby, to help keep track of things. To uncover this kind of evidence, you may need to search an employee's desk, locker, or other workspace, or to look inside an employee's personal belongings, such as a purse or knapsack. But whenever you conduct a workplace search, you risk violating your employees' privacy rights, particularly if you don't have the right policies in place.

When judges evaluate whether a particular workplace search is legal, they usually try to balance two competing concerns. First, the law considers the employer's justification for performing the search: An employer with a strong, work-related reason for searching has the best chance of prevailing. The court balances the employer's reason for searching against the worker's reasonable expectations of privacy. An employee who reasonably expects—based on the employer's policies, past practices, and common sense—that the employer will not search certain areas has the strongest argument here.

The court considers the relative strengths of these two competing interests to decide whether a particular search passes legal muster. The more steps employers take to lessen their workers' expectations of privacy and the stronger the employer's reason to search, the more likely a court is to find the search legal.

EXAMPLE 1: The owner of a large jewelry store notices that several expensive rings are missing from the display case. He immediately cuts the locks on every employee's locker and rifles through the employees' personal belongings. The store has no search policies, employee lockers have never been searched before, and the store has made no efforts to warn employees that their lockers might be searched. This search might violate employees' privacy rights.

EXAMPLE 2: Now assume that the jewelry store has a search policy, warning employees that all company property, including lockers, is subject to search. The store also requires employees to give the store owner a copy of their locker combination or a duplicate key to their locker. In this situation, the store has a much better argument that the search is legal. By warning employees that their lockers might be searched and by driving this point home by insisting that employees provide the store with a means of entering their lockers, the store has done all it can to diminish the employees' expectations of privacy.

 Privacy is a highly volatile legal issue.

Each year, workers bring lawsuits claiming that an employer invaded their privacy by conducting an improper search. The outcome of these cases depends on the judge's view of the worker's misconduct and the employer's methods for getting to the bottom of things, as well as the effect of any state laws on the topic. If a court rules against your company in an invasion of privacy lawsuit, you may have to pay financial damages or be subjected to a court order prohibiting you from taking similar action in the future. Because there are no guarantees in this area of the law, most employers should consult with a lawyer before conducting any but the most routine searches.

Here are a few tips that will help you stay on the right side of the law:

- **Adopt a policy before you need to search.** If you warn your employees in advance that certain areas (like desks or lockers) may be subject to search, employees will have lower expectations of privacy in those areas— and less reason to complain about a particular search.

- **Search only when necessary.** You need the strongest possible justification for your search—and that means you should have a very compelling reason for digging through your employee's belongings.

- **Never search an employee's body.** Some employers become so zealous that they want to physically search their workers for stolen items. This is always a bad idea. Your workers have a very strong privacy interest in their own bodies and the clothing worn on them. Before you frisk workers, talk to a lawyer—or call in the police.

- **Restrooms and changing areas are off limits.** Most workers legitimately expect that they will not be watched while using the bathroom or changing their clothes—and this expectation is highly reasonable. Some states even have laws prohibiting surveillance of these private areas. If you really think you'll need a bathroom monitor to catch your workplace thief, talk to a lawyer.

Going Undercover

Many private investigators and investigation firms advise placing an operative undercover to unravel complicated employee theft schemes. For example, if you suspect an employee of stealing expensive merchandise for resale, an undercover investigator could pose as a potential purchaser. If you are facing a kickback/bribe scheme, the investigator could pose as a vendor. Or, if you believe several of your employees are working together in a theft ring, the investigator could come in as a crooked employee hoping to get in on the deal.

However, using an undercover agent can get fairly complicated. Because the agent must be someone unknown to your employees, you will have to bring in an outsider. And because undercover work is difficult and nuanced, you'll want to bring in a professional—which will quickly run up some significant costs. Only in situations where you are being robbed of substantial assets will this make financial sense.

There are also legal pitfalls to watch out for. Remember, you are legally responsible for actions taken on your behalf by an outside agency. This means that if the undercover worker invades an employee's privacy rights by, for example, conducting an illegal search or getting too involved in an employee's life outside the workplace, you could be on the hook for damages. For all these reasons, if you are seriously considering using an undercover operative, you should hire an experienced and highly recommended investigation firm. For more information on using undercover agents, see *Undercover Investigations in the Workplace,* by Eugene F. Ferraro (Butterworth Heinemann, 2000).

Polygraph Tests

As discussed in Chapter 1, Section B10, a federal law called the Employee Polygraph Protection Act (EPPA) generally prohibits employers from requiring or even asking employees to take a polygraph test. However, the law carves out several exceptions, and one of them applies to investigations of workplace theft.

Under the EPPA, a private employer may ask an employee to take a polygraph if all of these conditions are met:

- The test is administered in connection with an ongoing investigation of economic loss or injury to the employer's business (see "What the Ongoing Investigation Exception Doesn't Cover," below).

- The employee had access to the property that is the subject of the investigation.

- The employer has a reasonable suspicion that the employee was involved in the incident or activity under investigation.

- The employer gives the employee, at least two working days before the test, a written statement that:

  ✓ describes the specific incident or activity under investigation and the basis for testing the employee

  ✓ identifies the specific loss or economic injury under investigation

  ✓ states that the employee had access to the property in question

  ✓ describes the basis for the employer's reasonable suspicion of the employee

  ✓ is signed by someone who is authorized to legally bind the employer, such as an officer or directory of the company, and indicates the time and date when the employee received the statement, and

  ✓ is signed by the employee.

What the Ongoing Investigation Exception Doesn't Cover

The ongoing investigation exception applies to many types of workplace theft, but not all of them. Because the exception applies only to an investigation into a specific incident or activity, an employer cannot rely on the exception to require polygraphs to find out whether theft has occurred or to look into a continuing loss, such as regular inventory shortages that occur all of the time. Testing is allowed only in response to a specific, identifiable incident of loss.

In addition, you can test only in response to an economic loss or injury to the employer's business, not to a customer, client, or coworker. So if your workplace thief is stealing from other employees or from clients, the exception probably doesn't apply.

Even if your situation fits within this exception, you still have to follow a lengthy list of technical requirements, from giving the employee extensive written notices before the test (including an exact list of every question to be asked), to observing a number of rules during the test, to providing the employee with a copy of the test results. You must also use a polygraph examiner who meets specified qualifications. And you can't take any action based on the test results alone, even if you follow all of these rules—you must have additional evidence of the employee's guilt.

Given all of these rules, it probably isn't worth using a polygraph in most theft investigations. If you think that a polygraph is necessary to get to the bottom of things, talk to a lawyer who is familiar with the law—and hire an experienced polygraph examiner.

5. Gather Documents and Other Evidence

Many theft schemes require—or create—paper trails. Think about what types of documents might be generated by the theft you suspect. An employee engaged in lapping, for example, will probably need a personal set of books to keep track of how much money has been deposited, how much is owed, which checks have been cashed, and so on. A refund or void scheme will yield paperwork in the form of cash register tapes and excessive void or refund slips. A phony vendor scheme generally requires invoices or other requests for payment listing the false vendor name.

Depending on what type of theft you suspect, you may want to look at some of these documents:

- cash register tape and receipts
- void slips
- refund slips
- credits
- purchase orders
- invoices
- deposit slips
- cancelled checks
- bank statements
- vendor records
- financial statements
- tax returns
- expense reimbursement forms
- balance sheets, or
- accounting documents, including ledgers and journals

You can also collect documents and information outside of the workplace. For example:

- If you suspect an employee of stealing, find out whether the employee is spending lots of money outside the workplace—and where that money came from. Is the employee suddenly buying a vacation home or luxury cars, taking expensive trips, wearing valuable jewelry or clothes? If the employee claims that the money came from a legitimate source, look into it. For example, if an employee claims to have inherited a large amount of money, you could check public probate court records—and obituaries in back issues of the newspaper.

Stick to public records and observable facts.

You might be tempted to start covert surveillance of an employee who seems to be living beyond her means, but that's generally a bad idea. To avoid violating the employee's privacy, limit your investigation to documents that are publicly available—such as records filed with a court or agency—and information that is plainly evident. Noticing that an employee is showing up to work in a brand new Lexus is fair game; calling every real estate agent in town to find out whether an employee is in the market to buy a new home probably is not.

- If you suspect an employee of a phony vendor scheme, check secretary of state filings. Is the business listed? If so, find out the name(s) of the owners—if it is a phony vendor, your employee or his friends or relatives will probably be listed. Check the business address to see if it matches the employee's address. And if the vendor is supposed to be licensed, you can check with your state's licensing agency to find out whether this requirement has been met.

6. Interviews

Once you've gathered and examined relevant documents, you're ready to begin your interviews. In a theft investigation, you'll want to interview your suspect(s) last. Unlike a harassment or discrimination investigation, which begins with the victim, moves to the accused employee, then goes to witnesses and other third parties to confirm or contradict the stories of the main players, a theft investigation moves from the outside in. You'll start your interviews with the most peripheral witnesses, then conclude by interviewing the suspect. That way, you'll have all of the evidence you can possibly gather before confronting the potential thief.

a.　Interviewing Witnesses

The types of witnesses who may be available will depend on the nature of the theft. Once you have a sense of what kind of theft you're dealing with, think about who might have helpful information to offer. In a bribe or kickback scheme, for example, you might want to interview your vendors, other employees who are involved in the vendor selection process, the suspect's supervisor, and anyone who might have had an opportunity to witness shady deals (for example, a coworker who accompanies the suspect on sales calls). If you suspect an employee of skimming at a cash register, you might talk to your bookkeeper and to employees who work the same register shifts as the suspect.

Getting Started

As in any investigation, it's best to begin your interviews with an opening statement to put the witness at ease and set the tone for your questions. However, unlike other investigations, you may want to keep your purpose secret at the beginning of the interview, to encourage the witness to reveal as much as possible and to try to prevent the suspect from learning of your interest. Because employees are so reluctant to finger their coworkers for theft, you may want to build up to the topic of your interview slowly, to give yourself time to establish a rapport with the witness.

Experienced investigators advise taking a somewhat vague approach when opening a witness interview. Rather than explaining their purpose in detail, they'll simply say, "The company has asked me to look into something, and I'm hoping you can help me out by answering a few questions. Is that OK?" Or, they might be a bit more specific about the topic: "I've been asked to gather information about our procedures for selecting vendors. Can I ask you some questions about that?"

Of course, if you're dealing with a complaint from a known person, whether employee or outsider, you can be less circumspect in your approach. For example, you might start an interview with a vendor who complained that one of your employees solicited a bribe by saying, "I understand that you've spoken to _____ about a problem with one of our employees. I've been asked to look into the matter. Can you tell me what happened?"

Questions

The questions you ask the witness will depend on the purpose of the interview. However, your approach should be the same with most witnesses: Move from the general to the specific. If you believe a witness may have seen a coworker stealing from a register, for example, start by finding out what shifts the witness works, when she is on the register, and who usually works the registers near her. You might then ask a general question about theft, such as "Have you ever seen anyone steal from the company?" If the employee responds negatively, get more specific by asking, "Have you ever seen anyone steal from a register?"

 Be more direct with a witness who has complained of theft.

If the witness has made a complaint about theft, you can start right in with the facts of the complaint. However, you'll want to make sure to cover basic background questions at some point in the interview, to make sure the witness had the opportunity to see or hear the incidents and to find out about any existing animosity between the witness and the suspected employee.

Closing the Interview

Once you have finished your questions, review your notes with the person you interviewed. Make sure you got everything right and that your notes include all of the important details. Ask the employee not to talk about what you've discussed with any coworkers. And ask the employee to come to you immediately with any new information.

 Perhaps no theft occurred.

Theft is not the cause of every shortage or loss a business suffers. In some investigations, you will conclude at this point that you are not dealing with theft. After examining relevant documents and talking to knowledgeable witnesses, you may decide that accounting mistakes, shoplifting, or faulty inventory procedures explain the apparent discrepancies or shortages in question. If you find yourself in this situation, be sure to take steps to shore up any security or procedural problems your investigation uncovered.

b. Interviewing Suspects

You may find yourself in one of two situations when interviewing a suspect. In some cases, your review of documents and interviews with witnesses will lead you to believe that a particular employee is the culprit. In other cases, you may have narrowed down the range of suspects to two or three employees who had the opportunity to commit the theft. Either way, you'll want to carefully structure your interview to give yourself the best chance of eliciting a confession.

 You may have more than one thief.

Most workplace thieves operate alone. Every once in a while, however, more than one employee is in on the scheme. If you have more than one suspect, remember that all of them may be guilty. In this situation, getting one to confess will probably bring down the whole operation.

Refusing to Name Names May Be a Sign of Guilt

If you have more than one suspect, ask this question: "Who do you think might have done this?" Experts agree that the employee who's guilty very rarely names someone else. Innocent employees often think through the situation, trying to figure out who could have done it. For example, an employee might say, "Well, I put the receipts in the safe every weekday night, and Claire, Frank, and I are the only ones who have a key to the safe. I didn't take the money, so it must have been Claire or Frank." The employee who's guilty, on the other hand, will often go to great lengths to avoid naming names: "Anyone could have taken money from the safe. Someone could have borrowed a manager's key and put it back before it was noticed, or maybe a manager left the safe open by mistake and a customer somehow saw it and took the money."

There are many theories about the reason for this reluctance. Some say the guilty party wants the list of suspects to be as broad as possible and so will pose explanations that suggest anyone could have done it. Others say that guilty employees don't want to name a specific coworker, either because they don't want to get an innocent person in trouble or because they know that it will eventually become clear that the coworker didn't do it, which will cast suspicion back on them.

Getting Started

As with witnesses, you should begin your interviews with suspects in an innocuous way. This will allow you to develop some rapport with the employee before you start in on the hard questions. Start by saying something like "I've been asked to take a look at our accounting practices" or "I'm gathering some information on sales and inventory procedures," then tell the suspect that you need to ask a few questions.

 Preserve the element of surprise.

When you're interviewing suspects, time your approach carefully. Make sure that the employee doesn't have something pressing to take care of or a scheduled appointment. Once you tell the employee you want to ask questions, you should conduct the interview immediately. If you delay, the employee may suspect the true reason for your interest—and take steps to foil the investigation (such as destroying documents or getting rid of other evidence of theft) or hide the proceeds of the theft.

Questions

The questions you ask a suspect will, of course, depend on what type of theft you're dealing with and what you already know about it. Because there's such a wide variety of types of theft, it's impossible to provide a list of sample questions, as has been included in other chapters. Instead, let's follow the hypothetical case of Mary the bookkeeper.

EXAMPLE: Sarah, the workplace investigator at GetGo Enterprises, believes that Mary the bookkeeper is running a lapping scheme. There have been significant lags in posting customer payments; in fact, several customers have complained of receiving a second notice of payment due after they've already paid their bills. To make certain that these discrepancies weren't due to simple errors, Sarah compares the payments the company actually received in the last week (by looking inside the envelopes, already opened in the company mail room, that are being routed to Mary and adding up the checks she found inside) to the amounts Mary has deposited. There is a shortfall of several thousand dollars.

A witness, whose desk is near Mary's, has told Sarah that Mary often writes in a notebook other than the company's ledger and journals, and that she takes this notebook with her everywhere, including to lunch and home at night.

Most interviews will follow the same general pattern:

- Start with general, open-ended questions. This will help you get the suspect talking, hopefully before she realizes the true purpose of the interview. It will also give you a chance to observe the suspect's body language under fairly normal circumstances. You can compare this to the suspect's demeanor when you start in on the tough topics.

EXAMPLE: Sarah approaches Mary as she's returning from her lunch break. "Hi Mary," she says. "I've been asked to gather some information on our internal accounting procedures. Could you help me out by answering a few questions?" Mary says that she has to get back to work. "I won't keep you too long," Sarah responds. "Let's go to my office."

Once both are settled, Sarah begins with a few general questions, such as "Please describe your job responsibilities," "Describe a typical day as the company bookkeeper," and "Could you briefly explain what books you keep for the company? What kind of information goes in each of them?"

- Hone in on the particular procedures or transactions at issue. Begin with general questions.

EXAMPLE: After Mary has described general bookkeeping procedures, Sarah is ready to ask about customer payments. "You're responsible for processing customer payments, right? Please explain how that works." Sarah's goal is to get Mary to walk her through the process, step by step. Once she's committed herself to a set procedure, she'll have a harder time explaining why she deviated from that procedure for particular customers.

- Get more specific, and be prepared to lay out documents or other evidence, bit by bit, that contradicts the suspect's statements. Give the employee a way to confess that is not too humiliating.

EXAMPLE: Mary has explained the procedure for recording and depositing customer payments. Sarah reiterates what Mary has said: "So, you post customer payments on the same day you receive them, do I have that right? And then you deposit the checks immediately?" Mary confirms what she has already said. Sarah then says, "But Mary, you waited several days to deposit this customer's check," and shows her the document. At this point, some employees will realize that the jig is up and will confess. Others will give a justification for the discrepancy. Mary offers an innocent explanation, so Sarah continues presenting evidence: "Last Thursday, the company took in over $6,000 in payments, but you deposited only $3,575. I know that because I added up the checks myself. And here's the deposit slip, filled out in your handwriting." Mary doesn't respond. Sarah says, "Mary, I know you've worked for this company for a long time, and you would only have done something like this if you really needed the money. You wouldn't do this just out of greed, would you?" At this point, Mary—like most suspects in a similar situation—admits to at least some role in the theft.

Convincing a Suspect to Confess

So how do you get from making the suspect uncomfortable to actually eliciting a confession? It varies from person to person, of course, but here are a couple tips from experienced investigators:

- Keep your documents and other evidence hidden, and lay them out one piece at a time. Virtually every workplace theft results in some kind of evidence, and the only person who knows exactly what evidence is available is the thief. If you show your hand only a little at a time, the thief won't know how much evidence you have—and may anticipate evidence you didn't know about.

- Give the suspect an out. Try to think of some way to make confessing to the theft more palatable to the suspect. For example, you could say, "I know you wouldn't do this unless you had a very good reason. Is money especially tight right now?" Or, you might frame the issue as a choice between two explanations, one more favorable than the other, but both implicating the suspect in the theft. For example, "Did you plan to steal from the company, or did you just act on the spur of the moment?"

- If the employee confesses, gather as much information as you can about the scope of the theft, whether anyone else was involved, and, perhaps most important, what happened to the proceeds. Get the basics of the confession in writing, if possible. Seek this information right away; once the employee leaves the room, the chances of cooperation voluntarily diminish significantly.

EXAMPLE: Mary has broken down and admitted that she has "borrowed" money from the deposits on occasion, but only because she was financially strapped after her divorce. Now's the time for Sarah to ask questions like these: "When's the first time you borrowed money from a customer payment? This must be hard to keep track of—do you have a written record of which payments you've deposited and which you've withheld? I understand you keep a personal notebook at your desk. Is this why? May I see it now? What have you done with the money? Do you still have any of it?" Mary is reluctant to talk, so Sarah prods her further by adding, "Mary, you can understand that we could run into serious problems with our customers if we don't credit their accounts properly. In fact, several customers have already complained. The first step towards making this right is to undo the damage to our customer relations. For that, we need to know which accounts have been affected."

Getting the Money Back

This interview may be your only chance to convince the suspect to volunteer information that will help you recapture the stolen money or goods. Here are some sample questions that should help you get what you need:

- What happened to the money?
- Is there anything left, or have you spent it? What have you spent it on? Do you still have the items you purchased with the money?
- Have you deposited any of the money in a bank account? Where do you bank? Would you be willing to sign an authorization for us to look at your bank records? (Have such an authorization available, or have one written up while sitting in the interview.)
- You understand that this is the company's money. If you return whatever's left voluntarily, that might help the situation. Will you do that?

7. Evaluate the Evidence

In theft cases, you will almost always have a strong sense of what happened and who did it by the end of your investigation. If you were successful in getting the suspect to admit to stealing, you will also have a confession. Obviously, in these situations, you won't have to spend much time sifting through the evidence you gathered.

It's relatively rare to close a theft investigation by concluding that you can't decide who, among a group of people, committed the theft. More common is a conclusion that you aren't sure whether you have enough proof that the person you suspect is guilty. For example, if a relatively small amount of money or property is missing, and the loss may be due to shoplifting, accounting errors, or shoddy inventory procedures, it might be tough to pin the blame on an employee you suspect of theft.

If you really can't figure out whether an employee is guilty, your best course of action is to close the investigation without reaching any conclusions (see Chapter 4 for more on how to do this) and take immediate steps to tighten workplace controls. Section B10, below, offers some tips on making it more difficult for thieves to prosper in your workplace; you should also consider hiring an accountant or auditor to help you identify and fix trouble spots.

8. Take Action

If you find that employee theft occurred, often the only appropriate response is to fire the employee. There may be exceptions to this general rule—for example, if the employee's actions were condoned by management and the employee had reason to believe they were not serious. But these situations will be rare. Remember, two-thirds of employees will steal if they see others stealing and getting away with it. To show your employees that you mean business, you should generally fire anyone who steals from you.

Pay Yourself Back by Keeping Minor Thieves on the Payroll

Sometimes, it makes sense not to fire a guilty employee, especially if the theft involved several employees and some are more culpable than others. By all means, get rid of the ringleader(s), but give some thought to retaining an employee who played a more minor role. If you keep a thief on the payroll, you know that person will have a source of income—and therefore, access to money that can be used to pay you back. (Of course, this strategy only makes sense if you can count on the employee to give you a solid day's work—and to stop stealing from you.)

Talk to a lawyer to find out your state's rules about taking deductions from an employee's paycheck. Some states allow an employer to withhold money from an employee to repay a debt. If you do business in one of these states, you could ask the employee to sign a promissory note (see Section B10, below) that authorizes you to withhold some amount of money each month for restitution.

9. Document the Investigation

Document the investigation, following the guidelines in Chapter 4. Make sure to stick to the facts—theft investigations can lead to defamation lawsuits, in which employees accused of theft claim that you spread false and damaging information about them (in other words, that you called them thieves). Avoid this unhappy result by recounting the facts that your investigation uncovered and detailing the reasons for your conclusions.

10. Follow Up

When you've finished your investigation, it's time to think about the future: how to get the company's money or property back (if possible) and how to prevent theft going forward.

a. Recouping Your Losses

Unfortunately, there's no surefire way to get back money or property a workplace thief has stolen. If you're dealing with a thrifty thief who has carefully deposited theft proceeds in a savings account, you might be in luck. In most situations, however, the thief will have spent most of the money already—that's usually why people steal, after all.

There are several avenues of recovery that might be available to you, depending on your situation. This section will give you some basic information about each. If you're facing major losses, however, you should talk to a lawyer before you decide how to proceed.

Criminal Prosecution

A criminal prosecution may offer you the best opportunity to get your money back. Many judges will order a thief who is convicted (or pleads guilty) to make restitution—that is, to pay back what was stolen—to the victim, as part of the sentence. Restitution may also be ordered as a condition of probation. This gives you tremendous leverage to get your money back, because the thief risks going to jail for failure to pay. Even if the criminal case never goes to trial, you can ask the district attorney to require restitution to you as a condition of any plea bargain or settlement of the charges.

If you are interested in having the thief prosecuted, you will need to show the police—and the district attorney—that there is a case to be made against the thief. Among other things, this will require you to be able to present evidence that there was a theft (as opposed to an accounting error, a loss, or a mistake), to reliably demonstrate the amount of the theft, and to show that the suspect committed the theft. A lawyer can help you figure out how best to convince those in the criminal justice system that yours is a case worth prosecuting.

Civil Lawsuits

Another method for recouping your losses is to file a civil lawsuit. The most obvious candidate to sue is the thief, but only if he or she either has the assets to pay a judgment or is likely to land a job in the near future (which would allow you to garnish his or her wages to guarantee repayment). There's not much point in paying the costs of a lawsuit if you're dealing with an indigent thief whose financial prospects look dim.

If the thief is unlikely to be able to pay a judgment, you might consult with an attorney to figure out whether any third parties could be liable for your losses. For example, someone who bought obviously stolen goods from the thief, or a financial institution whose loose controls allowed the thief unauthorized access to your accounts, might be legally responsible for at least some of your losses.

Agreement With the Employee

An employee who has confessed to theft may agree to restitution, or to sign a promissory note for the stolen amounts. However, such agreements often aren't worth the paper they're written on. Some employees sign such agreements with no intention of ever making good on their promises. Even if they do intend to pay you back when they sign the agreement, they might quickly change their mind once the feelings of the moment have passed.

If you try to come up with a restitution agreement, remember these tips:

- **Don't agree to payments over time.** The more time the employee has to pay you back, the less likely you are to collect the money. Instead of agreeing to installment payments, require the employee to pay you back, in full, within a few days or a week of signing the agreement. Put the burden on the employee to come up with the money, through a loan, help from friends and relatives, or some other source.

- **Write a binding contract.** Make sure that your agreement will be enforced as a contract if you ever have to show it to a judge—and explain to the employee that you will go to court to enforce the agreement if he or she fails to pay as promised. (For help drafting a binding promissory note, see *101 Law Forms for Personal Use*, by Ralph Warner and Robin Leonard (Nolo), or speak to a lawyer).

- **Negotiate carefully.** Remember the old adage about a bird in the hand? It applies to restitution as well as fowl hunting. If the employee can scrape together a large amount of what you're owed, it may make sense to accept that money as payment of the debt. But don't give up too easily—consider the employee's ability to pay and your chances of collecting through a lawsuit to decide whether you're willing to settle for less than you are owed. Remember, you can always take whatever the employee can give right now and retain your right to go after the rest.

Insurance Claims

If you have a fidelity bond or some other type of employee theft or employee dishonesty insurance, you may be able to recover at least part of your losses from the insurance company. (See Section B2, above, for more information on insurance against theft.) However, it can be pretty tough to get an insurance company to pay up. Often, the insurance company is more interested in finding ways to deny your claim than in paying out on the policy.

In order to recover, you'll have to follow the company's requirements carefully, and you'll have to be able to prove that you suffered a covered loss—that is, you'll have to prove the amount of the loss and prove that it was caused by theft. If your losses have been substantial and may be covered by insurance, you will probably want to retain a lawyer to represent your interests in negotiating with the insurance company.

If You Can't Recover a Loss, Deduct It

You may be able to take a tax deduction for losses suffered through theft or embezzlement, including stealing by employees. Generally, the IRS will allow businesses to deduct theft-related losses from their income for tax purposes if the business lost more than $100, the loss wasn't repaid from some other source (such as restitution or insurance), and the theft was illegal under the laws of the state where the business is located.

To deduct a business loss due to theft, you'll have to fill out IRS Form 4684, *Casualty and Theft,* and file it with your tax return. For instructions on filling out the form and more information on qualifying for the deduction, see IRS Publication 547, *Casualties, Disasters, and Theft* and Publication 584b, *Business Casualty, Disaster, and Theft Loss Workbook*. You can find these materials on the IRS's website, at www.irs.gov.

b. Minimize Opportunities for Theft

Now is also a good time to think about how you can prevent theft in the future. An accountant, auditor, or fraud examiner can review your internal systems for weaknesses that give thieves an opportunity to go to work. Here are some basic steps you can take to reduce your risk of theft:

- **Segregate job duties.** Make sure that no employee is solely responsible for any financial transaction from start to finish. In other words, make sure that every financial transaction requires the involvement of more than one employee. Requiring a second signature on checks, making sure that the employee who counts a deposit is not responsible for taking it to the bank, and requiring a second employee to count out cash register drawers are all examples of segregation of duties.

- **Require authorizations.** Don't let money leave your company through the back door. Adopt rules that require the signature or oversight of a high-ranking official (or the owner) for major transactions.

- **Adopt a proper accounting system.** Loose accounting procedures give employees all kinds of opportunities to steal. An outside accountant or auditor can help you set up a system that leaves less room for money to disappear.

- **Conduct regular audits.** The simple truth is that employees are less likely to steal if they believe they may be caught. Periodic audits of your books and inventory will deter theft—or at least, help you discover theft in its earliest stages.

- **Impose paperwork requirements.** Put some extra roadblocks in the way of workplace thieves by requiring documentation for cash outflows. Require receipts for reimbursements for expenses or petty cash. Make employees submit licenses and other paperwork from new vendors, to make sure they're on the up and up. Don't allow refunds unless an employee fills out a form that includes the customer's name, address, and phone number.

- **Get involved.** Remember the old saying, "When the cat's away, the mice will play"? You're the cat in this scenario, so avoid problems by making your presence known. Don't allow any checks to leave the building without your approval and signature. Have all bank statements sent to your home address, and reconcile the figures every month. The greater (and more public) role you play in the company's finances, the fewer problems you will have with theft.

- **Don't bend the rules.** Some companies that follow all of the tips listed above still have significant theft problems. The reason is that they allow employees to ignore or override the rules. It's not hard to avoid this mistake— simply insist that employees tow the line, and discipline any who don't.

- **Make your employees happy.** Surveys show that employee satisfaction plays a major role in deterring workplace theft. Employees who feel appreciated are less likely to steal—and more likely to report a coworker for theft. ∎

CHAPTER

Investigating Threats and Violence

Every employer has heard horror stories about violence in the workplace: A disgruntled employee, a worker's former lover, or an enraged client bursts through the door, shooting first and asking questions later. Although workplace violence is not as common as the news might lead us to believe, it is a major problem in the United States. Government studies estimate that there are about two million assaults and threats of violence made against workers each year. And according to the Workplace Violence Research Institute (www.noworkviolence.com), workplace violence costs businesses more than $36 billion each year.

Sometimes, violence comes out of the blue, without warning. Much more often, however, violent workplace incidents are preceded by threats, verbal bullying, and/or physical intimidation. This means that, in most cases of violence by employees and former employees, you will have an opportunity to avert more serious problems if you immediately investigate threats and other signs of aggression.

An immediate investigation of every potentially violent situation, no matter how minor it may seem, sends the message that violence will not be tolerated. You also give yourself an opportunity to nip serious problems in the bud. Because workplace violence often escalates from threats, explosive outbursts, or an obsession with weapons to physically harming others, you have a chance to stop this cycle if you investigate at the first sign of trouble.

However, investigating threats and violence by employees can be distressing. After all, you don't want your investigation to be the very thing that triggers a violent outburst, and you certainly don't want to make yourself a target for a violent employee's rage. You will have to move very quickly, act decisively, and often rely on outside experts to help you assess the situation and figure out how to handle it.

This chapter will help you navigate this rough terrain. Section A explains the types of workplace violence and when an employer will be held legally responsible for violence in the workplace. Section B describes the ten steps to an effective investigation of violence and threatening behavior.

This book covers workplace violence by current or former employees only.

This book focuses on investigating employee misconduct, not problems caused by people outside the workplace. For this reason, it includes only limited information about third-party assailants—people who come to your workplace solely to commit theft or other crimes, angry customers or clients, or family members or acquaintances of employees. There are certainly steps you can take to prevent third-party violence—Section A1, below, briefly discusses these other sources of violence and suggests resources that can provide more information.

A. Threats and Violence in the Workplace

The trick to a successful investigation of workplace violence is to start your inquiry at the very first sign of trouble. This means, in turn, that you have recognize the early warning signs that often precede violence. If you wait until an employee has seriously injured or killed someone, all you'll have to investigate is what went wrong and what you should have done differently.

Sections 1 and 2, below, will help you recognize common types of workplace violence and the warning signs that are often precursors to a violent incident. Section 3, below, explains when an employer will be legally responsible for the harm caused by workplace violence.

I. Types of Workplace Violence

Contrary to popular belief, the great majority of violent incidents in the workplace are perpetrated by outsiders—strangers intending to commit a crime—rather than employees. For example, according to the Bureau of Labor Statistics, most workplace homicides are committed by robbers trying to steal from the business, not by current or former workers.

However, employees (particularly former or soon-to-be former employees), people who know employees (such as romantic partners or family members), and customers or clients also commit workplace violence. This section explains some common types of workplace violence.

a. Violence by Outsiders

Nonemployee assailants commit most workplace homicides, as well as a substantial proportion of workplace assaults. Motives for this type of workplace violence run the gamut from robbery to revenge to a misguided sense of honor or principle. Consider these examples:

- In 1994, Paul Hill killed a doctor and one of the doctor's escorts as they arrived at the Pensacola Ladies Clinic. Hill claimed that he killed the doctor to prevent him from performing abortions.

- In 1993, Gian Luigi Ferri, a former client of the law firm Pettit & Martin, entered the firm's offices at 101 California Street in San Francisco. Ferri killed eight people and wounded six more before taking his own life.

- In 2003, a doctor was beaten and strangled to death during a physical examination of a patient at a psychiatric hospital in San Leandro, California.

- In 2000, seven workers at a Wendy's restaurant in Flushing, Queens were shot and five of them killed during a robbery. One of the men convicted in the shooting was a former employee.

High-Risk Occupations

Government statistics certify what most of us already know: Workers who deal with the public are more likely to fall victim to outsider violence. Those at particularly high risk include workers who exchange money with the public, deliver goods or services, work alone or in small numbers during the late evening/early morning hours, or work in jobs where they have extensive contact with the public. Certain industries—including health care, security (including police officers), and retail—are targeted more frequently than others.

It's difficult to predict and prevent violence by outsiders. While some acts of violence (particularly those committed by angry customers or clients, or by those who oppose a company's practices) may be preceded by threats and acts of vandalism, most are committed without warning.

However, there are a few things you can do to reduce the odds that an outsider will target your business. The Occupational Safety and Health Administration (OSHA) offers tips for employers hoping to protect their workers from violence. These include:

- training employees on how to recognize and respond to threatening situations

- securing the workplace by installing surveillance cameras, extra lighting, and alarm systems and by minimizing workplace access by outsiders through the use of identification badges and guards

- limiting the amount of cash kept on hand, particularly at night

- giving outside workers cell phones and alarms, and requiring them to keep in touch with a contact person throughout their shift, and

- telling employees not to go anywhere where they do not feel safe, and providing an escort in potentially dangerous areas.

 For more information on preventing violence by third parties, go to the OSHA's website, at www.osha.gov.

There, you'll find fact sheets and tips on how to prevent and minimize violence in various types of businesses, including retail stores and business that specialize in health care. For information on your state's workplace safety rules, contact your state's occupational safety and health agency. You can also find articles and resources on violence and violence prevention at the website of the Workplace Violence Research Institute, at www.noworkviolence.com.

b. Domestic Violence

According to the American Institute on Domestic Violence (www.aidv-usa.com), partners and boyfriends commit 13,000 acts of violence every year against women in the workplace. And sometimes these incidents go beyond the intended victim to harm other employees as well.

Experts tell us that domestic violence frequently follows a fairly predictable cycle, in which pressure, threats, and coercion precede acts of violence. By the time a batterer shows up at the victim's workplace intending to do harm, chances are good that he has already made threats and committed other acts of violence or property damage. If you encourage your employees to come forward and let you know when they fear an abusive partner, you can take steps to prevent that violence from entering your workplace.

Among the strategies you can adopt are:

- Establishing a confidential way for employees to report domestic violence. Victims of domestic violence are often extremely reluctant to come forward, so you must encourage employees to report abuse—and to report any potential new problems or developments (if the employee's abuser is getting out of jail or has threatened to come to the workplace, for example).

- Increasing workplace security by, for example, requiring workplace visitors to sign in and have an escort at all times, installing a locking door between your reception or greeting area and the rest of the workplace, and providing secure, well-lit parking facilities for your employees.

- Getting a restraining order on behalf of the victim and/or your company, requiring the abuser to stay away from the workplace. (See Section B2, below, for more information.)

- If you know that an employee has been threatened, making sure that the security staff in your office or building are aware of any outstanding restraining orders or threats against your employees—and know what the abuser looks like. You may also want to move the victim so she cannot be easily located by her abuser (for example, to a different floor, wing, or worksite), which will protect her and buy you some time to defuse a potentially violent encounter.

If both partners to the relationship work for you, you can investigate using the tips and strategies described in Section B, below. You also have the option of immediately suspending the abuser, to get him out of the workplace. (See Section B2, below.) Most often, however, the perpetrator won't be your employee. If you're facing this situation, you may need help from the police or a violence consultant.

Need more information on domestic violence?

There are a number of websites that offer information, training, sample policies, and strategies for dealing with domestic violence in the workplace. They include:

- the National Organization of Women's Legal Defense and Education Fund, at www.nowldef.org

- the Safe at Work Coalition (a project of the Altria Group, Inc.), at www.safe@workcoalition.org

- the National Domestic Violence Hotline, at www.ndvh.org (click "DV in the Workplace")

- the American Institute on Domestic Violence, at www.aidv-usa.com.

c. Violence by Employees and Former Employees

This chapter focuses on investigating incidents in which a current or former employee threatens or assaults others in the workplace. This is the most foreseeable (and therefore, preventable) type of violence. After all, the perpetrators are people you know, sometimes people you see every day. And very few of them simply snap one day and go on a rampage—instead, the problem builds up slowly, and the perpetrator usually sends up a few red flags that violence may in the offing. (See Section A2, below, for more on warning signs of violence.) Here are some examples:

- After the receptionist at the Housing Authority in Richmond, California was fired, he pulled out a gun and opened fire on his coworkers. In the days before he was fired, he told a coworker that he felt like committing a mass murder. The coworker reported his comments, and the receptionist was fired—but was allowed to return to his desk (where he kept his gun) on the way out the door. (*Bulletproof Practices*, by Robert J. Grossman (HR Magazine, November 2002).)

- Honeywell, Inc. decided to rehire Randy Landing as a custodian—after he was released from prison, having served five years for strangling a Honeywell coworker to death. After he was rehired, Landin sexually harassed female coworkers, challenged a male coworker to a fight, and threatened to kill another coworker—he was transferred twice because of these confrontations. After a female coworker spurned his romantic overtures, he harassed and threatened her, scratched a death threat on her locker door at work, then shot and killed her. *Yunker v. Honeywell, Inc.*, 496 NW2d 419 (Minn. Ct. of Apps., 1993).

- In 1978, former supervisor Dan White shot and killed supervisor Harvey Milk and Mayor George Moscone in San Francisco's City Hall. Although White would later famously claim that he was temporarily insane at the time of the shootings from eating too much junk food (the so-called "Twinkie defense"), he confessed to police that he planned to kill his targets (and others) because they had conspired against his reappointment to the city's board of supervisors.

- In 1999, Byran Uyesugi opened fire on his coworkers at Xerox in Honolulu, killing seven. Uyesugi had been hospitalized six years earlier, after kicking in an elevator door and threatening to kill his supervisor. According to news reports, Uyesugi, a gun collector, was scheduled to attend a meeting to discuss his work performance on the day of the killings.

- In 2000, Michael McDermott, a software developer, killed seven coworkers with an assault rifle at Edgewater Technology. McDermott was having financial problems; the human resources department had just complied with an order to garnish his wages. On the day of the shootings, his car was repossessed from the company parking lot.

Workplace violence runs the gamut from vague threats ("They'll be sorry if they fire me") to pointed threats ("I'm going to bring in a gun tomorrow and take out my supervisor"), bullying, physical and verbal intimidation, stalking, assault, and killing.

Tips for Preventing Violence

Investigating threats and aggressive behavior will help you limit opportunities for violence in your workplace. Other ways to prevent violence include:

- **Screen applicants before hiring.** Check for past criminal convictions (if your state allows it), restraining orders, or a history of difficulties with coworkers.

- **Conduct evaluations—and impose discipline only when it's warranted.** Experts say that employees are more likely to become violent if they believe they have been treated unfairly, taken by surprise, or sandbagged. Prevent these reactions by giving your employees fair warning and a chance to improve on minor problems.

- **Treat your workers with respect.** Always treat your workers decently, especially when you have to discipline or fire them. Depriving a worker of dignity—by disparaging the person in front of coworkers or calling the employee names—can trigger violent behavior.

- **Adopt a workplace violence policy.** Create a policy that states that violence of any kind will not be tolerated.

- **Never allow weapons in the workplace.** Unless your employees have a compelling need to be armed (for example, they work as security guards), don't allow weapons in the workplace.

- **Consider an employee assistance program.** Workplace violence often begins offsite—with a failing marriage, a substance abuse problem, or money troubles. Help your employees manage these difficulties with an employee assistance program (EAP). An EAP might include counseling, rehabilitation services, or anger management classes.

- **Develop a safety plan.** Instruct your employees on what to do if violence starts. Plan escape routes and know where first aid supplies are. And have the telephone numbers of local police or building security handy—preferably on speed dial.

- **Encourage reporting.** Ask your employees to come forward and report any incident of violence that they witness.

- **Train managers.** Make sure that your managers know the warning signs of violence, the safety plan, and the requirements of your policies.

2. Warning Signs of Violence

Experts agree that an employee or former employee who commits a violent act often exhibits certain signs of trouble before becoming violent. This is "good" news for employers—it means that you have a chance to prevent violence if you can read these signals and take action immediately. Of course, no single one of these signs, taken alone, is a sure indicator that an employee may turn violent. And some employees resort to violence without any warning. But employers should be on the lookout for clues that intervention and investigation may be necessary. These include:

- an unexplained rise in absences
- substance abuse
- outbursts at coworkers and customers; poor impulse control
- verbal abuse or threats towards coworkers and customers; harassing phone calls or email communications
- strained workplace relationships
- overreaction or resistance to even minor changes in workplace routine; insubordination and belligerence
- lack of attention to personal appearance, including hygiene
- interest in firearms or other weapons; access to weapons
- signs of paranoia ("everyone's out to get me") or withdrawal
- fascination with violent acts or fantasies, or a history of violence
- seeing oneself as a victim and others as persecutors; blaming others for one's problems
- obsessive behavior towards a coworker or customer, up to and including stalking
- comments about suicide
- mood swings, and
- domestic problems, including money troubles or family disputes.

> ## The Workplace Violence Profile
>
> Experts warn that relying on a profile to determine which employees might act violently is dangerous. Although perpetrators tend to be white men in their 30s or 40s who have few family ties, workplace violence can be committed by anyone, male or female, of any racial and ethnic background, marital status, and age. Using a profile rather than looking at an employee's actual behaviors can cause employers to miss important clues that violence may be in the offing—and can lead to suspicions about employees who have no violent intentions.

Violence is often a response to stress, whether in the workplace or in other areas of life. In many cases of workplace violence, there is some kind of triggering incident—the last straw for the perpetrator, who then decides to resort to violence. Often, this last straw is a disciplinary action or termination; in some cases, it may be a complaint against the employee for harassment or violation of another work rule. Some violent incidents are triggered by layoffs, economic difficulties outside of work, or an emotional crisis.

3. Employer Liability for Violence

Generally, employers are legally liable for workplace violence only if they failed to take reasonable steps to prevent or discourage it. Courts have allowed victims of workplace violence (and their survivors) to sue under several different legal theories, explained below.

a. OSH Act Violations

Under the Occupational Safety and Health Act (OSH Act), employers must provide employees with a workplace free of recognized hazards that are causing or are likely to cause serious harm or death. Traditionally, this requirement has applied primarily to hazards created by machinery, poor ventilation, dangerous chemicals, and so on. More recently, however, the Occupational Safety and Health Administration (OSHA), which interprets and enforces the OSH Act, has said that workplace violence may constitute a hazard under this rule. This means that employers who don't take reasonable steps to prevent or abate a recognized violence hazard can be punished by OSHA.

OSHA suggests that employers take a number of steps to prevent workplace violence (some are described in Section A1, above). Foremost among these is adopting a zero-tolerance policy toward workplace violence and enforcing that policy through prompt investigation of violence claims and immediate corrective action.

b. Harassment Laws

In some situations, workplace violence and threats may constitute legally actionable harassment or discrimination. For example, an employee who touches a coworker against her will, or threatens to harm her if she dates someone else, may be guilty of both sexual harassment and violence. Or, an employee who gets in a fistfight with another worker after calling him racist names could be committing both racial harassment and violence. For information on the laws that prohibit harassment and on investigating harassment claims, see Chapter 6.

c. Negligent Hiring, Retention, and Supervision

In some situations, a person who is injured by one of your employees can sue you if you failed to take reasonable care in selecting and retaining your workers. Under the legal theories of negligent hiring, retention, and supervision, employers can be sued if they knew or should have known that an applicant or employee was unfit for the job yet did nothing about it. Here are a few situations in which employers have been found liable:

- A pizza company hired a delivery driver without looking into his criminal past—which included a sexual assault conviction and an arrest for stalking a woman he met while delivering pizza for another company. After he raped a customer, he was sent to jail for 25 years—and the pizza franchise was liable to his victim for negligent hiring.

- A car rental company hired a man who later raped a coworker. Had the company verified his resume claims, it would have discovered that he was in prison for robbery during the years he claimed to be in high school and college. The company was liable to the coworker.

- A furniture company hired a deliveryman without requiring him to fill out an application or performing a background check. The employee assaulted a female customer in her home with a knife. The company was liable to the customer.

- An Amtrak employee who had a history of violent workplace incidents shot his supervisor twice after the supervisor reprimanded him for being absent from work. A jury found that Amtrak's failure to take action after the earlier incidents led to the shooting and ordered it to pay the supervisor $3.5 million in damages.

 Background checks are a conscientious employer's best friend.

If you want to avoid liability for negligent hiring—and make sure that you aren't being fed a line by job applicants—run a background check before you hire anyone. Especially if you are hiring for a position that will have a lot of public contact, you must do a background check to make sure that you aren't putting anyone at risk. For tips on background checks, see *Dealing With Problem Employees*, by Amy DelPo and Lisa Guerin (Nolo).

Although these lawsuits have not yet appeared in every state, the clear trend is to allow injured parties to sue employers for hiring or keeping on a dangerous worker.

Workers' Compensation Laws May Prevent Your Employees From Suing You

In every state, workers' compensation laws require employers to purchase insurance that provides benefits to employees who suffer work-related injuries or illnesses. The system strikes a compromise between employers and employees. Employees are entitled to benefits no matter who caused their injury: themselves, a coworker, or a customer. In return, the employer gets protection from personal injury lawsuits. If a workplace injury or illness is covered by workers' compensation, the worker may not sue the employer over it.

Not all workplace injuries are covered by workers' compensation, however. The injury must be connected to the job—for example, an accident that occurs hours after an employee leaves the workplace probably is not covered. And an employer cannot use the workers' compensation system to escape responsibility for its own intentional or reckless acts.

How does this relate to workplace violence? Some violent incidents are covered by workers' compensation—which means that the victims cannot sue their employers for their injuries (although they may still be able to sue the person who attacked them). However, if the violence is committed by a supervisor, manager, or officer of the company, or if the company has acted recklessly in allowing violence to occur (for example, by ignoring threats to an employee or retaining an employee who has already engaged in violence), then the incident probably won't be covered by workers' compensation. This means that the victim can sue the employer if one of the legal theories described in this section applies.

The rules on what workers' compensation does and does not cover vary from state to state. To find out about your state's laws, contact your state's workers' compensation office or talk to a lawyer.

B. Ten Steps to a Successful Investigation of Violence

This section explains how to apply the basic investigation steps covered in Part I of this book to an investigation of workplace threats or violence. If you haven't read Part I, you should do so before getting into this more specific material—the discussion that follows assumes that you are already familiar with basic investigation procedures.

If serious violence has already taken place.

This section assumes that you have learned of threats or relatively minor incidents of violence in time to prevent escalation and that your investigation will be taking place in this context. However, if serious injuries have already occurred, you are in a different predicament. In this situation, you should immediately contact the police—and emergency medical personnel, if necessary. Make sure that victims receive immediate medical treatment. You will also want to provide some counseling for your workers and discuss ways to prevent similar incidents in the future.

At some point (and probably with the help of the police), you will have to investigate what happened, to try to figure out what you could have done differently and what you should do, going forward, to prevent further violence. However, that is a very different investigation from the type covered in this section—and you may well be investigating in the shadow of legal actions against the perpetrator and/or your company. In this situation, you will definitely want professional help. See Section 2, below, for information on finding a workplace violence consultant.

I. Decide Whether to Investigate

Whenever you learn of a threat or aggressive behavior by one of your employees, you need to look into it. Remember, most employees who commit violence give some warning, often in the form of threats, intimidation, and minor acts of physical violence. If you ignore these early warning signs, you are only allowing the problem to escalate towards violence. And if you take a "wait and see" attitude, you might miss your chance to head off a disaster.

 Your employees will appreciate your efforts.

Employees are very concerned about workplace violence—and understandably fearful about working with someone who has made threats or seems to be out of control. If you don't do anything in the face of this kind of misconduct, workplace morale will suffer, absentee rates will rise, and productivity rates will drop. If you take action right away, on the other hand, your employees will see that you are concerned about their well-being and that you take their safety seriously.

So you can't ignore violence—but you also can't take action based solely on a complaint. Not every employee who makes a threat or loses his or her temper moves on to commit violence, and, of course, the truth may be somewhat different from what was first reported.

Some employers are so fearful that violence might erupt immediately that they fire first and ask questions later. This is a big mistake. If you are too quick to judge, you might mistakenly assume that an employee who poses no actual threat is violent. This kind of mistake may have disastrous consequences for the employee—and possibly for your company, if the employee decides to sue. You might even provoke the employee into committing a violent act that could have been avoided.

The solution is to investigate every threat and potentially violent act, but to do so very quickly (and often, with professional assistance). The sections that follow will explain how.

Learning About Threats

Sometimes, you'll learn about a threat of violence directly from an employee who has been threatened or treated aggressively. That employee might file a formal complaint, talk to a supervisor, or confide in a coworker. Even if no threat has been made, employees might come forward to report that a coworker is acting strangely: talking to him or herself, mentioning violence, losing control, or looking unusually disheveled and scattered.

You may also hear of anonymous threats: email messages or written notes that threaten harm but don't indicate the author. Some acts of violence—such as defacing an employee's car, vandalizing someone's workspace, or ruining equipment—might also be committed anonymously.

And in some situations, a concerned friend or family member might report the employee. If the employee is ranting to family and friends that he or she wants to kill coworkers or has a plan to harm the boss's children, someone might decide to tip off the company. These reports are sometimes made anonymously—perhaps in a message on the owner's voice mail or an unsigned letter.

2. Take Immediate Action, If Necessary

Once a threat or violent incident has been reported, your first concern is safety. To ensure the safety of your workplace while you investigate, there are a few things that you'll need to take care of right away. If the threat is serious and immediate, start by contacting a workplace violence consultant to help you plan your next moves. Next, you'll have to decide what to do with the suspect while you investigate. And you must figure out whether the company needs to step up security until the matter is resolved.

a. Lining Up Expert Help

Unless you have an in-house expert on workplace violence (as some larger companies do), your first decision after hearing about a violent or threatening incident should be whether to bring in a consultant. Sometimes called "workplace violence consultants" or "threat assessment specialists," these experts are trained and experienced in figuring out whether or not a particular employee poses a real danger to others.

They can also help you with other aspects of the investigation, including investigation planning, interviewing employees (including the accused employee), giving advice on what disciplinary action to take (and how to deliver the news), following up with police and security personnel, developing antiviolence training and policies, and helping you figure out how to avoid violent incidents in the future.

Generally, you should call in a specialist whenever you feel like you are in over your head or don't know what to do. Although hiring a consultant can get pricey, it will be well worth the money you spend to head off a violent incident. You should probably talk to an expert if:

- an employee brings a weapon to work, shows a weapon to other employees, talks frequently about owning weapons, or otherwise shows a serious fascination with weaponry

- an employee threatens serious physical violence against another employee or makes repeated references to the possibility of committing violence

- an employee physically harms another employee, in a situation that is neither an accident nor the product of mutual aggression (such as a fist fight or horseplay that gets out of hand)

- an employee stalks or follows another employee, or

- an employee shows a dramatic decline in mood, mental acuity, or awareness, or appears to be losing control.

 Finding a consultant.

The best way to find a workplace violence consultant—and any other workplace expert—is to ask those you know and trust for a referral. Of course, not every company will have used a workplace violence expert, but some larger companies may have one on call. Another good source of referrals is your business or employment lawyer. Your local or state police may also be able to help you find a workplace violence expert.

b. Dealing With the Suspect

In every situation involving workplace conflict, you will want to separate the alleged offender and the alleged victim while you sort out what happened. Workplace violence presents a slightly different scenario, however. If a worker has threatened or committed violence against another worker, separating the two won't necessarily solve the problem, even temporarily. For one thing, a worker bent on committing violence can follow through, no matter how far away the victim works. The violent worker can accost the victim in a parking lot, a common space, or the victim's work area. And an employee who has been threatened or treated violently isn't likely to feel much safer if you simply move the offending worker to a different floor or shift.

 Refer an employee accused of violence to your EAP program.

If your company has an Employee Assistance Program (EAP), let the accused employee know about it. Many larger companies have these programs, designed to help employees with problems from anger management to relationship difficulties to debt counseling and more. Particularly if the accused employee admits to feeling stress or having difficulties off the job, providing immediate help through the EAP could help head off any further workplace incidents.

A worker who has resorted to threats or violence is likely to do so again. Even if separating the workers offers temporary protection to the first victim, it does nothing for the employees who work in the area to which the potentially violent employee is moved, who may quickly become the latest targets of his or her rage and frustration.

All things considered, the best course of action is to immediately suspend an employee accused of violence or threats. When you tell the accused employee about the suspension, emphasize that it's a temporary situation, that no conclusions have been reached about the truth or falsity of the allegations, and that the transfer or suspension is not intended to be punitive. Explain that the alleged acts violate company policy and that you must investigate the situation before deciding what to do. Explain that the employee is not to return to the worksite until further notice and that you will be in touch to arrange an interview as part of the investigation. And don't allow the employee to return to the work area after the meeting, except under the escort of a security guard.

 Don't suspend workers without pay.

From a legal standpoint, you generally can't suspend exempt, salaried employees—those who are not entitled to overtime if they work extra hours—without pay. And even though you can suspend hourly, nonexempt workers without pay, it's not a good idea. A suspension without pay is punitive: It improperly signals that you have made up your mind about the allegations before you've even begun to investigate. A worker who is suspended without pay will probably be angry about it—and you don't want to add fuel to the fire if the worker has a potential for violence. If the allegations turn out to be false, you may be inviting a lawsuit. And unpaid suspensions can be an administrative hassle, as they require you to interrupt your usual payroll system. Avoiding these problems will be worth the wages you pay out to a temporarily suspended employee.

Keeping the Accused Employee in the Loop

In a violence investigation, it's especially important to let the accused employee know exactly what's going on, what you plan to do, and why. After all, as the warning signs of violence (described in Section A2, above) indicate, employees who commit violent acts are often suspicious and distrustful of others. They sometimes feel that others are out to get them. They are under stress, and they feel isolated to the point that violence seems like a viable solution to their problems.

One key to preventing a violent reaction to the investigation itself is to keep the accused employee informed. Rather than forcing him or her out of the workplace without an explanation or sending security to march him or her out the door, meet with the accused employee immediately; describe the allegations; tell the employee that the allegations, if true, violate company policy; explain that you will investigate and interview anyone who might have relevant information (including the accused employee) and that the company will make a decision only when all the information has been gathered; and convey that the employee will be immediately suspended, with pay, until the situation is cleared up.

By taking this approach, you accomplish two important objectives: You let the employee know that his or her behavior has been noticed and may result in discipline, and you include the employee in the process, thereby counteracting the employee's feelings of isolation and persecution.

Of course, there may be situations when you have to act more precipitously. For example, if you learn that an employee has gone to the parking lot to retrieve a weapon or has threatened to harm a supervisor when he or she returns from lunch, you won't have a chance to hold this meeting—you'll need to immediately dispatch security to deal with the danger. But, in most cases, you should meet directly with the accused employee to explain where things stand. For information on safety concerns during the meeting, see Section B5, below.

c. Restraining Orders

Some states allow employers to get a restraining order against anyone who has threatened or committed violence against their employees. Generally, a restraining order is a court order that prohibits someone from doing something. The prohibited actions depend on the reason for the order—restraining orders are used for a number of purposes, from preventing a neighbor from cutting down a shared tree to prohibiting the government from allowing a particular law to go into effect.

In the last few decades, restraining orders have been used as a tool to fight domestic violence. A victim of violence fills out court papers explaining the incidents or threats that have taken place and why she fears further harm. If a judge signs the order, the person accused of violence must stay a specified distance away from the victim (and sometimes must also stay away from locations where the victim spends time, like her home or school). If the abuser violates the restraining order (for example, by approaching the victim on the street or coming to her home), the police can arrest the abuser for violating the order before any violence takes place.

In recent years, a number of states have passed laws that allow employers to get restraining orders against anyone who has threatened or committed violence against employees. State laws differ regarding what the employer has to prove to get an order, whom the order can protect (that is, if it applies to all employees or only to those whom the offender has threatened), and other details. (To find out whether your state has a law—and what the law requires— check out the website of the National Organization for Women's Legal Defense and Education Fund, at www.nowldef.org. From the home page, click "Violence Against Women," then "Working Women and Violence.")

EXAMPLE: Lynette, a department manager at USS-Posco Industries, learned that Ezell, one of her employees, violated work rules. Lynette warned Ezell that he would be disciplined for any further violations. Lynette later heard that Ezell had threatened the employees who brought the violations to her attention. Ezell had also made other threats towards his coworkers and bragged that he kept a gun in his car. Ezell was later fired.

The company got a restraining order requiring Ezell to stay away from Lynette and from the workplace. Ezell challenged the order, claiming that he shouldn't be required to stay away from Lynette because he hadn't threatened her directly. The court denied Ezell's challenge, finding that his general threats of violence against employees was enough to allow the company to get the order on behalf of itself and Lynette.

Restraining orders are most effective against terminated employees and other outsiders. It makes sense to apply for an immediate restraining order (if your state allows you to) if you are facing a threat of imminent violence from a former employee or another person who is offsite (such as a customer or the domestic partner of an employee). However, you'll have to weigh the information you have to go on and the severity of the threat. If the threat looks serious and you have credible information to back it up (for example, several employees heard the threat), you may want to get a restraining order even before you investigate. On the other hand, if the threat is unclear and witnesses' stories are conflicting, it may be wiser to wait until you've dug a little deeper. After all, when you seek a restraining order, you are telling a court that you have legitimate reason to fear another person; if you don't have evidence to back that up, you won't get the court order, and you may have some legal trouble with the accused ex-employee.

Restraining orders are not as useful for current employees—because they are required to come to work, a legal order prohibiting them from doing so won't do you much good. In this situation, it's best to complete your investigation before deciding whether a restraining order is necessary (and it may well be, if you decide to terminate the worker for violence). If you suspend the worker while you investigate, you can instruct the worker not to come to the workplace—and enforce that instruction by telling guards and reception personnel that the worker is not to be admitted until you instruct them otherwise.

d. Security Measures

You will probably want to step up security at the workplace, at least until you complete the investigation. Depending on the nature of the threat (and how extensive your existing security measures are), you may want to adopt some of all of the following precautions:

- Require all workplace visitors to check in, receive a security badge, and be escorted at all times.
- Require all employees to wear a badge or picture ID while at work.
- Install surveillance cameras (check your state's laws first—some prohibit cameras in certain workplace areas), extra lighting, and alarm systems.
- Install a locking door between the entrance or reception area and the rest of the workplace.

- Make sure every employee knows what to do in an emergency.

- Bring in security guards (or additional security guards); if you suspect a particular person, give security a recent photograph and a complete description, with instructions not to allow that person into the workplace.

3. Choose the Investigator

Chapter 2, Section D, explains the qualities that make an investigator particular effective—such as professionalism, experience, and impartiality. Those considerations always apply, no matter what type of problem you're investigating. However, there are some additional issues to consider in a violence investigation.

a. Using an Outside Investigator

If you are dealing with a workplace violence or threat assessment consultant, that person may be able to handle the investigation. Of course, the consultant can't make decisions on behalf of the company—most important, what discipline should be imposed on the violent employee. However, the consultant should be well equipped to handle the interviews, review documents, and write a report summarizing his or her conclusions. Most experts will also be able to help you decide what to tell your other employees, whether you need changes to your security plans or personnel policies to deal with violence, and how to train your workforce to prevent future violence.

Getting the assistance of a consultant is a very good idea in any investigation of serious threats of violence or violent incidents. Experts tell us that much can be learned from reading the nuances of a suspected employee's presentation: key phrases, body language, facial expressions, and gestures. Consultants have years of experience deciphering these signals—and have interviewed many employees who have committed or are suspected of violence. On the other hand, you and/or your human resources staff may have no training or experience in dealing with violent employees, up until now. Given the very high stakes, it's often a good idea to have an expert on hand to help you out.

Some consultants will want to handle the whole investigation, while others will be willing to advise you throughout the investigation without taking over the whole process. For example, the consultant may give you advice about what steps to take right away to secure the workforce, how to get the suspected employee out of the workplace, what documents to gather, and how to handle the interviews (and interpret the responses). Or, the consultant may interview the suspect and victim, while leaving other interviews to you. During your initial contact with a consultant, ask whether the consultant is willing to handle any of the investigative chores—or to be available to advise you throughout the investigation.

b. Investigator Qualities

In a violence investigation, two of your most important goals are:

- **Laying down the law with the accused employee.** Violence happens, in part, because it is allowed to happen. An employee who has been getting away with intimidating and threatening coworkers may not fully understand that these actions are unacceptable. The longer this situation continues, the more resistant and resentful the employee will be towards any efforts to correct it. The person who interviews the accused employee must be able to clearly explain why the alleged behavior violates company policy and why the company is obligated to take action. This will convey that the employee's actions will have consequences—which, in turn, can diminish the chances for further violent incidents.

- **Including the accused employee in the process.** Remember, employees who commit violent acts often feel persecuted and misunderstood. Part of the investigator's job is to convey to the accused employee what is going to happen and why—to make the investigation a transparent process, so the employee doesn't feel that the outcome is inevitable or the company is engaged in a plot against him or her. An accused employee who is included in the process is less likely to see the investigation as a reason to escalate the violence.

The investigator must be able to successfully handle both of these goals. To set limits for the employee, the investigator must have a certain amount of gravitas within the company. This means that a lower-level supervisor or human resources representative might not be the right person for the job; a member of upper management or a company officer might be in a better position to get this message across.

To make sure that the employee sees the investigation as fair and open, you must take care not to choose an investigator who has had any run-ins or unpleasant dealings with the accused employee. If your investigator has a "past" with the accused employee, the employee may see the investigation as just another workplace conspiracy against him or her. Even more distressing, the accused employee may fixate on the investigator as a source of his or her problems in the workplace—which means that the investigator may become a target for violence.

4. Plan the Investigation

If violence has been threatened or committed, your investigation will have to be especially speedy. With this in mind, you should limit your investigation planning to the bare minimum once you've taken dealt with any immediate safety concerns. (See Section B2, above.)

As always, your first step is to consider what you already know. What happened? If a threat was made, what were the exact words used? If aggressive, intimidating, or violent acts are alleged, what was done? Do you know who made an alleged threat or committed a violent act, or was it done anonymously? Where did it take place? Who was the victim? Who else had the opportunity to witness it?

Your answers to these questions will help you plan your next moves. Specifically, you'll need to figure out:

- **Whom to interview.** The victim or recipient of threats should be first on your list. You'll also want to interview anyone who saw or heard the incidents and, of course, the suspected employee. Other possible candidates include the suspected employee's supervisor or manager and anyone else who may have had an opportunity to witness the work relationship between the victim and the suspect.

- **What documents and evidence to gather.** Start off with the personnel files of the suspected employee and the victim, to see if anything similar has been reported before. If any threats have been put in writing, collect those as well. You'll also want to secure any physical objects that relate to the situation—such as defaced or damaged property (or photographs of the property), weapons, or unsolicited gifts or other objects left for the victim.

- **Whether you will need to review other records.** For example, it may be prudent to run a background check on the accused employee, to find out if he or she has a criminal record, a history of violent behavior, or prior incidents of violence or similar trouble at previous employers. (See Section B6, below, for more information).

5. Interviews

Once you've finished your investigation planning, you're ready to start your interviews. Generally, you'll want to interview the victim first, followed by witnesses, and save the accused employee for last. This will give you a chance to gather as much information as possible, so you can get the accused employee's response to every allegation.

No matter whom you're interviewing, you should start the interview with some opening remarks to set the employee at ease and explain the process. Next, proceed to your specific questions, remembering to follow up on any new information raised by the witness's responses. Close the interview by letting the witness know what will happen next and inviting him or her to come to you with any concerns or additional information. And conduct follow-up interviews if any new information comes to light.

a. The Victim

The purpose of your interview with the victim is to find out as much as you can about what happened: what was said or done, when, in what context, how the victim responded, whether similar incidents have happened in the past, and so on. However, most victims will have a different goal during the interview: to find out what is being or can be done to secure their own safety. This is an entirely reasonable concern, and you should address it at the start of the interview.

Getting Started

At the outset, explain that the company is investigating the complaint or incident and that the purpose of the meeting is to gather as much information as possible. Make sure to cover any measures the company has taken to keep the employee safe, such as increasing security, placing the accused employee on leave, consulting with a violence expert, getting a restraining order, and so on. Cover safety measures the employee can take outside the workplace, such as changing established routines, not going out alone, and improving home security—the local police or a violence consultant can help come up with a comprehensive list of security measures for the victim.

Explain how the investigation will proceed and that you will discipline any employee who has committed misconduct. Ask the victim to come to you immediately if anyone retaliates against him or her for coming forward. Explain that the victim must not talk about the investigation with others in the workplace and that you will protect the victim's confidentiality to the extent possible. Finally, find out if the victim has any questions or concerns about the investigation.

Questions

When you question the victim, you want to find out exactly what happened. Being attacked or threatened is obviously a very upsetting experience; as a result, some victims may be so caught up in how the incident made them feel that they will have trouble relating the facts. For example, a victim might say, "He threatened to kill me!" or "I can't work with someone who attacked me," but this doesn't really tell you very much about what was actually said or done. Although it's important to find out how the victim felt and reacted, remember not to lose sight of the basic facts: who, what, where, when, and how.

Here are some sample questions to consider (of course, the actual questions you ask will depend on the facts of your case):

- What happened?
- What did [the accused employee] say or do to you?
- How did you respond?
- Did [the accused employee] touch you in any way?
- Did [the accused employee] threaten you? What were his or her exact words?
- What was [the accused employee]'s demeanor? Did he or she make any gestures? What was his or her facial expression? Did he or she yell, speak loudly, use a normal tone of voice?
- Did anyone else see or hear the confrontation?
- What was going on immediately before the incident? Were you interacting with [the accused employee] at all?
- Where and when did the incident take place?
- Has [the accused employee] ever threatened or intimidated you before? Please describe each incident.
- Did anyone witness these prior incidents?
- Have you experienced any unexplained acts of vandalism or property damage? Have you received any unsolicited gifts or other items?
- Do you work with [the accused employee]? What is your working relationship (that is, are you coworkers, does one of you report to the other, do you work together on projects)?

- For how long have you worked together? Describe what your working relationship has been like. Have you worked well together in the past? Have you had difficulty working together in the past?

- Do you know of anyone else who has had similar problems with [the accused employee]? If so, please describe what happened to them.

- Is there anything else you want to tell me about [the accused employee] or about this incident?

- How have the incidents affected you? Did you take any time off as a result of the incidents? Did you seek medical treatment or counseling?

- Are there any documents or other kinds of evidence relating to the incidents? Did you take notes or keep a journal recording these incidents?

- Have you spoken to anyone about this? Whom, and what did you say?

Closing the Interview

Once you have finished your questions, review your notes with the person you interviewed. Make sure you got everything right and that your notes include all of the important details. Ask the employee not to discuss the complaint or the investigation with any coworkers. Remind the employee about retaliation. Ask the employee to come to you immediately with any new information. And let the employee know what will happen next.

b. Witnesses

Witnesses might be coworkers who heard or saw the incident, others who have had trouble with the accused employee in the past, or the accused employee's supervisor or manager. Like the victim, witnesses may also be concerned about safety—and may be very reluctant to tell you anything that they feel might make them a target.

Getting Started

For witnesses, your opening remarks can be brief. The witness doesn't need to know who complained, who is accused, or what the specific allegations are (although they may already know). Once you have explained that you are investigating a workplace problem and talked about confidentiality and retaliation, you can begin asking your questions.

If the witness raises safety concerns, explain some of the measures you have taken to improve security in the workplace.

Questions

When questioning witnesses, your goal is to gather information without giving too much away. To plan your questions, consider who suggested the witness and why. Did the witness see or hear the incident? Was the witness told about the incident? Is the witness privy to some details of the relationship between the victim and the accused?

Start with general questions about the witness's work; these questions will help you figure out if the witness could have seen or heard the alleged incidents. Next, move on to the specifics of the alleged incidents. Here are some sample questions to consider:

- Describe your typical workday or workweek. Who is your supervisor? Where is your workstation? What time do you typically arrive at work each day? What time do you leave?

- Do you work with [the victim] and/or [the accused employee]? How would you describe their work relationship? What is your work relationship like with each of them?

- Has [the victim] ever spoken to you about [the accused employee]? Has [the accused employee] ever spoken to you about [the victim]?

- Have you seen any incidents or heard any communications between [the victim] and [the accused employee] that made you uncomfortable? Describe them to me.

- If the witness may have seen or heard any incidents, ask questions to figure out whether the witness was there and what happened.

EXAMPLE: The victim claims that the witness heard the accused employee say, "If you were smart, you'd give me a higher rating. I know you work late sometimes, and it's a long, dark walk to where you park your car. Anything could happen to you." The victim says the accused employee made this statement in the hallway outside her office, late Monday afternoon.

You should start by asking general questions to figure out if the witness was there. For example: Were you in the office on Monday? What did you do on Monday afternoon? Did you see the victim and the accused employee in the hallway? What time? What did each of them say?

If these questions don't get you the information you need, you'll have to ask more specific questions, like: Did the accused employee say anything about his rating? Did he say anything about the victim's work hours? Did he say anything that you considered threatening?

- Have you heard this or other incidents discussed in the workplace? When, where, and by whom?
- Have you ever had any problems working with [the victim] or [the accused employee]?
- Do you know of anyone else who might have information about the incident? Are there any documents or other evidence that you know of relating to the incident?

Closing the Interview

Once you have finished your questions, review your notes with the witness. Make sure you got everything right and that your notes include all of the important details. Ask the employee not to discuss the complaint or the investigation with any coworkers. Remind the employee about retaliation. And ask the employee to come to you immediately with any new information.

c. The Accused Employee

You have several goals in mind when you interview the accused employee. Of course, you want to hear that person's side of the story, so you can figure out what actually happened. But your primary goal should be threat assessment: determining whether the accused employee really poses a violent threat (and if so, to whom).

 Get expert help.

Although this point has already been made in this chapter, it's worth repeating: Assessing whether a particular person will act violently is difficult work, and the consequences of guessing wrong can be disastrous. You should hire an expert for help and advice in any situation that has the potential for violence. The material in this section provides general guidelines, not the comprehensive and individualized assistance that only an expert can provide. For information on working with a violence consultant, see Section B2, above.

Getting Started

At the outset, explain the purpose of the meeting. Emphasize that the company has not reached any decisions about what happened and that you are interested in hearing what everyone involved has to say before making a decision or taking any action. Because you will probably have to reveal the name of the complaining employee, spend some extra time discussing retaliation: what it is, that the company prohibits it, and that employees who engage in retaliation will be subject to discipline.

Keep the Interview Safe

Any time you meet with an employee who has the potential for violence, you'll want to take steps to maintain your own safety. First and foremost, you should hold the interview in a room that offers you an escape route—for example, a door that opens directly to the outside of the building. If there is only one door to the room, make sure that the employee doesn't sit between you and that door (rearrange furniture, if necessary).

During the interview itself, be sure to listen to the employee and let the employee know that you are interested in what he or she has to say. Acknowledge the employee's feelings about the allegations, but explain that you need to find out what happened in order for the company to deal with the situation. If the employee becomes agitated or upset, make a special effort to stay calm and focused, to avoid letting the situation escalate. Don't be confrontational in your questioning—maintain the demeanor of an objective fact-gatherer. Don't crowd the employee physically or make any agitated movements.

If you have any concerns about safety, bring another person into the interview with you. And make sure that you have security waiting nearby, available to come in if things get out of hand. You should have a telephone in the interview room and a prearranged signal that will let security personnel know that you need some help.

Questions

Let the accused employee know that you are investigating alleged threats or violent behavior—and that this behavior, if it happened, violates company policy and will result in discipline. Be very clear that violent behavior has consequences; this will not only set the proper tone for the interview, but will also help dissuade the accused employee from resorting to violence during the interview.

Although the accused employee will probably want to know the specific allegations right away, you are better off postponing this discussion until later in the interview, after you have had a chance to gather some important background information. Assure the accused employee that he or she will have the opportunity to hear and respond to the allegations before the interview is over.

Here are some sample questions to consider:

- When did you start working for the company? What was the first position you held? Who was your supervisor? What were your job responsibilities? For how long did you hold that position?

- What was the next position you held at the company? [Ask the same questions for each position, up to the current job.]

- What is your current job? Who is your supervisor? What do you think of your coworkers? Do you like your current position? What are some of the things you like about it? Is there anything you dislike about it?

- What is your typical workday or workweek like? What time do you arrive, what time do you leave? What are your job responsibilities?

- Do you supervise any employees? What are their names and positions?

- How would you characterize your working relationship with your direct reports? Your coworkers? Your supervisor?

- [Tell the accused employee what misconduct is alleged or suspected.] What is your response to these allegations?

 You must allow the accused employee to respond to the allegations.

Some investigators are so eager to keep the interview civil—or to protect the complaining employee's privacy—that they never actually get around to confronting the accuser with the allegations against him or her. This is a big mistake, one that could undermine the legitimacy of the entire investigation. Courts have held that accused employees who never learn precisely what they are accused of haven't had a fair opportunity to tell their side of the story, to offer the names of relevant witnesses, or to explain why the victim might have made the accusations. You don't necessarily have to say who complained, but you should say whom the employee is accused of threatening or harming. And don't worry about privacy concerns—you have a very compelling business reason for revealing this information.

- Did these things happen? [if the accused employee does not completely deny the allegations] What did happen? When and where?
- How did [the victim] respond?
- Did anyone witness these incidents?
- Have you told anyone about these incidents?
- Have you kept any notes or a journal about these incidents?
- What is your work relationship like with [the victim]?
- [if the accused employee denies the allegations] Could another person have misunderstood your actions or statements? Do you think someone made up these incidents? Why?
- Have you ever used foul language in the workplace?
- Have you ever threatened anyone in the workplace? Have you ever had a physical confrontation with another employee? Where and when?
- Do you own any weapons? Do you own any guns? Have you ever used a gun?
- Has anyone ever filed a restraining order against you? Have you ever had any dealings with the police? Please describe the circumstances.
- [for complaints of stalking or romantic obsession] Have you ever seen [the victim] outside of work? Have you ever had a social relationship with each other? A romantic relationship? Have you ever asked [the victim] out on a date? What was [his or her] response?
- Have you ever been accused of making threats or acting violently before, at this job or at previous jobs you've held? Where and when? How were the accusations resolved?
- Do you know of anyone who might have information about these incidents?
- Do you know of any documents or other evidence relating to these allegations?
- How do you think this situation should be resolved?

Need interviewing tips?

For more information on interviewing the accused employee, check out *Dealing With Workplace Violence: A Guide for Agency Planners,* available from the federal Office of Personnel Management, at www.opm.gov/ehs/workplac/. Written for federal government agencies, this informative resource is now widely used by private companies as well. It offers case examples, planning tips, policy guidance, advice on handling the aftermath of a violent incident, and much more. Although some of the information is relevant only to government workplaces, you'll find most of it to be extremely useful.

d. Follow-Up Interviews

If any new information comes up during your investigation, you should conduct follow-up interviews with the victim or accused employee. Both employees should have the opportunity to respond to new allegations or defenses, to make sure that you have a complete understanding of the facts when you make your decision and to give you the opportunity to gauge credibility. It is especially important to let the accused employee know of any additional allegations that come up during the investigation. If you don't, you may be accused of unfairness for refusing to give him or her an opportunity to respond.

6. Gather Documents and Other Evidence

Except in very rare circumstances, workplace violence generally escalates from threats, conflicts with coworkers, and intimidation to actual violent acts. This means that, if your company is doing its job right, there may be a paper trail. Check the accused employee's personnel file for any history of problems working with others, abusive behavior, physical altercations, and so on. Find out if anyone has complained about the accused employee before. And review the personnel files of any other employees involved in the incident as well, to see if there's any indication of prior problems with the accused employee.

In addition to official company records, there may be other types of documents and evidence that will help you reach a decision. Here are some examples:

- **Records of threats by the accused employee.** For example, if the threats were made in writing—either on paper or in email—you can get those documents. If threatening messages were left on an answering machine or voice mail service, see if you can get copies. And make sure to ask the victim and witnesses if they've kept any records—for example, a log of threatening phone calls or notes of an intimidating encounter.

- **Medical records or records of treatment sought by the victim.** If a physical assault has occurred, the victim's medical records (if the victim sought treatment) can help you assess what happened. And if the victim has sought counseling or other help to deal with stress created by the accused employee, you might ask for a note from the treatment provider to that effect. (The victim will have to consent to the release of any medical records.)

- **Items collected by the accused employee.** Sometimes, an employee with a propensity for violence will collect news articles on other violent incidents, weapons paraphernalia, photographs of or information about the victim, or other items. If the accused employee keeps these things at work, you may be able to collect them for your investigation. (See Chapter 7, Section B4, for information on conducting workplace searches.)

- **Nondocumentary evidence.** For example, if the victim's property has been damaged or defaced, you might collect that property (if it's small), or take photographs of the damage. The victim may have received gifts, photographs, or other items from the accused employee, which you can gather and review.

- **Official records.** You may wish to find out whether the accused employee has a criminal record, has been subject to restraining orders, or has been sued for harassment or injuring someone. Many of these records are publicly available; some states restrict an employer's ability to review criminal records (check with your state's department of labor or ask a lawyer to find out about your state's laws).

7. Evaluate the Evidence

In some violence investigations, the accused employee admits that the incident happened as the victim described. An accused employee who acted under extreme stress and realizes that his or her actions were wrong may be willing to own up to the misconduct, while explaining what led to the problem.

EXAMPLE: Marjorie is accused of suddenly turning on a coworker who was walking behind her in a hallway, pushing him away, and screaming, "Just stay away from me! Don't crowd me!" She then ran down the hall to her office and slammed the door. Marjorie's coworkers have noticed that she's been acting strangely for the last month or so—she's been showing up late, falling behind on her assignments, crying, and appearing to be out of it some of the time.

When Marjorie is interviewed, she begins crying. She admits that the hallway incident happened just as her coworker described but explains that her ex-husband has been stalking her and threatening to kill her. She is fearful and jumpy, and she thought momentarily that her coworker was her ex-husband; when she realized her mistake, she was so embarrassed that she ran away.

An employee who feels justified in resorting to violence or intimidation may also admit to the incident—claiming, in effect, that the victim deserved it. In this situation, the employee feels, inappropriately, entitled to bully others.

EXAMPLE: Marcus is accused of threatening his boss, Sharon, after she promoted one of his coworkers instead of him. Sharon says that Marcus told her, "You'll be sorry for passing me over. You're going to find out what it means to be on my hit list."

When Marcus is interviewed, he readily admits to making the statement but claims that he didn't intend to threaten her with physical violence. "She's been hard on me ever since I started reporting to her, and she never even gave me a chance for that promotion. I wanted her to know that she'd made a mistake and that I wasn't going to forget it."

In many cases, however, the accused employee will deny the allegations, or at least some part of them. For example, the accused employee might claim to have been joking, to have said something slightly different, or to have spoken in a calm tone of voice rather than a shout. To figure out what really happened, consider the factors listed in Chapter 4. In cases of threats and violence, plausibility, demeanor, corroboration, and prior incidents are often especially important.

- **Plausibility.** Whose story makes sense? Does one story defy common sense—or (as may be true in a threat situation) ordinary rules of conversation?

EXAMPLE 1: Charlotte claims that Harry has threatened her and that she has seen him parked outside her house. Harry first denies knowing where Charlotte lives; when confronted with a photograph her husband took of his car, he admits that he may have been in the neighborhood, but it was to visit a friend. He refuses to give his friend's name or address.

EXAMPLE 2: Jamal says that Larry has been angry with him ever since he received a promotion that Larry wanted. Most recently, Jamal claims that Larry told him, "You better hope you don't run into me in a dark alleyway—like the one where you park your car." Larry denies intending to threaten Jamal; he claims that he said, "I worry about you walking to your car at night. You could get hurt." Larry can't explain why he was worried about Jamal, or why he thought Jamal wouldn't be safe walking to his car alone.

- **Corroboration.** Did anyone else hear or see the incident? Should someone else have been able to see or hear it, if it happened the way the victim or accused employee claimed it did?
- **Demeanor.** Victims or recipients of threats or violence are often pretty stressed out and frightened by the situation. Does the victim's demeanor make sense, given the allegations? Does the accused employee exhibit the behaviors attributed to him by the victim?

EXAMPLE 1: Karen says that Curtis threatened to bring a gun to work and open fire on his coworkers. She says that Curtis said he felt like he was going to explode and couldn't take the pressure of work any more. Karen related these statements in a calm tone of voice, then asked, "Can you really keep someone like Curtis here? I mean, what if he goes through with it?" Curtis appeared to be under no particular stress—until told of Karen's allegations, which he vehemently denied, saying, "Why would she say something like that?" Curtis denies owning a gun and points out the bumper sticker on his car in support of strict gun control. In this case, there may be more to Karen's story than meets the eye.

EXAMPLE 2: John says that Rex has been physically intimidating towards him and other coworkers. John claims that Rex blocks their way in the halls, looms over John when he's sitting at his desk, and gets in John's face whenever he is upset about something. Lately, John says Rex has threatened to harm him. John looks pretty freaked out; he has dark circles under his eyes and is very concerned that Rex might hurt him if he finds out that John has complained. During Rex's interview, he crowds the interviewer, raises his voice, and tries to talk over the interviewer. Both John and Rex are acting in ways that support John's story.

- **Prior incidents.** Because violence is usually preceded by warnings, prior incidents of threats or abusive behavior is important evidence. Although it isn't conclusive evidence that the incident in question occurred, a history of violence lends a lot of weight to the victim's version of events.

8. Take Action

If you conclude that the accused employee is capable of violence, deciding what discipline to impose won't be your only concern. The danger to the victim and your other employees doesn't necessarily end once the accused employee is out of the workplace; in fact, firing the accused employee, if handled improperly, could actually increase the risk of a violent incident. In addition to any discipline you might want to impose, you need to come up a plan to deal with the accused employee and keep the target employee (and workplace) safe.

a. Disciplinary Action

In some cases, you may conclude that no discipline is warranted for the accused employee. For example, if the allegations turn out to be false, you may decide to discipline the complaining employee instead. (See Chapter 4 for more on false accusations.) If there appears to have been a genuine verbal misunderstanding, you may reasonably decide to simply end the matter with warnings all around and renewed training about workplace violence. (See Section B10, below.)

In some circumstances, you may decide that some form of aggressive behavior occurred but that the accused employee should be excused to some degree. For example, consider the case of Marjorie, discussed in Section B7, above, who pushed a coworker but was under extreme stress because of threats and stalking by her ex-husband. Because Marjorie understands that her behavior was inappropriate, it has never happened before, and her current situation is highly unusual, you might choose to give Marjorie a written warning and direct her to some sources of help for her problem with her ex-husband (such as the police and an employee assistance program).

However, if you decide that the accused employee made a threat or committed violence absent special circumstances, you will have to decide whether firing is warranted. Generally, you will probably have to fire most employees who actually threaten someone or physically assault someone else—you have a legal obligation to keep your workplace safe, and retaining an employee who has shown a propensity for violence is not in keeping with that obligation. If the accused employee recognizes that his or her conduct was wrong, is willing to seek help with anger control and appropriate workplace behavior, and can work with you to figure out how to prevent similar problems in the future, it might be worthwhile to keep the employee on board—as long as the behavior was not extreme and you are willing to commit to monitoring the situation closely. If you are considering keeping on an employee who has made threats or committed violence, consult with a lawyer and/or workplace violence consultant first.

b. Coming Up With a Safety Plan

Once you've decided whether to take disciplinary measures, you'll have to come up with a plan to keep the workplace safe going forward. This is especially important if you are firing the accused employee—remember, termination just gets the employee off your payroll; it doesn't necessarily solve the underlying problem of the employee's willingness to resort to violence.

How Serious Is the Threat?

Experts say that it is often possible to tell, from the language of a threat or the nature of aggressive behavior, how likely it is that a person will commit violence. Of course, there are no absolutes here—this is all a matter of interpretation and degree, not an exact science. However, history has shown that certain types of statements and conduct are more indicative of violence than others.

Here are some examples:

- An employee who has focused his or her attention and anger on a particular person is more dangerous than an employee who has vague, general complaints against the company.

- An employee who has threatened someone is more dangerous than an employee who has not.

- An employee who has followed or approached the intended victim, or who has gathered information (such as home address, a favorite route home, or where children go to school), is more dangerous than one who has not.

- An employee who owns or has practiced with weapons is more dangerous that one who has not.

- An employee who conveys a detailed plan for harming the victim (such as how the victim will come to harm, what type of weapon the employee will use, when and where the assault will take place) is more dangerous than one has not.

- An employee who has rehearsed committing violence is more dangerous than one who has not.

- An employee who feels that he or she must act right away is more dangerous than one who threatens to act at some undefined point in the future.

Consider whether you should pursue any criminal law options—such as informing the police, getting a restraining order (see Section B2, above), or reporting the accused employee for violating weapons, stalking, or assault and battery laws. Consider taking additional steps to enhance workplace security (see Section B2, above)—talk to your local police for ideas. And make sure to inform your workplace security staff that the accused employee is no longer welcome on company property and that police should immediately be called if he or she shows up. A workplace violence expert can help you craft an effective safety plan.

c. Breaking the News

You will have to inform the accused employee and the victim of the results of the investigation. If you have decided to fire the accused employee, you will want to have security available to assist you, if necessary. Explain what your investigation revealed and why the company decided to fire the employee. Explain exactly what you expect of the employee in the future—that he or she stay away from the workplace, in particular. Give the employee the name of someone in the company to call to wrap up final details, such as continuing health insurance, getting the final paycheck, and so on.

If the employee becomes agitated or threatening, bring in security immediately. Explain that this kind of behavior won't be tolerated and that the employee will be escorted from the workplace immediately. If a termination meeting ends in further threats or aggression, you should probably contact your local police to report the incident.

Always Be Respectful

It is extremely important to treat an employee you are firing with respect and dignity. Hold the termination in private, and don't belabor the employee's failings. Never belittle an employee, and be sure to mention the employee's hard work for the company. Studies show that the way a termination is handled plays a major role in how the fired employee views the company—and if you're dealing with an employee who has the potential to commit violence, you'll want him or her to view the company in the best possible light.

When you meet with the victim, explain the action you have taken and why. Describe the safety plan, including steps you have taken to enhance security, and any criminal proceedings you've set in motion. Make sure the victim knows what to do if he or she sees or hears from the accused employee—for example, if there is a restraining order in effect, the victim should call the police immediately and inform you of the incident.

Find out whether the victim has concerns about his or her own safety—if so, offer to put the victim in touch with someone who can help develop a safety plan for outside the workplace (your local police or a violence consultant can help with this). Ask about the victim's feelings about what happened; in some cases, the victim may be traumatized by the incidents. If the victim needs time off work to recuperate, make that available as an option. You might also offer to pay for a few counseling sessions, if the victim wishes.

9. Document the Investigation

Document your violence investigation just as you would any other workplace investigation. (See Chapter 4 for details.) Be sure to include any legal actions taken, such as applying for a restraining order or reporting the incident to the police. Also, include your plans for following up with the accused employee or the victim. (See Section B10, below.)

10. Follow Up

Even after you've finished your investigation, there will be quite a few things to do. First of all, you'll want to check in with the victim from time to time, to make sure that he or she feels secure in the workplace and is satisfied with your efforts to ensure safety. If you've decided to retain the accused employee, you'll also want to meet frequently with him or her, to make sure that any required counseling is completed and to keep track of the accused employee's progress.

In addition to these follow-up meetings, there are several steps you should take to get the workplace back to normal and prevent violence in the future.

a. Counseling

If actual violence or significant threats have taken place, your employees may be traumatized. In addition, after handling the investigation, you may also be feeling some stress. If you or your workers appear to need some help getting back to business as usual, you might consider bringing in some trauma counselors or other workplace advisers, so employees have a chance to express their feelings and have their questions answered.

b. Policies, Planning, and Training

Most companies learn at least a few thing they should be doing differently after investigating a violent incident. Try to use this as an opportunity to figure out how better to prevent and address violence in the future. As part of your violence prevention efforts, consider the following strategies:

- **Adopt an antiviolence policy.** Every organization, no matter how small, should have a clear policy prohibiting all kinds of workplace violence, from horseplay and intimidation to threats and assault. You can find a sample policy in Appendix A.

- **Assemble a workplace violence team.** Experts agree that the best way to prevent and address violence is to put together a team from different areas of the company—human resources, security, legal, labor, and so on—to figure out what the company should do. The team can work together to develop an antiviolence policy, come up with a security plan, decide how to respond to violent incidents, audit potential trouble spots, develop a working relationship with a violence consultant or local police, and figure out how to handle the aftermath of a violent incident.

- **Train your team, managers, and employees.** Once you've got a team in place, consider bringing in a violence consultant to train you in violence prevention and response techniques, including threat assessment. Your managers and employees should also be trained on the company's anti-violence policy, how the company will handle reports of violence, the warning signs of potential violence, and so on.

- **Do a workplace security audit.** Ask the police or a workplace violence consultant to do a walk-through of your workplace and give you ideas on how you can improve employee safety. ■

APPENDIX

Workplace Policies

Complaint Policy

Open-Door Policy

Antidiscrimination Policy

Antiharassment Policy

Antiviolence Policy

Complaint Policy

Your policy should describe the conduct about which employees can complain, how to make a complaint, and what will happen once a complaint is filed.

- **Prohibited conduct.** A complaint policy should spell out, in simple terms, what conduct will be investigated. If you have a progressive discipline policy, sexual harassment policy, or other written guidelines describing unacceptable workplace behavior, you can use those policies for reference. List the types of misconduct that you would like your employees to report (for example, harassment, discriminatory conduct or comments, violent behavior or threats of violence, safety violations, theft, and/or misuse of company property). Include a catchall category at the end of your list, allowing employees to raise concerns about any type of behavior that makes them feel uncomfortable, upset, or unsafe.

- **How to make complaints.** Next, tell your workers how to make a formal complaint if they are victims of, or witnesses to, any of these prohibited behaviors. Make sure that employees can also complain to someone outside of their chain of command: a human resources manager, another supervisor, or even the head of the company. If an employee is being harassed or mistreated by his or her own supervisor, this allows the worker to bypass that person and complain to someone who isn't part of the problem. Even if the employee's direct supervisor is not the source of the complaint, workers may simply feel more comfortable talking to someone who won't be responsible for evaluating their performance and making decisions on promotions, raises, and assignments. However, don't designate too many people. The more people responsible for taking complaints, the greater the likelihood that a complaint could fall through the cracks. Generally, it's sufficient to give employees two or three people to choose from, rather than designating all of your supervisors or managers to hear complaints.

Make sure that the people you designate to take complaints are accessible to employees.

For example, if your human resources department is located in a distant office or your local human resources manager works a part-time schedule, you should choose alternate complaint takers who are local and available.

- **Investigation.** While you need not describe your investigative procedures in detail, your policy should assure your employees that serious complaints will be investigated quickly, completely, and fairly.

- **Retaliation.** Your complaint policy should assure employees that no action will be taken against them for complaining in good faith. Promise to take all necessary steps to prevent and discourage retaliation. Encourage employees to come forward if they feel retaliated against, and assure employees that you will act quickly to prevent any further harassment or mistreatment while the investigation is pending.

- **Managers' responsibilities.** Your policy should state that managers and supervisors are responsible for reporting violations of company rules and for forwarding any complaints they hear to the appropriate complaint takers.

- **Confidentiality.** Your policy should make clear to your employees that you will keep the complaint confidential *to the extent possible*. You cannot reasonably promise not to tell anyone about the complaint; after all, you will have to tell the alleged wrongdoer about the complaining employee's statements and perhaps interview witnesses about the incident.

- **Corrective action.** Your policy should state that you will take immediate disciplinary action against employees who violate company policy, following a thorough investigation.

Sample Complaint Policy

[Company Name] is committed to providing a safe and productive work environment, free of threats to the health, safety, and wellbeing of our workers, including but not limited to harassment, discrimination, violations of health and safety rules, and violence.

Any employee who witnesses or is subject to inappropriate conduct in the workplace may complain to _____ or to any company officer. Any supervisor, manager, or company officer who receives a complaint about, hears of, or witnesses any inappropriate conduct is required to immediately notify _____. Inappropriate conduct includes any conduct prohibited by our company policies about harassment, discrimination, discipline, workplace violence, health and safety, and drug and alcohol use. In addition, we encourage employees to come forward with any workplace complaint, even if the subject of the complaint is not explicitly covered by our written policies.

We encourage you to come forward with complaints immediately, so we can take whatever action is needed to handle the problem. Once a complaint has been made, _____ will determine how to handle it. For serious complaints alleging harassment, discrimination, and other illegal conduct, we will immediately conduct a complete and impartial investigation. All complaints will be handled as confidentially as possible. When the investigation is complete, the company will take corrective action, if appropriate.

The company will not engage in or allow retaliation against any employee who makes a good-faith complaint or participates in an investigation. If you believe that you are being subjected to any kind of negative treatment because you made or were questioned about a complaint, report the conduct immediately to _____.

Open-Door Policy

An open-door policy can be very informal; indeed, adopting a friendly, informal tone will help encourage your employees to come forward with their concerns and ideas. The most important components of an open-door policy are:

- **Purpose.** Describe the reasons for your open-door policy (for example, to facilitate communication between employees and management, to encourage employees to report work-related concerns, to find out what your employees are thinking).

- **Appropriate topics.** Explain what types of issues employees might want to raise—you can also give some examples (such as if you're having a problem with a coworker or supervisor, you want to share a good idea, or you want to propose topics for a company meeting or training).

- **Whose door is open.** Tell employees who they should talk to (for example, a supervisor or manager, the company president or CEO, company officers, the human resources department).

- **Encouragement.** Let employees know that you are eager to hear their concerns. If your employees don't use the policy, it won't do you any good.

Sample Open-Door Policy

We want to maintain a positive and pleasant environment for all of our employees. To help us meet this goal, [Company Name] has an open-door policy, by which employees are encouraged to report work-related concerns.

If something about your job is bothering you, or if you have a question, concern, idea, or problem related to your work, please discuss it with your immediate supervisor as soon as possible. If for any reason you don't feel comfortable bringing the matter to your supervisor, feel free to raise the issue with any company officer.

We encourage you to come forward and make your concerns known to the Company. We can't solve the problem if we don't know about it.

Antidiscrimination Policy

Your antidiscrimination policy should explain your company's commitment to equal opportunity. Here are some issues your policy should cover:

- **Prohibited conduct.** Your policy should explain what types of discrimination are prohibited (for example, race, sex, and so on). To find out what antidiscrimination laws you must follow—and therefore, which types of prohibited discrimination you should list in your policy—see Chapter 5, Section A1. You'll find a list of state antidiscrimination laws in Appendix A.

- **Complaint procedures.** Your policy should explain how employees can complain about discrimination.

- **Retaliation.** Let employees know that retaliation will not be permitted, and ask employees to report retaliation.

- **Managers' responsibilities.** Your policy should indicate that managers are required to report discriminatory conduct.

- **Corrective action.** The policy should state that you will take immediate and appropriate disciplinary action against any employee who violates the policy.

Antidiscrimination Policy

[Company Name] is strongly committed to providing equal employment opportunity for all employees and all applicants for employment. For us, this is the only acceptable way to do business.

All employment decisions at our Company—including those relating to hiring, promotion, transfers, benefits, compensation, placement, and termination—will be made without regard to [prohibited bases for discrimination].

Any employee or applicant who believes that he or she has been discriminated against in violation of this policy should immediately file a complaint with _____, as explained in our Complaint Policy. We encourage you to come forward if you have suffered or witnessed what you believe to be discrimination—we cannot solve the problem until you let us know about it. The Company will not retaliate, or allow retaliation, against any employee or applicant who complains of discrimination, assists in an investigation of possible discrimination, or files an administrative charge or lawsuit alleging discrimination.

Managers are required to report any discriminatory conduct or incidents, as described in our Complaint Policy.

Our Company will not tolerate discrimination against any employee or applicant. We will take immediate and appropriate disciplinary action against any employee who violates this policy.

Antiharassment Policy

A harassment policy should include the following:

- **Definition of harassment.** The policy should explain what harassment is, and list the prohibited bases for harassment—that is, race, sex, age, and so on. To find out what antidiscrimination laws you must follow—and therefore, which types of prohibited harassment you should list in your policy—see Chapter 5, Section A1. You'll find a list of state antidiscrimination laws in Appendix A.

- **Harassment is prohibited.** State clearly that harassment will not be tolerated.

- **Complaint procedure.** Explain how to make complaints of harassment, and encourage employees to come forward.

- **Retaliation.** Explain that retaliation is prohibited.

- **Managers' responsibilities.** State that managers are required to report harassment.

- **Investigation and corrective action.** State that complaints will be investigated and that anyone who is found to have violated the policy will be disciplined.

Antiharassment Policy

It is our policy and our responsibility to provide our employees with a workplace free from harassment. Harassment on the basis of [prohibited bases for discrimination] undermines our workplace morale and our commitment to treat each other with dignity and respect. Accordingly, harassment will not be tolerated at our Company.

Harassment can take many forms, including but not limited to touching or other unwanted physical contact, posting offensive cartoons or pictures, using slurs or other derogatory terms, telling offensive or lewd jokes and stories, and sending email messages with offensive content. Unwanted sexual advances, requests for sexual favors, and sexually suggestive gestures, jokes, propositions, email messages, or other communications all constitute harassment.

If you experience or witness any form of harassment in the workplace, please immediately notify the company by following the steps outlined in our Complaint Policy. We encourage you to come forward with complaints—the sooner we learn about the problem, the sooner we can take steps to resolve it. The Company will not retaliate, or allow retaliation, against anyone who complains of harassment, assists in a harassment investigation, or files an administrative charge or lawsuit alleging harassment. All managers are required to immediately report any incidents of harassment, as set forth in our Complaint Policy.

Complaints will be investigated quickly. Those who are found to have violated this policy will be subject to appropriate disciplinary action, up to and including termination.

Antiviolence Policy

Here are some of the issues an antiviolence policy should address:

- **Violence is prohibited.** State that violence will not be tolerated. Explain what violence is and that threats or comments about violence will be taken seriously.

- **Weapons are prohibited.** Indicate that weapons are not allowed in the workplace. (If some of you workers must carry weapons, you will have to modify this provision.)

- **Procedures.** Explain what employees should do if they witness a threat or violence. Explain how employees can make a complaint about violence.

- **Investigation.** State that all complaints of violence will be investigated and that appropriate corrective action will be taken.

- **Retaliation.** Explain that retaliation is not permitted.

Antiviolence Policy

We will not tolerate violence in the workplace. Violence includes physical altercations, coercion, pushing or shoving, horseplay, intimidation, stalking, and threats of violence. Any comments about violence will be taken seriously—and may result in your termination. Please do not joke or make off-hand remarks about violence.

No Weapons

No weapons are allowed in our workplace. Weapons include firearms, knives, brass knuckles, martial arts equipment, clubs or bats, and explosives. If your work requires you to use an item that might qualify as a weapon, you must receive authorization from your supervisor to bring that item to work or use it in the workplace. Any employee found with an unauthorized weapon in the workplace will be subject to discipline, up to and including termination.

What to Do in Case of Violence

If you observe an incident or threat of violence that is immediate and serious, IMMEDIATELY DIAL 9-1-1 and report it to the police. If the incident or threat does not appear to require immediate police intervention, please contact _____ and report it as soon as possible, using the Company's complaint procedure. All complaints will be investigated and appropriate action will be taken. You will not face retaliation for making a complaint. ■

APPENDIX B

Forms and Checklists

Ten Steps to a Successful Investigation

Avoiding Common Investigation Mistakes

Sample Complaint Reporting Form

Document Checklist

Credibility Checklist

Discipline Checklist

Investigation Report Checklist

Ten Steps to a Successful Investigation

1. Decide whether to investigate.

2. Take immediate action, if necessary.

3. Choose an investigator.

4. Plan the investigation.

5. Conduct interviews.

6. Gather documents and other evidence.

7. Evaluate the evidence.

8. Take action.

9. Document the investigation.

10. Follow up.

Avoiding Common Investigation Mistakes

Avoiding Mistake 1: Failing to Investigate

- ✓ Never ignore complaints.
- ✓ Make sure the problem is minor before you decide not to investigate further.

Avoiding Mistake 2: Delay

- ✓ Get started right away.
- ✓ If you have a good reason for waiting, put it in writing.

Avoiding Mistake 3: Inconsistency

- ✓ Don't punish one employee more severely than another for similar misconduct.
- ✓ Investigate misconduct if you've investigated similar problems in the past.
- ✓ Make sure your own biases aren't influencing your decisions.

Avoiding Mistake 4: Retaliation

- ✓ Warn employees that retaliation will not be tolerated.
- ✓ Ask the complaining employee to immediately report retaliation.
- ✓ If you must separate workers, move the accused worker, not the worker who complained.

Mistake 5: Half-hearted Efforts

- ✓ Investigate every serious complaint or problem thoroughly and carefully.

Avoiding Mistake 6: Talking Too Much

- ✓ Reveal investigation information only on a need-to-know basis.
- ✓ Avoid making negative statements about current or former employees.
- ✓ Don't say anything unless you know it's true.

Avoiding Mistake 7: Losing Objectivity

- ✓ Remember your role: You work for the company.
- ✓ Get help if you need it.

Avoiding Common Investigation Mistakes, *continued*

Avoiding Mistake 8: Strong-Arm Investigation Tactics

✓ If an employee wants to end an interview, let the employee leave.

✓ Don't physically restrain employees by locking doors or blocking the exit.

✓ Discipline employees who fail to cooperate with the investigation.

Avoiding Mistake 9: Invading Privacy Rights

✓ Ask or search for only what you legitimately need to know.

✓ Adopt workplace policies reserving the right to search.

✓ Make sure you have a sound business reason for searching, questioning, or monitoring any employee.

Avoiding Mistake 10: Using Polygraphs Improperly

✓ Skip the polygraph altogether—the law is too complicated and the results might not be very revealing.

✓ If you use a polygraph, hire a qualified examiner who knows how to comply with the law's technical requirements.

Sample Complaint Reporting Form

Date of Complaint: _____

Name of Complaining Employee: _____

Telephone Number (work): _____

Telephone Number (home): _____

Email address: _____

Complaining Employee's Position: _____

Name(s) of Accused Employee: _____

Accused Employee's Position: _____

Incident(s) at Issue: _____

_____

_____

Potential Witnesses: _____

_____

_____

Has Complaining Employee Told Others of Incident(s): _____

_____

_____

Documents Relating to Complaint: _____

_____

_____

Other Issues: _____

_____

_____

Name of Intake Person: _____

Signature of Intake Person: _____

Document Checklist

✓ Company policies

✓ Email messages

✓ Postings to company bulletin boards (electronic or corkboard)

✓ Correspondence

✓ Performance evaluations

✓ Work samples

✓ Written warnings and other disciplinary records

✓ Customer complaints or comments

✓ Commendations

✓ Documents signed by the employees involved
(such as hiring agreements, employment contracts, and other agreements)

✓ Attendance records
(for work generally, required meetings, or training sessions, for example)

✓ Payroll records

✓ Time cards or other records showing hours worked

✓ Work schedules

✓ Inventory records

✓ Expense reports

✓ Computer records (of Internet sites visited, productivity, and so on)

✓ Cash register receipts

✓ Purchase orders

✓ Productivity reports
(such as records of sales completed, deadlines met, or projects finished)

✓ Sales receipts

✓ Equipment logs

✓ Notes taken by an employee involved
(for example, if an employee made a record of threatening or harassing comments
by another employee, or kept a diary or journal of workplace incidents)

✓ Files from any previous investigations of the same employees or same types of incidents

Credibility Checklist

✓ **Plausibility:** Whose story makes the most sense? Could the employees involved have heard and seen what they claimed to have witnessed? Should they have heard and seen things that they did not admit?

✓ **Source of Information:** Did the witness see or hear the event directly? Did the witness report firsthand knowledge, or rely on statements from other employees or rumors?

✓ **Detail:** How general or specific was each person's statement? Were details supported by other evidence? Did the accused or suspected employee deny the allegation in detail or only generally?

✓ **Corroboration and Conflicting Testimony:** What witnesses or documents support each side of the story? Does the evidence contradict one person's statements? Do the witnesses support the person who suggested you interview them? If there are conflicts, are they over minor or significant issues?

✓ **Contradictions:** Was each person's story consistent throughout your questioning or on a second telling? Did any of the witnesses contradict themselves? If so, did the change involve a minor issue or a matter of substance?

✓ **Demeanor:** How did the witnesses act during the interview? Did they appear to be telling the truth or lying? Did the accused employee have a strong reaction to the complaint or no reaction at all? Did the complaining employee seem genuinely upset? Were any witnesses' reactions unusual, based on their ordinary demeanor or behavior?

✓ **Omissions:** Did anyone leave out important information during the interview? Is there a reasonable explanation for the omission?

✓ **Prior Incidents:** Does the accused employee have a documented history of this type of misconduct? Has the complaining employee made previous complaints? Have there been other incidents between the complaining and the accused employee?

✓ **Motive:** Does anyone have a motive to lie about, exaggerate, or deny the incident? Is there any history between the employees involved that affects their credibility? Do any of the witnesses have a special loyalty to—or grudge against—anyone involved in the incident?

Discipline Checklist

✓ **Severity:** How serious was the misconduct? If there was a victim, how was the victim affected by the accused employee's actions? What effect did the accused employee's actions have on the workplace?

✓ **Consistency:** Have other employees committed similar misconduct in the past? How were these incidents handled?

✓ **Policy:** Does the company have a progressive discipline policy, in which you spell out the types of misconduct that might result in particular disciplinary consequences? Where does this misconduct fall on your company's scale?

✓ **History:** Have there been any similar prior incidents involving this employee? Does the employee have a history of disciplinary problems?

✓ **Knowledge:** Did the employee know that this conduct was prohibited? Did workplace rules and policies clearly spell out the company's expectations? Was the behavior clearly inappropriate, regardless of whether it was explicitly prohibited?

✓ **Evidence:** How strong is the evidence of misconduct? Do you have powerful, firsthand, corroborated evidence of wrongdoing?

Investigation Report Checklist

✓ The date of the incident under investigation

✓ If there is a complaint, the date of the complaint and name of the employee who complained

✓ Why the investigation was initiated (for example, an employee complained, a fight broke out, or an employee was suspected of being under the influence of drugs at work) and the basic facts to be investigated

✓ Who conducted the investigation

✓ When the investigation began

✓ What documents or other evidence were gathered

✓ Where documents or evidence were found (for example, in an employee's personnel file, pinned to the company bulletin board, or in an employee's desk drawer)

✓ When documents or evidence were gathered

✓ Any company policies that are relevant to the incident under investigation

✓ Who was interviewed

✓ The date of each interview

✓ A summary of each witness's statement

✓ A summary of any other important facts (for example, things you may have noticed when visiting the scene of the incident)

✓ Your conclusions and how you came to them

✓ Any important issues left unresolved

✓ Any action taken in the workplace (for example, discipline against the wrongdoer or workplace training) ■

APPENDIX C

Resources

State Laws Prohibiting Discrimination in Employment

Agencies That Enforce Laws Prohibiting Discrimination in Employment

State Occupational Safety and Health Offices

State Workers' Compensation Offices

State Laws Prohibiting Discrimination in Employment

State	Law applies to employers with	Age	Ancestry or national origin	Disability	AIDS/HIV	Gender	Marital status	Pregnancy, childbirth, and related medical conditions	Race or color	Religion or creed	Sexual orientation	Genetic testing information	Additional protected categories
Private employers may not make employment decisions based on													
Alabama Ala. Code §§ 21-7-1, 25-1-20	20 or more employees	40 and older											
Alaska Alaska Stat. §§ 18.80.220, 47.30.865	One or more employees	40 and older	✓	Physical and mental	✓	✓	✓ (Includes changes in status)	✓ Parenthood	✓	✓			Mental illness
Arizona Ariz. Rev. Stat. § 41-1461	15 or more employees	40 and older	✓	Physical	✓	✓			✓	✓		✓	
Arkansas Ark. Code Ann. §§ 16-123-101, 11-4-601, 11-5-403	9 or more employees		✓	Physical and mental		✓		✓	✓	✓		✓[1]	
California Cal. Gov't. Code §§ 12920, 12941; Cal. Lab. Code § 1101	5 or more employees	40 and older	✓	Physical and mental	✓	✓[2]	✓	✓	✓	✓	✓	✓	• Medical condition • Political activities or affiliations
Colorado Colo. Rev. Stat. §§ 24-34-301, 24-34-401, 27-10-115	Law applies to all employers	40 to 70	✓	Physical, mental, and learning	✓	✓		✓	✓	✓			• Lawful conduct outside of work • Mental illness
Connecticut Conn. Gen. Stat. Ann. §§ 46a-51, 46a-60	3 or more employees	40 and older	✓	Present or past physical, mental, or learning	✓	✓	✓	✓	✓	✓		✓	Mental retardation
Delaware Del. Code Ann. tit. 19, § 710	4 or more employees	40 to 70	✓	Physical or mental	✓	✓	✓	✓	✓	✓		✓	
District of Columbia D.C. Code Ann. §§ 2-1401.01, 7-1703.03	Law applies to all employers	18 and older	✓	Physical or mental	✓	✓	✓	✓ Parenthood	✓	✓	✓		• Enrollment in vocational or professional or college education • Family duties • Perceived race • Personal appearance • Political affiliation • Smoker

[1] Employees covered by FLSA
[2] Includes gender identity

State Laws Prohibiting Discrimination in Employment

State	Law applies to employers with	Age	Ancestry or national origin	Disability	AIDS/HIV	Gender	Marital status	Pregnancy, childbirth, and related medical conditions	Race or color	Religion or creed	Sexual orientation	Genetic testing information	Additional protected categories
Florida Fla. Stat. Ann. §§ 760.01, 760.50, 448.075	15 or more employees	No age limit	✓	"Handicap"	✓	✓	✓		✓	✓			• Sickle cell trait • Family status
Georgia Ga. Code Ann. §§ 34-6A-1, 34-1-23, 34-5-1	15 or more employees (disability) 10 or more employees (gender)	40 to 70		Physical or mental		✓³							
Hawaii Haw. Rev. Stat. § 378-1	One or more employees	No age limit	✓	Physical or mental	✓	✓	✓	✓ Breastfeeding	✓	✓	✓	✓	Arrest and court record (unless there is a conviction directly related to job)
Idaho Idaho Code § 67-5909	5 or more employees	40 and older	✓	Physical or mental		✓		✓	✓	✓			
Illinois 775 Ill. Comp. Stat. §§ 5/1-101, 5/2-101; Ill. Admin. Code tit. 56, § 5210.110	15 or more employees	40 and older	✓	Physical or mental	✓	✓	✓	✓	✓	✓			• Arrest record • Citizen status • Military status • Unfavorable military discharge • Victim of domestic violence or sexual assault
Indiana Ind. Code Ann. §§ 22-9-1-1, 22-9-2-1	6 or more employees	40 to 70	✓	Physical or mental		✓				✓	✓		
Iowa Iowa Code § 216.1	4 or more employees	18 or older	✓	Physical or mental	✓	✓		✓	✓	✓			
Kansas Kan. Stat. Ann. §§ 44-1001, 44-1111, 44-1125, 65-6002(e)	4 or more employees	18 or older	✓	Physical or mental	✓	✓			✓	✓		✓	Military status
Kentucky Ky. Rev. Stat. Ann. §§ 344.040, 207.130, 342.197	8 or more employees	40 or older	✓	Physical (Includes black lung disease)	✓	✓			✓	✓			Smoker or non-smoker

³ Wage discrimination only

State	Law applies to employers with	Age	Ancestry or national origin	Disability	AIDS/HIV	Gender	Marital status	Pregnancy, childbirth, and related medical conditions	Race or color	Religion or creed	Sexual orientation	Genetic testing information	Additional protected categories
State Laws Prohibiting Discrimination in Employment													
Private employers may not make employment decisions based on													
Louisiana La. Rev. Stat. Ann. §§ 23:301 to 23:352	20 or more employees		✓	Physical or mental		✓		✓ (Applies to employers with 25 or more employees)	✓	✓		✓	Sickle cell trait
Maine Me. Rev. Stat. Ann. tit. 5, §§ 4551, 4571	Law applies to all employers	No age limit	✓	Physical or mental		✓		✓	✓	✓	✓	✓	
Maryland Md. Code 1957 Art. 49B, § 15	15 or more employees	No age limit	✓	Physical or mental		✓	✓	✓	✓	✓	✓	✓	
Massachusetts Mass. Gen. Laws ch. 151B, § 4	6 or more employees	40 or older	✓	Physical or mental	✓	✓			✓	✓	✓	✓	
Michigan Mich. Comp. Laws §§ 37.1201, 37.2201, 37.1103	One or more employees	No age limit	✓	Physical or mental	✓	✓	✓	✓	✓	✓		✓	• Height or weight • Arrest record
Minnesota Minn. Stat. Ann. §§ 363A.03, 363A.08; 181.974	One or more employees	18 or older	✓	Physical or mental	✓	✓	✓	✓	✓	✓	✓	✓	• Member of local commission • Perceived sexual orientation • Receiving public assistance
Mississippi Miss. Code Ann. §§ 25-9-149, 33-1-15, 43-6-15	All employers seeking small business assistance		✓	Physical (Employers receiving any public funding)		✓			✓	✓			Military status (all employers)
Missouri Mo. Rev. Stat. §§ 213.010, 191.665, 375.1306	6 or more employees	40 to 70	✓	Physical or mental	✓	✓		✓	✓	✓		✓	
Montana Mont. Code Ann. §§ 49-2-101, 49-2-303	One or more employees	No age limit	✓	Physical or mental		✓	✓	✓	✓	✓			
Nebraska Neb. Rev. Stat. §§ 48-1101, 48-1001, 20-168	15 or more employees	40 to 70 [4]	✓	Physical or mental	✓	✓	✓	✓	✓	✓		✓	

[4] Employers with 25 or more employees

State Laws Prohibiting Discrimination in Employment

Private employers may not make employment decisions based on

State	Law applies to employers with	Age	Ancestry or national origin	Disability	AIDS/HIV	Gender	Marital status	Pregnancy, childbirth, and related medical conditions	Race or color	Religion or creed	Sexual orientation	Genetic testing information	Additional protected categories
Nevada Nev. Rev. Stat. Ann. §§ 613.310 and following	15 or more employees	40 or older	✓	Physical or mental		✓		✓	✓	✓	✓	✓	• Lawful use of any product when not at work • Use of service animal
New Hampshire N.H. Rev. Stat. Ann. §§ 354-A2 and following, 141-H:3	6 or more employees	No age limit	✓	Physical or mental	✓	✓		✓	✓	✓	✓		
New Jersey N.J. Stat. Ann. §§ 10:5-1 to 10:5-12; 34:6B-1	Law applies to all employers	18 to 70	✓	Past or present physical or mental	✓	✓	✓ (Includes domestic partner)	✓	✓	✓	✓	✓	• Hereditary cellular or blood trait • Military service or status • Smoker or nonsmoker
New Mexico N.M. Stat. Ann. § 28-1-7	Law applies to all employers	40 or older	✓	Physical or mental		✓	✓ (Applies to employers with 50 or more employees)	✓	✓	✓	✓[5]		• Gender identity (employers with 15 or more employees) • Serious medical condition
New York N.Y. Exec. Law § 296; N.Y. Lab. Law § 201-d	4 or more employees	18 and over	✓	Physical or mental	✓	✓	✓	✓	✓	✓	✓	✓	• Lawful use of any product when not at work • Military status • Observance of Sabbath • Political activities
North Carolina N.C. Gen. Stat. §§ 143-422.2, 168A-1, 95-28.1, 130A-148	15 or more employees	No age limit	✓	Physical or mental	✓	✓			✓	✓			• Lawful use of any product when not at work • Sickle cell trait
North Dakota N.D. Cent. Code §§ 14-02.4-01, 34-01-17	One or more employees	40 or older	✓	Physical or mental		✓	✓	✓	✓	✓			• Lawful conduct outside of work • Receiving public assistance
Ohio Ohio Rev. Code Ann. §§ 4111.17, 4112.01	4 or more employees	40 or older	✓	Physical, mental, or learning		✓		✓	✓	✓			

[5] Employers with 15 or more employees

State Laws Prohibiting Discrimination in Employment

Private employers may not make employment decisions based on

State	Law applies to employers with	Age	Ancestry or national origin	Disability	AIDS/HIV	Gender	Marital status	Pregnancy, childbirth, and related medical conditions	Race or color	Religion or creed	Sexual orientation	Genetic testing information	Additional protected categories
Oklahoma Okla. Stat. Ann. tit. 25, § 1301; tit. 36, § 3614.2; tit. 40, § 500; tit. 44, § 208	15 or more employees	40 or older	✓	Physical or mental		✓			✓	✓		✓	• Military service • Smoker or nonsmoker
Oregon Or. Rev. Stat. §§ 659A.100 and following, 659A.303	One or more employees	18 or older	✓	Physical or mental[6]		✓	✓	✓	✓	✓		✓	
Pennsylvania 43 Pa. Cons. Stat. Ann. § 953	4 or more employees	40 to 70	✓	Physical or mental		✓		✓ (Pregnancy not treated as a disability in terms of benefits)	✓	✓			• Familial status • GED rather than high school diploma
Rhode Island R.I. Gen. Laws §§ 28-6-17, 28-5-11, 2-28-10, 23-6-22, 23-20.7.1-1	4 or more employees	40 or older	✓	Physical or mental	✓	✓		✓	✓	✓	✓	✓	• Domestic abuse victim • Gender identity or expression • Smoker or nonsmoker
South Carolina S.C. Code Ann. §§ 1-13-20 and following	15 or more employees	40 or older	✓	Physical or mental		✓		✓	✓	✓			
South Dakota S.D. Codified Laws Ann. §§ 20-13-10, 60-12-15, 60-2-20, 62-1-17	Law applies to all employers		✓	Physical, mental, and learning		✓			✓	✓		✓	Preexisting injury
Tennessee Tenn. Code Ann. §§ 4-21-102, 4-21-401 and following; 8-50-103, 50-2-202	8 or more employees	40 or older	✓	Physical or mental		✓		✓ (Full-time employee who worked the previous 12 months entitled to 4 months' maternity leave. Pay at discretion of employer.)[7]	✓	✓			

[6] Employers with 6 or more employees

[7] Employers with 100 or more employees

State Laws Prohibiting Discrimination in Employment

Private employers may not make employment decisions based on

State	Law applies to employers with	Age	Ancestry or national origin	Disability	AIDS/HIV	Gender	Marital status	Pregnancy, childbirth, and related medical conditions	Race or color	Religion or creed	Sexual orientation	Genetic testing information	Additional protected categories
Texas Tex. Lab. Code Ann. §§ 21.002, 21.101, 21.401	15 or more employees	40 or older	✓	Physical or mental		✓		✓	✓	✓		✓	
Utah Utah Code Ann. § 34A-5-106	15 or more employees	40 or older	✓	Follows federal law	✓[8]	✓		✓	✓	✓			
Vermont Vt. Stat. Ann. tit. 21, § 495; tit. 18, § 9333	One or more employees	18 or older	✓	Physical, mental, or learning	✓	✓			✓	✓	✓	✓	Place of birth
Virginia Va. Code Ann. §§ 2.2-3900, 40.1-28.6, 51.5-3	Law applies to all employers	No age limit	✓	Physical or mental		✓	✓	✓	✓	✓		✓	
Washington Wash. Rev. Code Ann. §§ 49.60.040, 49.60.172 and foll.; 49.12.175, 49.44.090; Wash. Admin. Code § 162-30-020	8 or more employees	40 or older	✓	Physical, mental, or sensory	✓	✓	✓	✓	✓	✓		✓	• Hepatitis C infection • Member of state militia • Use of guide dog or service animal
West Virginia W.Va. Code §§ 5-11-3, 5-11-9, 21-5B-1	12 or more employees	40 or older	✓	Physical or mental	✓	✓[9]			✓	✓			Smoker or non-smoker
Wisconsin Wis. Stat. Ann. §§ 111.32 and following	One or more employees	40 or older	✓	Physical or mental	✓	✓	✓	✓	✓	✓	✓	✓	• Arrest or conviction • Lawful use of any product when not at work • Military service or status
Wyoming Wyo. Stat. §§ 27-9-105, 19-11-104	2 or more employees	40 or older	✓			✓			✓	✓			• Military service or status • Smoker or nonsmoker

[8] Follows federal ADA statutes

[9] Equal pay laws apply to employers with one or more employees

Current as of March 2004

State Agencies That Enforce Laws Prohibiting Discrimination in Employment

United States Government
Equal Employment Opportunity
Commission (EEOC)
Washington, DC
202-663-4900
800-669-4000
www.eeoc.gov
Field office locations and phone numbers
www.eeoc.gov/offices.html

Alabama
EEOC District Office
Birmingham, AL
205-731-0082/0083
http://eeoc.gov/birmingham/index.html

Alaska
Commission for Human Rights
Anchorage, AK
907-274-4692
800-478-4692
www.gov.state.ak.us/aschr/aschr.htm

Arizona
Civil Rights Division
Phoenix, AZ
602-542-5263
www.attorneygeneral.state.az.us/
civil_rights/index.html

Arkansas
Equal Employment Opportunity Commission
Little Rock, AR
501-324-5060
www.eeoc.gov/littlerock/index.html

California
Department of Fair Employment and Housing
Sacramento District Office
Sacramento, CA
916-227-0551
800-884-1684
www.dfeh.ca.gov

Colorado
Civil Rights Division
Denver, CO
303-894-2997
800-262-4845
www.dora.state.co.us/Civil-Rights

Connecticut
Commission on Human Rights
& Opportunities
Hartford, CT
860-541-3400
800-477-5737
www.state.ct.us/chro

Delaware
Office of Labor Law Enforcement
Division of Industrial Affairs
Wilmington, DE
302-761-8200
www.delawareworks.com/industrialaffairs/
services/LaborLawEnforcement.shtml

District of Columbia
Office of Human Rights
Washington, DC
202-727-4559
www.ohr.washingtondc.gov/main.shtm

Florida
Commission on Human Relations
Tallahassee, FL
850-488-7082
800-342-8170
http://fchr.state.fl.us

Georgia
Atlanta District Office
U.S. Equal Employment Opportunity
Commission
Atlanta, GA
404-562-6800
800-669-4600
www.eeoc.gov/atlanta/index.html

State Agencies That Enforce Laws Prohibiting Discrimination in Employment, *continued*

Hawaii
Hawai'i Civil Rights Commission
Honolulu, HI
808-586-8640 (Oahu only)
800-468-4644 x68640 (other islands)
www.state.hi.us/hcrc

Idaho
Idaho Human Rights Commission
Boise, ID
208-334-2873
www2.state.id.us/ihrc

Illinois
Department of Human Rights
Chicago, IL
312-814-6200
www.state.il.us/dhr

Indiana
Civil Rights Commission
Indianapolis, IN
317-232-2600
800-628-2909
www.in.gov/icrc

Iowa
Iowa Civil Rights Commission
Des Moines, IA 50309
515-281-4121
800-457-4416
www.state.ia.us/government/crc

Kansas
Human Rights Commission
Topeka, KS
785-296-3206
www.ink.org/public/khrc

Kentucky
Human Rights Commission
Louisville, KY
502-595-4024
800-292-5566
www.state.ky.us/agencies2/kchr

Louisiana
Commission on Human Rights
Baton Rouge, LA
225-342-6969

Maine
Human Rights Commission
Augusta, ME 04333
207-624-6050
www.state.me.us/mhrc/index.shtml

Maryland
Commission on Human Relations
Baltimore, MD 21202
410-767-8600
800-637-6247
www.mchr.state.md.us

Massachusetts
Commission Against Discrimination
Boston, MA 02108
617-994-6000
www.state.ma.us/mcad

Michigan
Department of Civil Rights
Detroit, MI 48226
313-456-3700
800-482-3604
www.michigan.gov/mdcr

Minnesota
Department of Human Rights
St. Paul, MN 55101
651-296-5663
800-657-3704
www.humanrights.state.mn.us

Mississippi
Equal Opportunity Department
Employment Security Commission
Jackson, MS
601-961-7420
www.mesc.state.ms.us

State Agencies That Enforce Laws Prohibiting Discrimination in Employment, *continued*

Missouri
Commission on Human Rights
Jefferson City MO 65102
573-751-3325
www.dolir.state.mo.us/hr

Montana
Human Rights Bureau
Employment Relations Division
Department of Labor & Industry
Helena, MT 59624
406-444-2884
800-542-0807
http://erd.dli.state.mt.us/HumanRights/
HRhome.htm

Nebraska
Equal Opportunity Commission
Lincoln, NE 68509
402-471-2024
800-642-6112
www.nol.org/home/NEOC

Nevada
Equal Rights Commission
Reno, NV 89509
775-688-1288
http://detr.state.nv.us/nerc

New Hampshire
Commission for Human Rights
Concord, NH 03301
603-271-2767
http://webster.state.nh.us/hrc

New Jersey
Division on Civil Rights
Newark, NJ 07102
973-648-2700
www.state.nj.us/lps/dcr

New Mexico
Human Rights Division
Santa Fe, NM 87505
505-827-6838
800-566-9471
www.dol.state.nm.us/dol_hrd.html

New York
Division of Human Rights
Bronx, NY 10458
718-741-8400
www.nysdhr.com

North Carolina
Employment Discrimination Bureau
Department of Labor
Raleigh, N.C. 27601
919-807-2796
800-NCLABOR (625-2267)
www.dol.state.nc.us/edb/edb.htm

North Dakota
Human Rights Division
Department of Labor
Bismarck ND 58505
701-328-2660
800-582-8032
www.state.nd.us/labor/services/humanrights

Ohio
Civil Rights Commission
Columbus, OH 43205
614-466-2785
888-278-7101
www.state.oh.us/crc

Oklahoma
Human Rights Commission
Oklahoma City, OK 73105
405-521-2360
www.youroklahoma.com/ohrc

Oregon
Civil Rights Division
Bureau of Labor and Industries
Portland, OR 97232
503-731-4200
www.boli.state.or.us/civil/index.html

Pennsylvania
Human Relations Commission
Philadelphia, PA 19130
215-560-2496
www.phrc.state.pa.us

State Agencies That Enforce Laws Prohibiting Discrimination in Employment, *continued*

Rhode Island
Commission for Human Rights
Providence, RI 02903
401-222-2661
www.state.ri.us/manual/data/queries/
stdept_.idc?id=16

South Carolina
Human Affairs Commission
Columbia, SC 29204
803-737-7800
800-521-0725
www.state.sc.us/schac

South Dakota
Division of Human Rights
Pierre, SD 57501
605-773-4493
www.state.sd.us/dcr/hr/HR_HOM.htm

Tennessee
Human Rights Commission
Knoxville, TN 37902
865-594-6500
800-251-3589
www.state.tn.us/humanrights

Texas
Commission on Human Rights
Austin, TX 78711
512-437-3450
888-452-4778
http://tchr.state.tx.us

Utah
Anti-Discrimination & Labor Division
Labor Commission
Salt Lake City, UT 84111
801-530-6801
800-222-1238
http://laborcommission.utah.gov/
Utah_Antidiscrimination___Labo/
utah_antidiscrimination___labo.htm

Vermont
Attorney General's Office
Civil Rights Division
Montpelier, VT 05609
802-828-3657
888-745-9195
www.state.vt.us/atg/civil rights.htm

Virginia
Council on Human Rights
Richmond, VA 23219
804-225-2292
www.chr.state.va.us

Washington
Human Rights Commission
Seattle, WA 98101
206-464-6500
www.wa.gov/hrc

West Virginia
Human Rights Commission
Charleston, WV 25301
304-558-2616
888-676-5546
www.state.wv.us/wvhrc

Wisconsin
Department of Workforce Development
Madison, WI
608-266-6860
www.dwd.state.wi.us/er

Wyoming
Department of Employment
Cheyenne, WY
307-777-7261
http://wydoe.state.wy.us/doe.asp?ID=3

State Occupational Safety and Health Offices

Federal OSHA
United States Department of Labor
Occupational Safety & Health Administration
Washington, DC
800-321-OSHA (6742)
www.osha.gov

State OSHA Offices

AKOSH
Alaska Department of Labor and Workforce
Development
Labor Standards and Safety Division
Occupational Safety and Health Section
Juneau, AK
907-465-4855 (Juneau)
907-269-4955 (Anchorage)
www.labor.state.ak.us/lss/oshhome.htm

ADOSH
Industrial Commission of Arizona
Phoenix, AZ
602-542-5795 (Phoenix)
602-628-5478 (Tuscon)
www.ica.state.az.us/ADOSH/oshatop.htm

Cal-OSHA
California Department of Industrial Relations
San Francisco, CA
415-703-5100 (information about local
offices)
www.dir.ca.gov/DOSH

Conn-OSHA *(Public sector only)*
Connecticut Department of Labor
Wethersfield, CT
860-566-4550
www.ctdol.state.ct.us/osha/osha.htm

HIOSH
Hawaii Department of Labor and Industrial
Relations
Honolulu, HI
808-586-9100
http://hiosh.hawaii.gov

IOSHA
Indiana Department of Labor
Indianapolis, IN
317-232-2685
www.in.gov/labor/iosha

IOSH
Iowa Division of Labor Services
Des Moines, IA
515-281-3606
www.iowaworkforce.org/labor/iosh

KYOSH
Kentucky Labor Cabinet
Frankfort, KY
502-564-3070
www.labor.ky.gov/osh/index.htm

MOSH
Maryland Division of Labor and Industry
Department of Labor, Licensing, and
Regulation
Baltimore, MD
410-767-2215
www.dllr.state.md.us/labor/mosh.html

MIOSHA
Michigan Department of Consumer
& Industry Services
Bureau of Safety and Regulation
Lansing, MI
517-322-1814
www.michigan.gov/cis

MNOSHA
Minnesota Department of Labor and Industry
St. Paul, MN
651-284-5050
800-342-5354
www.doli.state.mn.us/mnosha.html

State Occupational Safety and Health Offices, *continued*

OSHES
Nevada Division of Industrial Relations
Henderson, NV
702-486-9044 (Henderson)
775-688-1380 (Reno)
http://dirweb.state.nv.us/oshes.htm

PEOSH *(Public sector only)*
New Jersey Department of Labor
Trenton, New Jersey
609-292-7036
www.state.nj.us/labor/lsse/lspeosh.html

Occupational Health and Safety Bureau
New Mexico Environment Department
Environmental Protection Division
Santa Fe, NM
505-827 4230
www.nmenv.state.nm.us/OHSB_Website
ohsb_home.htm

Division of Safety and Health
New York Department of Labor
Albany, NY
518-457-5508 (Albany)
212-352-6132 (New York City)
www.labor.state.ny.us/business_ny/
employer_responsibilities/safety_health.html

Occupational Safety & Health (OSH)
Division
North Carolina Department of Labor
Raleigh, NC
919-807-2900
www.dol.state.nc.us/osha/osh.htm

OR-OSHA
Oregon Occupational Safety and Health
Division
Department of Consumer & Business Services
Salem, OR
503-378-3272
800-922-2689
www.cbs.state.or.us/external/osha

OSHA
South Carolina Department of Labor,
Licensing, and Regulation
Columbia, SC
803-734-9669
www.llr.state.sc.us/osha.asp

TOSHA
Tennessee Department of Labor &
Workforce Development
Nashville, TN
615-741-2793
800-249-8510
www.state.tn.us/labor-wfd/tosha.html

UOSH
Utah Labor Commission
Salt Lake City, UT
801-530-6901
www.uosh.utah.gov

VOSHA
Vermont Department of Labor & Industry
Montpelier, VT
802-828-2765
www.state.vt.us/labind/vosha.htm

VOSH
Virginia Department of Labor & Industry
Richmond, VA
804-786-0574 (Health Compliance)
804-786-2391 (Safety Compliance)
www.doli.state.va.us/whatwedo/index.html

WISHA
Washington Department of Labor & Industries
Olympia, WA
360-902-5433
800-423-7233
www.lni.wa.gov/wisha

Wyoming Department of Employment
Workers' Safety/OSHA
Cheyenne, WY
307-777-7786
http://wydoe.state.wy.us/ doe.asp?ID=7

State Workers' Compensation Offices

Alabama
Workers' Compensation Division
Department of Industrial Relations
Montgomery, AL
334-242-2868
http://dir.state.al.us/wc

Alaska
Workers' Compensation Division
Department of Labor
Juneau, AK
907-465-2970
www.labor.state.ak.us/wc/wc.htm

Arizona
Industrial Commission
Phoenix, AZ
602-542-4661
www.ica.state.az.us

Arkansas
Workers' Compensation Commission
Little Rock, AR
501-682-3930
www.awcc.state.ar.us

California
Division of Workers' Compensation
Sacramento, CA
800-736-7401
www.dir.ca.gov/dwc/dwc_home_page.htm

Colorado
Division of Workers' Compensation
Denver, CO
800-390-7936 or 303-318-8700
www.coworkforce.com/DWC

Connecticut
Workers' Compensation Commission
Hartford, CT
860-493-1500
www.ctdol.state.ct.us

Delaware
Division of Industrial Affairs
Office of Workers' Compensation
Wilmington, DE
302-761-8200
www.delawareworks.com/divisions/
industaffairs/workers.comp.htm

District of Columbia
Department of Employment Services
Labor Standards Bureau
Office of Workers' Compensation
Washington, DC
202-671-1000
http://does.dc.gov/services/wkr_comp.shtm

Florida
Department of Financial Services
Division of Workers' Compensation
Tallahassee, FL
800-342-1741
http://www.fldfs.com/wc

Georgia
Board of Workers' Compensation
Atlanta, GA
404-656-3875
http://www.state.ga.us/sbwc

Hawaii
Disability Compensation Division
Department of Labor and Industrial Relations
Honolulu, HI
808-586-9174
http://dlir.state.hi.us

Idaho
Industrial Commission
Boise, ID
208-334-6000 or 800-950-2110
www2.state.id.us/iic

State Workers' Compensation Offices, *continued*

Illinois
Industrial Commission
Chicago, IL
312-814-6611
www.state.il.us/agency/iic

Indiana
Workers' Compensation Board
Indianapolis, IN
1-800-824-COMP or 317-232-3809
www.in.gov/workcomp

Iowa
Division of Workers' Compensation
Des Moines, IA
515-281-5387 or 800-562-4692
www.iowaworkforce.org/wc

Kansas
Division of Workers' Compensation
Department of Human Resources
Topeka, KS
785-296-3441
www.hr.state.ks.us/wc/html/wc.html

Kentucky
Department of Workers' Claims
Frankfort, KY
502-564-5550
http://labor.ky.gov/dwc

Louisiana
Office of Workers' Compensation Administration
Baton Rouge, LA
800-201-2499 or 225-342-7555
www.laworks.net

Maine
Workers' Compensation Board
Augusta, ME
207-287-3751 or 888-801-9087
www.state.me.us/wcb

Maryland
Workers' Compensation Commission
Baltimore, MD
800-492-0479 or 410-864-5100
www.wcc.state.md.us

Massachusetts
Department of Industrial Accidents
Boston, MA
800-323-3249 or 617-727-4900
www.state.ma.us/dia

Michigan
Bureau of Workers' and Unemployment
Compensation
Lansing, MI
517-322-1296 or 888-396-5041
www.michigan.gov/bwuc

Minnesota
Workers' Compensation Division
Department of Labor and Industry
St. Paul, MN
800-342-5354 or 651-284-5032
www.doli.state.mn.us/workcomp.html

Mississippi
Workers' Compensation Commission
Jackson, MS
601-987-4200
www.mwcc.state.ms.us

Missouri
Division of Workers' Compensation
Department of Labor and Industrial Relations
Jefferson City, MO
573-751-4231
www.dolir.state.mo.us/wc/index.htm

Montana
Department of Labor and Industry
Helena, MT
406-444-6543
http://dli.state.mt.us

State Workers' Compensation Offices, *continued*

Nebraska
Workers' Compensation Court
Lincoln, NE
402-471-6468 or 800-599-5155
www.state.ne.us/home/WC

Nevada
Division of Industrial Relations
Carson City, NV
775-684-7260
http://dirweb.state.nv.us

New Hampshire
Workers' Compensation Division
Department of Labor
Concord, NH
800-272-4353 or 603-271-3176
www.labor.state.nh.us/
workers_compensation.asp

New Jersey
Department of Labor
Division of Workers' Compensation
Trenton, NJ
609-292-2515
www.state.nj.us/labor/wc/wcindex.html

New Mexico
Workers' Compensation Administration
Albuquerque, NM
505-841-6000
http://www.state.nm.us/wca

New York
Workers' Compensation Board
Albany, NY
518-474-6674
www.wcb.state.ny.us/index.html

North Carolina
Industrial Commission
Raleigh, NC
800-688-8349
www.compstate.nc.us

North Dakota
Workers' Compensation Bureau
Bismarck, ND
800-777-5033 or 701-328-3800
www.ndworkerscomp.com

Ohio
Bureau of Workers' Compensation
Columbus, OH
800-644-6292
www.state.oh.us/odjfs/ouc/index.stm

Oklahoma
Workers' Compensation Court
Oklahoma City, OK
800-522-8210 or 405-522-8600
www.owcc.state.ok.us

Oregon
Workers' Compensation Division
Salem, OR
503-947-7810 or 800-452-0288
www.cbs.state.or.us/external/wcd

Pennsylvania
Bureau of Workers' Compensation
Harrisburg, PA
717-787-5279
www.dli.state.pa.us

Rhode Island
Department of Labor and Training
Division of Workers' Compensation
Cranston, RI
401-462-8100
www.dlt.state.ri.us/webdev/wc/default.htm

South Carolina
Workers' Compensation Commission
Columbia, SC
803-737-5700
www.wcc.state.sc.us

State Workers' Compensation Offices, *continued*

South Dakota
Division of Labor and Management
Department of Labor
Pierre, SD
605-773-3681
www.state.sd.us/dol/dlm/dlm-home.htm

Tennessee
Workers' Compensation Division
Labor and Workforce Development
Nashville, TN
615-532-2731
www.state.tn.us/labor-wfd/wcomp.html

Texas
Workers' Compensation Commission
Austin, TX
513-933-1899
www.twc.state.tx.us

Utah
Industrial Accident Division
Salt Lake City, UT
801-530-6800
www.ind-com.state.ut.us/indacc/indacc.htm

Vermont
Department of Labor and Industry
Workers' Compensation Division
Montpelier, VT
802-828-2286
www.state.vt.us/labind/wcindex.htm

Virginia
Workers' Compensation Commission
Richmond, VA
804-367-8600 or 877-664-2566
www.vwc.state.va.us

Washington
Department of Labor and Industries
Olympia, WA
360-902-5999
www.lni.wa.gov

West Virginia
Workers' Compensation Division
Charleston, WV
304-926-5000
www.state.wv.us/scripts/bep/wc

Wisconsin
Workers' Compensation Division
Madison, WI
608-266-1340
www.dwd.state.wi.us/wc/default.htm

Wyoming
Workers' Safety and Compensation Division
Cheyenne, WY
307-777-6763
http://wydoe.state.wy.us/doe.asp?ID=9 ■

Index

I

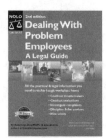

Remember:

Little publishers have big ears.
We really listen to you.

Take 2 Minutes & Give Us Your 2 cents

Your comments make a big difference in the development and revision of Nolo books and software. Please take a few minutes and register your Nolo product—and your comments—with us. Not only will your input make a difference, you'll receive special offers available only to registered owners of Nolo products on our newest books and software. Register now by:

PHONE
1-800-728-3555

FAX
1-800-645-0895

EMAIL
cs@nolo.com

or **MAIL** us
this registration card

fold here

Registration Card

NAME _____ DATE _____

ADDRESS _____

_____

CITY _____ STATE _____ ZIP _____

PHONE _____ EMAIL _____

WHERE DID YOU HEAR ABOUT THIS PRODUCT? _____

WHERE DID YOU PURCHASE THIS PRODUCT? _____

DID YOU CONSULT A LAWYER? (PLEASE CIRCLE ONE)   YES   NO   NOT APPLICABLE

DID YOU FIND THIS BOOK HELPFUL?   (VERY)   5   4   3   2   1   (NOT AT ALL)

COMMENTS _____

_____

_____

WAS IT EASY TO USE?   (VERY EASY)   5   4   3   2   1   (VERY DIFFICULT)

We occasionally make our mailing list available to carefully selected companies whose products may be of interest to you.

☐ If you do not wish to receive mailings from these companies, please check this box.

☐ You can quote me in future Nolo promotional materials.

Daytime phone number _____.

CMPLN 1.0

Nolo
in the
NEWS

"Nolo helps lay people perform legal tasks without the aid—or fees—of lawyers."
—USA TODAY

Nolo books are ..."written in plain language, free of legal mumbo jumbo, and spiced with witty personal observations."
—ASSOCIATED PRESS

"...Nolo publications...guide people simply through the how, when, where and why of law."
—WASHINGTON POST

"Increasingly, people who are not lawyers are performing tasks usually regarded as legal work... And consumers, using books like Nolo's, do routine legal work themselves."
—NEW YORK TIMES

"...All of [Nolo's] books are easy-to-understand, are updated regularly, provide pull-out forms...and are often quite moving in their sense of compassion for the struggles of the lay reader."
—SAN FRANCISCO CHRONICLE

fold here

- -

Place
stamp here

Nolo
950 Parker Street
Berkeley, CA 94710-9867

Attn: CMPLN 1.0